# THE
# BOARDGAME
# BOOK

# THE BOARDGAME BOOK

R C Bell

THE KNAPP PRESS   PUBLISHERS   LOS ANGELES
DISTRIBUTED BY THE VIKING PRESS NEW YORK

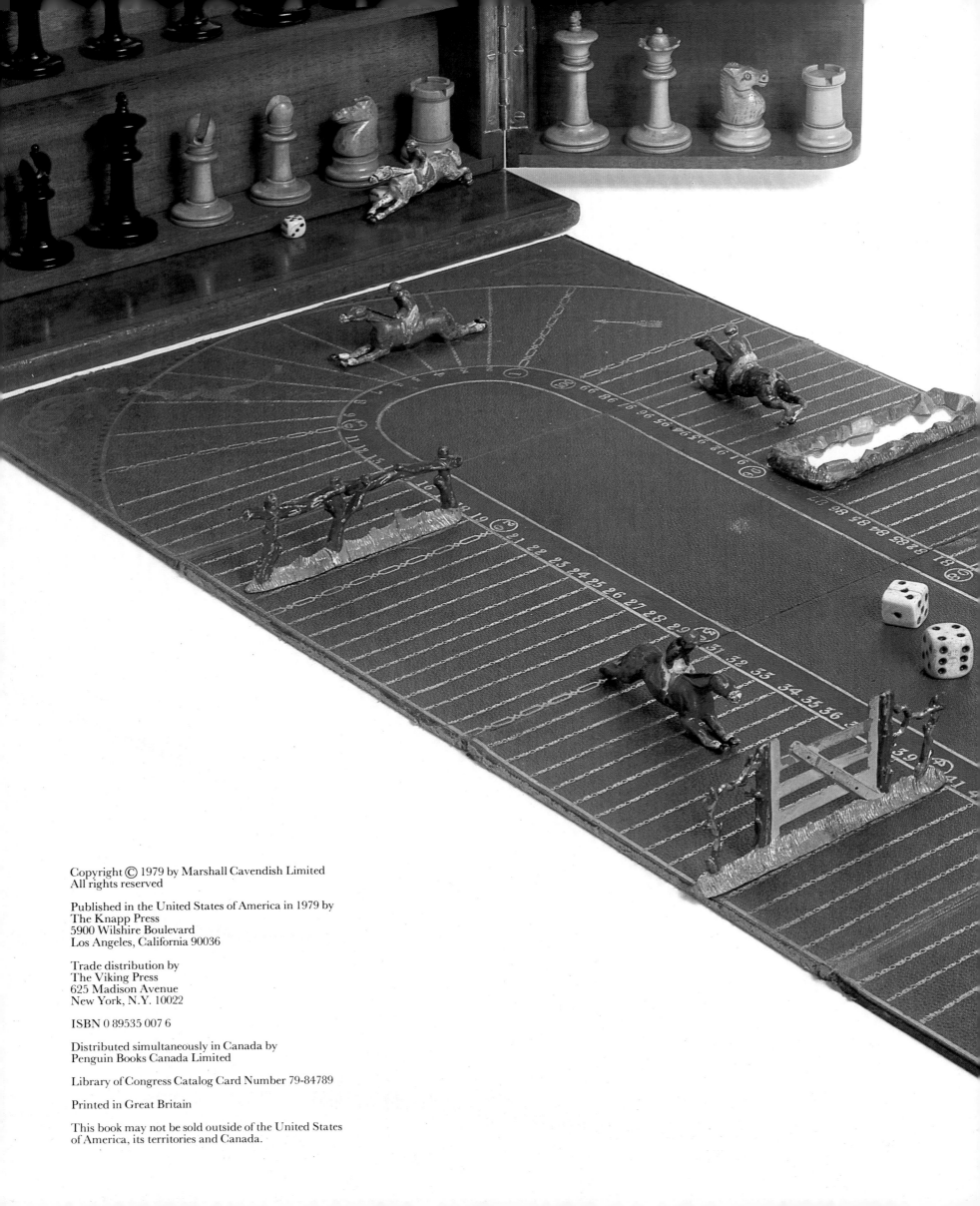

Published in the United States of America in 1979 by
The Knapp Press
5900 Wilshire Boulevard
Los Angeles, California 90036

Trade distribution by
The Viking Press
625 Madison Avenue
New York, N.Y. 10022

ISBN 0 89535 007 6

Distributed simultaneously in Canada by
Penguin Books Canada Limited

Library of Congress Catalog Card Number 79-84789

Printed in Great Britain

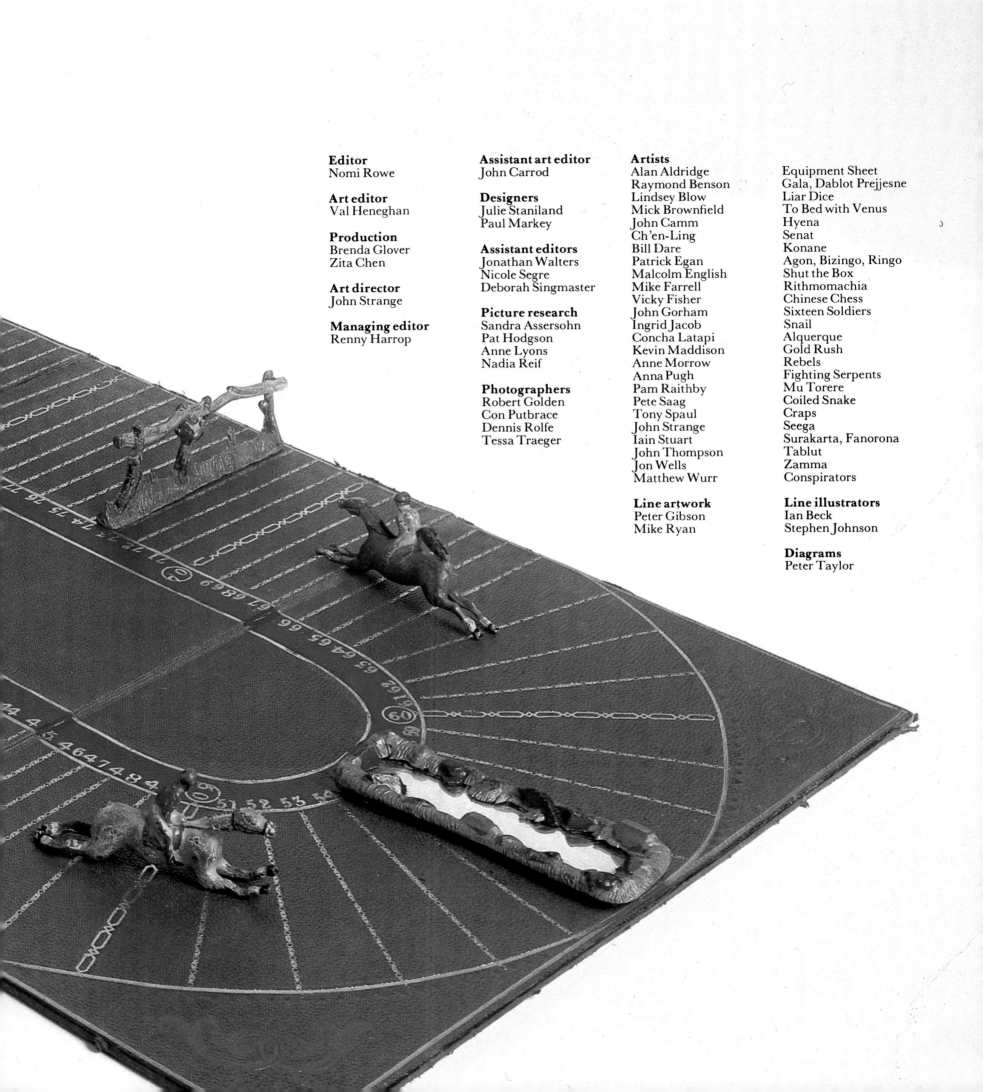

**Editor**
Nomi Rowe

**Art editor**
Val Heneghan

**Production**
Brenda Glover
Zita Chen

**Art director**
John Strange

**Managing editor**
Renny Harrop

**Assistant art editor**
John Carrod

**Designers**
Julie Staniland
Paul Markey

**Assistant editors**
Jonathan Walters
Nicole Segre
Deborah Singmaster

**Picture research**
Sandra Assersohn
Pat Hodgson
Anne Lyons
Nadia Reif

**Photographers**
Robert Golden
Con Putbrace
Dennis Rolfe
Tessa Traeger

**Artists**
Alan Aldridge
Raymond Benson
Lindsey Blow
Mick Brownfield
John Camm
Ch'en-Ling
Bill Dare
Patrick Egan
Malcolm English
Mike Farrell
Vicky Fisher
John Gorham
Ingrid Jacob
Concha Latapi
Kevin Maddison
Anne Morrow
Anna Pugh
Pam Raithby
Pete Saag
Tony Spaul
John Strange
Iain Stuart
John Thompson
Jon Wells
Matthew Wurr

Equipment Sheet
Gala, Dablot Prejjesne
Liar Dice
To Bed with Venus
Hyena
Senat
Konane
Agon, Bizingo, Ringo
Shut the Box
Rithmomachia
Chinese Chess
Sixteen Soldiers
Snail
Alquerque
Gold Rush
Rebels
Fighting Serpents
Mu Torere
Coiled Snake
Craps
Seega
Surakarta, Fanorona
Tablut
Zamma
Conspirators

**Line artwork**
Peter Gibson
Mike Ryan

**Line illustrators**
Ian Beck
Stephen Johnson

**Diagrams**
Peter Taylor

# Contents

# Introduction

troù Madame

Dant d'elephant

Torniquet

*A symbolic seventeenth century figure laden with a variety of games and holding the wood and ivory from which they are made.*

HERE IS A UNIQUE COLLECTION OF over eighty games from every part of the world and dating as far back as five thousand years. Some, though very popular in their countries of origin, are almost totally unknown abroad, and others are rarities only to be found in museums and private collections.

Many of the games reproduced in The Boardgame Book are from an especially fine collection built up by R. C. Bell over many years. All the games have been chosen as much for their interest and visual appeal as for their value as a pleasant and universal pastime. About one third of the boards reproduced in this book are completely new designs which have been specially commissioned, with all the details taking account of traditional models.

The pages of The Boardgame Book have been carefully designed to make it possible to play each of the games and their variants on a reproduction of the board. Facing each board the reader will find a brief description of the game and its origins, as well as detailed instructions for play in the form of rules and diagrams. In cases where games have survived without a complete set of rules, these have been reconstructed from the existing evidence.

Folded into the slipcase is an equipment sheet which supplies the players with counters and pieces necessary for all the games. The reader may either cut these from the sheet or trace them off onto card if the sheet is to be kept as a decorative wall hanging. Small objects which are easily available, such as buttons, coins or matchsticks broken in half (the half with the head can represent the black side), all make good substitute counters or could be used to supplement the equipment sheet if more players wish to take part. Six players have been provided for, as most games cannot be played easily by more.

The four other fold-out sheets enclosed in the slipcase reproduce eight nineteenth century games too detailed to be reduced and which are beautiful enough to be hung on the wall when they are not being used as boards. In addition, the dustcover (reproduced from an eighteenth century games box) can be removed and one side serves as a Backgammon board and the other side can be used for Chess and Nine Men's Morris – the rules for these games are included in the book.

Games with similar origins have been grouped together in historical sequence, but otherwise the main concern has been to achieve as much scope and variety within the book as possible. The selection includes simple race games like Ludo, gambling games like Faro, adapted for all the family, and complex games of skill like Chess and Go.

Special terms used in a single game have been explained within the text for that game, but certain terms common to many games can be found in the Glossary on page 160. Where these appear within the rules they are indicated by the use of italics, and, in the introductions to the games, by the use of double quotation marks.

# History of Boardgames

Boardgames have been invented and played in nearly all parts of the world, although the games played by the Indians of South America seem to be entirely of European or African origin. Only among the Eskimos and Australian Aborigines have no boardgames been found. This book provides a comprehensive selection of the world's boardgames and shows the different forms these take.

Some boardgames depend on chance – the player has to accept what destiny allots, without being able to influence the course of events. An example of this is the Game of the Goose (pages 140–141), and the numerous versions and adaptations of this game that have been developed since the eighteenth century, such as Universal History, Tramway Game, Panorama of Europe and Gathering of the Nations. Recent research suggests that in societies where games of chance are prevalent there is likely to be an emphasis on control of the supernatural, with a belief in gods and spirits that are benevolent, or at any rate can be coerced by performing certain actions.

Other boardgames are based on strategy, where no advantage is given to any player, but each can achieve mastery through exercising the necessary skill. The classic example of this type of game is Chess (pages 18–21), the logic and complexity of which has made it a perennial favourite – sometimes even an obsession – in both its Oriental and Western forms.

In between these two classes of games stands a group which combines elements both of chance and skill. Backgammon (pages 88–91) is such a game where a skillful player can exploit the throw of the dice so as to gain advantage even from a seemingly unpromising position.

Boardgames often reflect aspects of daily life in a play form. Some games, for example Draughts/Checkers (pages 26–29), are a form of standardized warfare, with two equal and opposing armies struggling for supremacy and power. In other battle-games, such as Go (pages 124–127) or Mu Torere (pages 42–43), the aim of each army is to blockade the other by seizing either territory or strategic points.

A second group of battle-games involves two sides of unequal numbers and different capabilities, so that the game takes the form of a hunt rather than a war. One family of these games, represented by Fox and Geese (pages 50–51), originated in northern Europe, while another, including games such as Cows and Leopards (pages 62–63), developed in southern Asia.

Another group of games is built around the idea of a race. Nyout (pages 32–33), Pachisi (pages 110–111) and Patolli (pages 108–109) are examples of this type of game. In these games, the players are not seeking to win by defeating each other by elimination or immobilization, but are competing to pass successfully along a fixed course from beginning to end. Sometimes the course is marked with pitfalls and dangers, while in other games the chief

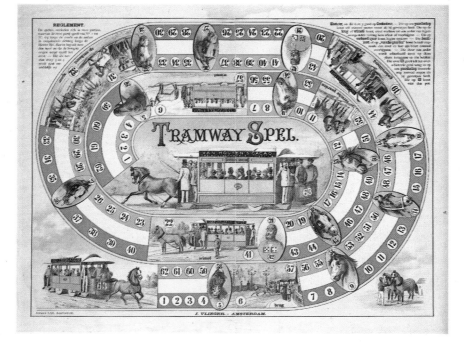

*Above: A race game which was published to commemorate the Great Exhibition of 1851, held in the Crystal Palace, London – shown in the centre panel of the game.*

*Left: A nineteenth century variation on the Game of Goose which reflects one aspect of contemporary Dutch social history by its depiction of horse-drawn trams.*

*Right: Another spiral race game, providing a potted history lesson, from an English viewpoint, from Adam and Eve to the beginning of Queen Victoria's reign.*

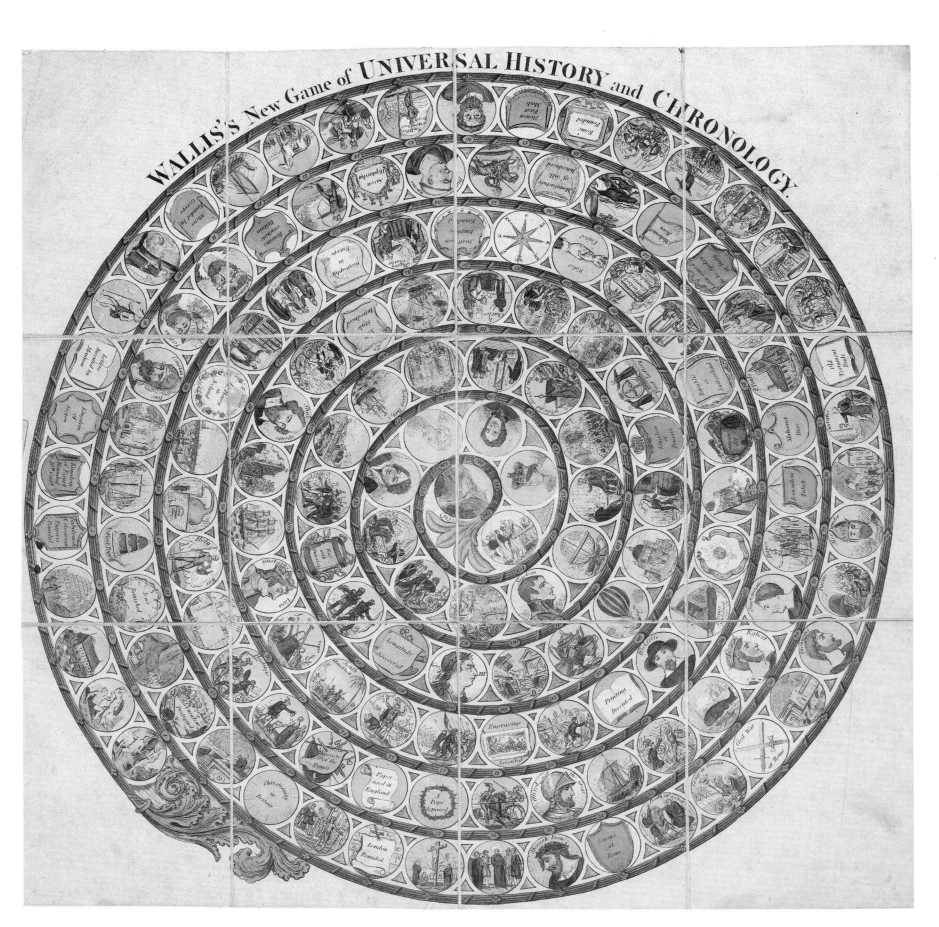

WALLIS'S New Game of UNIVERSAL HISTORY and CHRONOLOGY.

danger is the possibility of attack by an enemy piece. The three games mentioned above are all of the 'cross and circle' type, where the pieces go round the board like the hands of a clock and are taken off at a marked winning point.

During recent centuries in the West, one of the most common forms of race game has been based on the idea of reaching a goal in life, overcoming difficulties and hindrances on the way. This type of game developed in the eighteenth century, and the Game of the Goose (pages 140–141) is probably the original from which other variants are derived. The factors common to all this group are the spiral form of the board and the movement of the pieces from the outside towards the centre. The essential similarity of all these boards is disguised by their varied appearance and the many different aims that each displays; also the sets of difficulties or hazards involved being particular to every game.

A further group of boardgames is characterized by the fact that one person plays on his own without needing an opponent. This kind of boardgame presents a single player with the possibility of defeat or success in the solitary solving of a problem or set of problems in particular circumstances. Solitaire (pages 54–55) and Pentalpha (pages 60–61) are examples of boardgames for one player.

Mancala is the general name given to a large group of games. Although these are usually included in the category of boardgames, they have not been reproduced in the book, as it would be difficult for any of them to be played on a flat page. The main feature shared by all members of the Mancala group is that the board consists of two, or sometimes four, rows of shallow depressions into which a number of counters, mostly pebbles or seeds, are placed. These are then redistributed by each player in turn. Like a number of other games, the earliest examples of this game are from the ancient Middle East, in this case Egypt.

Several sets of hollows arranged for a Mancala game have been found cut into the roofing slabs of a temple built at Kurna on the west bank of the Nile in about 1400 B.C. It seems that these and a number of other boardgames were cut by the masons for use while working on the project and before the stones were finally positioned, since some have been cut away at the edges when the stones were fitted into place. Other sets have been found cut into a pylon built in front of the great temple at Karnak during the Ptolemaic period in the last three centuries before Christ. Other boards suitable for games of the Mancala type have been found in Arabia, predating the establishment of the Muslim religion. The game from which the whole family now takes its name was described by Edward Lane, an Englishman who spent a number of years living in Cairo in the 1830's. At this time traditional Egyptian society was only just starting to come under the influence of modern European civilization. Lane relates how this game was played in contemporary coffee-houses.

The rules of this fascinating game have been included here as the board may be marked out with the required number of hollows wherever the ground is suitable. For example, any sandy beach provides a good surface or the game may be played in a garden, or in the dust of a country path, which is one of the most familiar sites for the game in Africa.

RULES
1. The board is made by hollowing two rows of six shallow circular depressions: one row for each of two players.
2. Seventy-two pebbles or counters are used. One player, without counting them out, places about half in each row, either in the middle hollows of each row, or in the hollow which is on each player's extreme left.
3. The other player picks up all the counters from any one of his pits, and sows one in each pit rotating from left to right along the rest of his row and then down his opponent's row, continuing until all the counters have been placed. From A to F, F to a and f to A (see figure A).

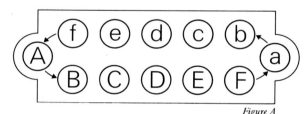

*Figure A*

4. If the last counter is sown into a pit already containing one or three counters, the player *bears off* those two or four (including the newcomer) and any counters there may be in the pit opposite. If one or more of the immediately preceding pits contains two or four counters, he *bears off* these too, together with any counters in the pit opposite.
5. If the last counter of a lap falls into a pit with an even number of counters already in it, the player lifts all these counters out and sows them rotating from left to right around the board.
6. If the last counter of a lap falls into an empty pit, that turn ends.
7. Each player plays in turn, continuing until his last counter lands in an empty pit.
8. If there is more than one counter in a player's row and his opponent has none on his side, the player must put one of these counters in the end pit of his opponent's row on his opponent's extreme left. However, if there are only two counters left on the board, they become the property of the first player to get them both in his row.
9. When there are no counters left in play the round ends and each player counts the counters in his possession. The difference between the two numbers is the score for that round.
10. A new round is begun and play continues until one player has a score of sixty.

*A game of Mancala is enjoyed by two girls from the Dan tribe in the hinterland of Liberia, West Africa.*

Forms of Mancala are found throughout Black Africa, but because the game is played using hollows scooped out of the ground, or perishable material like wood is used to make a board, it is not possible to determine exactly where this game originated. It may have developed in ancient Egypt and then spread south-west (there were extensive trade-links in the period of the Pharaohs between Egypt and both Central and West Africa), or the game may have originated in Black Africa and been taken to Egypt at a very early date. There are a number of different forms of Mancala played in the different regions of West Africa. The early seventeenth century traveller Richard Jobson described one form of the game, called Wari, in the Gambia territory:

'In the heat of the day, the men will come forth and sit themselves in companies, under the shady trees, to receive the fresh aire, and there passe the time in communication, having only one kind of game to recreate themselves with all, and that is a piece of wood, certaine great holes cut, which they set upon the ground betwixt two of them, with a number of some thirty pibble stones, after a manner of counting, they take one from the other, until one is possessed of all, whereat some of them are wondrous nimble.'

The inhabitants of West Africa who were

enslaved and taken to the Americas brought much of their culture with them. This included their religion, which survives in altered form in Brazil and as Voodoo in Haiti, and also a number of forms of Mancala such as Wari.

There are four variants of Wari found today in the West Indies and Guyana, one of which is known as Awari. Traditionally this game is played by men rather than women. However, some women do play it but if a woman becomes too expert at the game, most men will refuse to play her, since it is considered humiliating to lose to a woman. Another form of Mancala, known as Pallanguli, is played by the Tamils in southern India and Sri Lanka (Ceylon). Here it is usually played by women, but sometimes men use it as a gambling game. Unless this form of the game arose spontaneously without any connection with other Mancala games, which seems extremely unlikely, it is probable that it reached the Tamils either from Muslim invaders or through the trade links between India and Africa.

More complex forms of Mancala, involving four rows rather than two, are played in East and South Africa. Four-row Mancala boards made of stone have been found in and near the mines of Zimbabwe, the site of a civilization that flourished from about 1450 A.D. to about 1800 A.D., in the area now known as Rhodesia/Zimbabwe. One of these four-row Mancala games, called Hus, is played by the Hottentots. It is unusual in that the stones remain on the board and are not *borne off* by the players. The rules of this game for two players are given below.

## RULES

1. There are four rows of eight holes, two rows for each player.

2. Each player has two stones or counters in each of the holes of his back row and two in each of the right-hand four holes of his front row (see figure B).

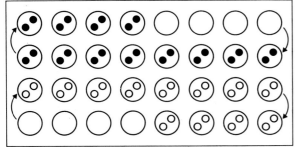

*Figure B*

3. All moves are made in a clockwise direction, each player moving only around his own two rows.

4. The first player is chosen by lot, lifts the counters from any one of his holes, and sows them one at a time into the following holes. If the last stone falls into an empty hole, that is the end of his turn, and his opponent takes a turn.

5. If the last counter is sown into a hole which already has counters in it, all of these counters,

*Ivory Chessmen: a mounted knight from Canton, China, standing twenty-three centimetres (nine inches) high and carved from a single tusk. The howdah-carrying elephant represents a king and was made about 1790 in Delhi, India. In the original Indian game an elephant was used in the same way as we now use a bishop. Its identity was changed by Muslim Arabs for a V-shaped piece which Europeans took to represent a bishop's mitre.*

including the one just thrown into it, are lifted up and sown one by one into the next holes.

6. If a player's sowing ends in a loaded front-row hole, and the corresponding hole in his opponent's front row has counters in it, he takes up those counters and sows them instead of his own. More than one of these captures can be made in the same turn of play.

7. If a player captures counters from one of his opponent's front holes, and the corresponding enemy back hole also contains counters, he takes up and sows these too and also captures and uses the counters from any other one of his opponent's holes.

8. A player must begin his turn from a hole which contains two or more counters: if he has only *singletons* he cannot play and loses the game.

9. If a player captures all his opponent's counters, that constitutes a double win.

10. The player who wins one game begins the next, and the overall winner is the player who wins the best of seven games.

As well as corresponding to certain important human situations in their basic structure, boardgames often refer to specific historical circumstances in their names and those of their

pieces. Dablot Prejjesne (pages 152–153), for example, mirrors the conflict between nomadic herders and settled agriculturalists, while Asalto (pages 52–53) is a version of Fox and Geese updated at the time of the Indian Mutiny.

Chess pieces have for centuries been carved in forms based on local political personalities. Napoleon, for example, is represented (always as the White King) in many chess sets made at the turn of the nineteenth-century. A chess set carved in the Soviet Union in 1930 shows one side as Communists and the other as Capitalists. An English set made in 1973 represents the British political scene of the time. The white pieces stand for the Conservatives, Mr. Heath and his cabinet, whereas the black pieces portray the Labour opposition led by Mr. Wilson.

The development of Chess also reflects in broader terms the different societies through which it has passed. In ancient India, where this game probably originated, the pieces stood for the different arms of warfare: chariots (which became rooks), cavalry (still recognisable as knights), elephants (changed into bishops), the king and his prime minister (now the queen). In Chinese Chess (pages 24–25) the king has altered into a general, the queen is a mandarin, and in addition to the other pieces there is a cannon, a reminder of the fact that it was the Chinese who invented gunpowder.

The changing identity of the piece now known as the bishop is particularly interesting, showing as it does how different cultures change and reinterpret what they adopt from the outside world in accordance with their own preconceptions and prejudices. In the original Indian game, this piece was an elephant, and was shown as such in the way it was carved. Taken from India to Persia, Chess was adopted by the Muslim Arabs in the seventh or eighth centuries after they had overrun Persia. The Islamic tradition, however, tends to be hostile to the artistic representation of any object, preferring art to be non-representational. A V-shaped nick was therefore cut into the top of the elephant-piece, so that it would remind players of an elephant with its big, flapping ears. When the game reached Europe, the form of the piece reminded western Christians of a bishop's mitre, and that is how the piece got its present name. It may seem strange to us that bishops should be part of a battle game, but in the Middle Ages it was not unheard of for churchmen to take an active part in fighting when they considered it necessary or appropriate. The old French epic 'Song of Roland', for instance, dating in its present form from the eleventh-century recounts how Archbishop Turpin joined in the battle against the Saracens, which was presumably perfectly acceptable to both the author and his audience.

Race-games of the Game of the Goose family are especially easy to adapt to particular circumstances, and both Up to Klondyke (pages 74–75) and Gold Rush (pages 72–73) focus on the excitement and enthusiasm that the nineteenth century gold-strikes aroused.

Up to Klondyke was almost certainly published within a couple of years of the discovery of gold in the Klondike in 1896. The story of how it was found, at Dawson off the Yukon river in north-western Canada, is a classic tale of gold prospecting. The three men who staked the claim at Fort Cudahy, the Mounted Police post eighty miles down the river, were George Carmack and two Indian companions called 'Skookum' Jim and 'Taglish' Charlie. The creek where the gold was found was soon renamed Bonanza Creek and rapidly became the centre of a mining camp. After a ship had called in at Seattle from Alaska in the spring of 1897, news of the Klondike was flashed round the world by telegraph. During the next fews months thousands of men and several women struggled to the Klondike over one of several difficult routes. One was by boat to Skagway or Dyea and then either over the Chilcoot Pass or via the White Pass to Lake Bennett, down the White Horse Rapids to the Yukon and on down to Bonanza Creek. Thousands died on the way. An even harder journey was from Edmonton northwards along the Mackenzie river and west down the Porcupine and up the Yukon.

Within a few years Dawson had grown from a few

shacks to a city of twenty-five thousand, and at the peak of the boom in 1900 gold to the value of over twenty-two million dollars was produced. Only the gold, however, kept people there and when that ran out the bulk of the population left, so that by the middle of this century Dawson was a sleepy town of a few hundred inhabitants.

Another kind of race-game, Snakes and Ladders (pages 134–135), with a particularly interesting history, was used to combine pleasure with instruction until the modern form which is purely for fun. It is based on a game called 'Moksha-Patamu' used in India for religious education. According to the Hindu sages, virtuous acts, represented by ladders, shorten the journey of a soul through a number of incarnations to Nirvana, the state of ultimate perfection. Human sin, symbolized by the head of the snake, leads to reincarnation in a lower, animal form. Thus Snakes and Ladders is a symbolic moral journey through life to heaven.

In the eighteenth and nineteenth centuries, many spiral games were produced to teach children history, geography, scripture, botany and other natural sciences. Simpler games were designed for amusement only and others commemorated important topical events, such as the Great Exhibition of 1851 held in London, England.

Almost certainly the first boardgames had a religious rather than a purely secular use. The earliest known game-board, now in the Musée du Cinquanténaire in Brussels, Belgium, dates back to between 4000 and 3500 B.C. It was found in a pre-dynastic cemetery at El-Mahasna, about eight miles north of Abydos in Upper Egypt, together with a large number of clay and ivory objects. The board was nearly eighteen centimetres (seven inches) long and seven centimetres (two and three-quarter inches) wide, standing on two crossbars. The surface was divided into three by six squares and with the board were eleven conical pieces. The archaeologists who found the grave believed that its occupant may have been a magician or soothsayer and the game used for divination and foretelling the future.

Other early game-boards include one from Beth Shemesh, Israel, dated about 2000 B.C., and the Royal Game of Ur, discovered by Sir Leonard Woolley in Iraq and dated about 3000 B.C. The divinatory use of boardgames has not only been confined to ancient times, nor to the Middle East. Zohn Ahl (pages 36–37) was used for fortune-telling in North America up to a century ago and in Madagascar, political and military decisions were taken with the help of Fanorona (pages 150–151) at the end of the nineteenth century. Linstron's Fortune Telling Game, dating from the early years of the twentieth century, is a modern example of the same idea. During play the curved end of the Linstron's board is raised slightly and marbles are propelled by a spring from the tunnel on the right, coming to rest either in a hole linked to a card, or out of play against the base line.

On the back of the board is an explanation of what each card represents as follows:

Hearts/Diamonds *good*
Clubs/Spades *bad*
Red picture cards *blondes*
Black picture cards *brunettes*
King *a married man*
Queen *a woman*
Jack *an unmarried man*
Ace *a letter*
Two *divorce*
Three *health*
(if red *good* if black, *poor*)
Four *a surprise*
(if black, *a disappointment*)
Five *a change*
Six *business affairs*
Seven *marriage*
Eight *travel*
Nine *love*
Ten *money*

Examples
Ace of Diamonds, Jack of Clubs, Four of Hearts.
Interpretation: *you will receive a letter from a dark young man which will be a pleasant surprise.*

Queen of Diamonds, Five of Spades, Nine of Diamonds, King of Spades.
Interpretation: *a woman will cause a change in the matrimonial affairs of a dark-haired young man.*

Ten of Diamonds, Six of Hearts.
Interpretation: *you will receive money, probably from a business deal enabling you to make a change for the better.*

Jack of Spades, Nine of Clubs, Jack of Hearts.
Interpretation: *two young men are in love with you, one is dark and the other fair. Both are unhappy, and the affair is ill-favoured.*

Ace of Hearts, Six of Diamonds, Ten of Hearts.
Interpretation: *you will receive a business letter relating to money. The transaction will be successful.*

Eight of Diamonds, Three of Hearts, Five of Clubs, Six of Spades.
Interpretation: *you will travel, your health will improve, but there will be an unfortunate change in your affairs.*

It seems that boardgames were not only used to divine the future, but were played in the afterlife. According to Ancient Egyptian belief, the souls of those who died had to pass through various trials before their final judgement. If successful, the souls entered the Blessed Fields of the Dead. Here they could enjoy life after death in such pleasant ways as playing a game of Senat, as shown in the illustration to the right. This is part of a papyrus text from the Book of the Dead, which was commissioned for Ani, a Royal Scribe (c. 1250 B.C.), to help him on his journey to the world of the dead.

As the gods are often believed to intervene in games of chance, it is not surprising that many cultures have a particular deity to whom gamblers may appeal when trying to influence their luck. Shown on the right is a reproduction of a Pre-Columbian statuette from the northern coast of Ecuador. This represents a god of gambling, comparable to Macuilxochitl, the Aztec deity who was also the god of sport and pleasure. Both cultures usually portray these figures wearing a helmet-mask in the shape of a bird's head. The Ecuador deity is shown playing pan-pipes, like his Greek counterpart, Dionysus. The vessel attached to the statuette's back was for holding a libation to the god when gamblers wanted to enlist his aid, just as the Aztec players of Patolli (pages 108–109) called on their god Macuilxochitl for help. Less powerful than the deities are the talismans and lucky charms used by gamesters over the centuries.

The notion underlying this supernatural aspect of boardgames is that the gods control what is otherwise called 'chance', or the random fall of the

*Above: In this Egyptian painting, Ani, a Royal Scribe during the nineteenth dynasty plays a game of Senat, watched by his wife.*
*Right: A god of gambling and music from the Jama-Coaque culture of Ecuador, which flourished from 500 B.C. to 500 A.D.*

dice. According to one Greek tradition, it was Palamedes who invented dice, to pass the time during the ten-year siege of Troy. In fact, however, dice go back long before the Trojan War. The earliest kinds of dice were probably casting sticks, made from split twigs – rounded on one side and flat on the other – used in a simple 'heads or tails' system with the odds changing subtly according to the number of sticks thrown. Cowrie shells, landing either mouth side up or mouth side down, serve the same purpose. Pyramid-shaped dice and long dice with four marked sides were both used by the Egyptians. Another early form of dice was the bone from a dog's or a sheep's foot, called an astragalus, whose different sides were numbered from one to six. Such astragali are probably referred to in the Bible in the expression 'casting lots', and are still used today by some Arabian and Amerindian tribes. Cubic dice probably developed from astraguli, but unlike the natural bones, the faces of accurately made cubic dice have equal chances of falling uppermost. The present arrangement, in which the spots on any two opposite faces add up to seven, dates from about 1400 B.C.

A poem called the 'Gamester's Lament' from the earliest Indian poetry, the 'Rig-Veda', refers to dice, which in this case were probably made from nuts:
'Don't play with dice, but plough your furrow!
Delight in your property, prize it highly!
Look to your cattle and look to your wife, you gambler!'
These lines are typical of the hostility that gamblers have mostly had to face, being accused of neglecting their duties in life and wasting their substance.

It is interesting to note that the passion for gambling is not prevalent throughout the world. There are several cultures where gambling is not practised. The Aborigines of Australia, traditionally indifferent to the accumulation of wealth, do not gamble, but neither do the Melanesians of Papua, who spend a lot of time acquiring property. Where gambling is common, though, it is often curbed. This can be by social disapproval, as in Victorian times, when the gaming-boards were made in the form of books for the sake of secret gamesters; or by legislation, which leads to ingenious devices like the whisky glass shown on page 17, where the dice could easily be concealed by the hand of an illegal gambler if the police came by.

Whatever the prevailing moral attitude towards dicing, it is clear that boardgames themselves are universally popular. This is proved by the substantial literature on the subject which, in the case of Chess, runs into many thousands of volumes. Of all the books written on boardgames, the first is still considered one of the best. This superb manuscript was compiled between 1251 and 1282 A.D., by command of Alfonso X, King of Leon and Castile. It is now in the monastery library of St. Lorenze del Escorial, a few miles from Madrid, Spain. It consists of ninety-eight pages, bound in sheepskin. The Spanish text, written in a beautiful script, is one of the first masterpieces of literature to be expressed in colloquial language. There are many illuminated initials and a hundred and fifty coloured drawings, ten being full plates. This 'Libro de Juegos' (Book of Games) is divided into four sections: the first part deals with Chess; the second with dice games; the third with varieties of Backgammon; the fourth contains a miscellany of games ranging from the complexities of Grande Acedrez, an enlarged variety of Chess, to the simplicity of Alquerque.

In his introduction, King Alfonso explained that God intended everyone to enjoy themselves with many games, especially boardgames for '. . . those who like to enjoy themselves in private to avoid the annoyance and unpleasantness of public places, or those who have fallen into another's power, either in prison, or slavery, or as seafarers, and in general all those who are looking for a pleasant pastime which will bring them comfort and dispel their boredom. For that reason, I, Don Alfonso . . . have commanded this book to be written.'

King Alfonso's high opinion of the enjoyment which boardgames provide continues to be endorsed by players of all ages everywhere.

*Right: The Spanish king, Alfonso X, from an illustration in the 'Book of Games', which was compiled at his command.*

*Below: Box-shaped boards, made in about 1890, simulate books to disguise their frivolous nature.*

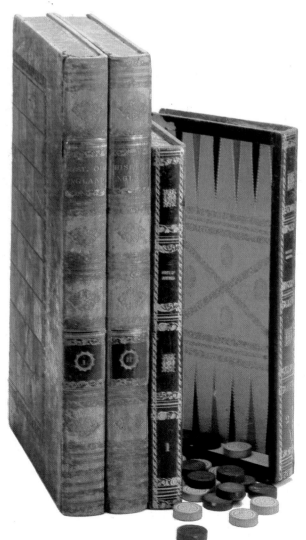

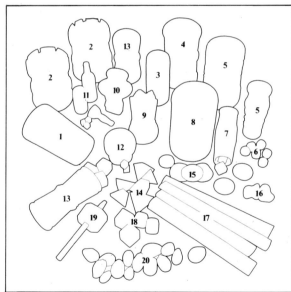

1. Whisky glass with three dice in a false bottom.
2. English wooden dicing cup and matching money-box (c.1800).
3. Mauchline-ware dicing cup (c.1910).
4. English ivory dicing cup.
5. Chinese dicing cups, carved ivory (c.1850).
6. Six modern Chinese dice.
7. English plain ivory dicing cup with three dice stamped GR as proof of tax paid (c.1790).
8. Tortoiseshell dicing cup (c.1880).
9. Ivory and teak dicing cup from India (c.1900).
10. Dicing cup disguised as a minstrel whose top hat contains two small red dice.
11. Two wooden dicing cups shaped like bottles, souvenirs from the Northeast Exhibition held at

Newcastle upon Tyne, England in 1929.
12. Dicing box for Thai Backgammon based on the same principle as the Roman pyrgus.
13. Crown and Anchor dice (c.1940) emerging from a wooden dicing cup, one of a pair (c.1850).
14. Six reproduction pyramidal dice based on originals from Sumer (c.3000 B.C.).
15. Various Roman coins.
16. Two modern astragali based on original examples from 4000 years ago.
17. Reproduction Amerindian dicing-sticks, (nineteenth century).
18. Modern red 'perfect dice' from a Reno casino in Nevada, U.S.A. and the more familiar white, round-cornered 'shop dice'.
19. Eight-sided teetotum.
20. Cowrie shells used as dice.

# Chess I

The origin of Chess, according to scholarly research, is traced back as far as sixth century India, making it a later invention than other board games, for example, Alquerque (see pages 146–147) or Backgammon (see pages 88–91). The Indian ancestor of Chess was known as Chaturanga, the sanskrit word for the four members or components of an Indian army: elephants, horses, chariots and foot soldiers. From India the game travelled to Persia where, according to the Persian national epic 'Shah-namah', it was brought as a gift to the king, Khosrau I Anushirvan, who was told he must divine the secrets of the game or pay a tribute. Seven days later one of his wise men arrived with the solution. The game was called Chatrang in Persian but when the Arabs invaded the country they changed this to Shantranj and became the first scientific exponents of Chess.

The Moors (as the Arabs were known in medieval Europe) introduced Shatranj into Spain and from here it spread northwards to France. It may have reached Italy through trade with Byzantium. The game was probably brought to much of northwest Europe by the Vikings. The beautiful Isle of Lewis Chess set, now in the British Museum in London, England, dates back to the twelfth century and was certainly brought to the Hebrides by the Vikings.

From its earliest recorded beginnings, Chess seems to have been capable of exercising an uncanny fascination over all who played it, which may account for the many colourful legends which have been woven around the game. Perhaps as a result of these spellbinding qualities chess was sometimes also considered diabolical. For example the Koran denounces the game in the fifth chapter because it employs graven images which are strictly forbidden in the Islamic faith. A monk in the twelfth century decreed that those who played Chess did so under pain of excommunication. In 1291, the Archbishop of Canterbury threatened the clergy of Coxford in Norfolk, England, with a diet of bread and water if they did not stop playing Chess. However, what some saw as a force for evil, others used as an instrument for preaching morality. An Italian monk, Jacobus de Cessolis, writing in the thirteenth century, used the strategy of the game as the basis for his sermons; this work forms the basis for the first English book on the subject, printed in the fifteenth century by William Caxton as The Game of Chesse.

Literary references to Chess are so numerous that they would fill a whole book by themselves. This would include quotations from the 'Roman de la Rose', Chaucer's 'The Boke of the Duchesse' and Castiglione's 'The Book of the Courtier'; and is evidence of the importance attributed to the game in European culture. It was considered an accomplishment to be a skilled Chess player. All the Tudor monarchs of England excelled at the game. Napoleon was also a keen player but, predictably, a bad loser.

Modern Chess bears little relation to the game of Chaturanga which was played in Hindustan in the sixth century. The chariots have become rooks, the horses changed to knights and the elephants to bishops. The most significant change has been the emergence of the queen, from a position of little consequence as the king's minister, into her present role as the most versatile and influential piece on the board. The strategy of the game has altered; originally it was slow and ponderous but with the increased mobility of the queen and bishop, and the optional opening pawn move of two squares instead of one, the tempo quickened. Perhaps the most direct link with the past is preserved in the term 'checkmate' which comes from the Persian 'shah' or king and 'mat' meaning helpless.

As the popularity of Chess grew, players of exceptional skill began to appear. One of the earliest of these 'masters' was the Italian, Paolo Boi, who toured Europe earning his livelihood by playing Chess. The stunt of playing Chess blindfolded was performed as early as the fifteenth century by a Mogul player, Ala'addin at-Tabrizi. But it was only in the last century that the game became an acknowledged way of life and 'Grandmasters' became figures of world renown. One of the outstanding names is that of an American, Paul Morphy (1837–1884), who resigned from the game at a comparatively early age and throughout his career displayed many of the temperamental characteristics we have come to associate with chess prodigies in recent years. Another international 'Grandmaster' was the Cuban, Jose Raoul Capablanca (1888–1942).

The first international chess tournament was held in London in 1851 and organized by the British player Howard Staunton. He also designed a board in 1843 which has since become the standard European board. In this century the player who has achieved most notoriety is Bobby Fischer, born in Chicago in 1943. He became a 'Grandmaster' at the age of fifteen. In 1972 he defeated Boris Spassky of Russia at Reykjavik, Iceland, to become the World Champion. A Hungarian engineer at the end of the eighteenth century invented a mechanical chess player known as 'The Turk' which provided an entertaining side-show. It was later discovered that a live player concealed beneath all the gadgetry had been working the pieces with magnets.

Recently small chess boards have appeared on the market with specially programmed computers built in for players to learn the game or exercise their skills in solitude.

The endless fascination of the game continues to attract Chess players and accumulates modern stories of legendary skill. Only one example of an ancient Mongolian fable from the vast store, can be retold here.

Long ago a hunter went alone up into a mountain valley and saw two old men playing Chess. The young man rode up to them, tethered his horse and stood unobserved by their side, so engrossed were they in their play. The spectator was a Chess enthusiast and he soon realised that this was no ordinary contest, indeed the subtlety of the play seemed inspired. The longer the young man watched, the more fascinating the game became. As it approached its climax the experts bent over the board, and the onlooker, oblivious of all else, followed in silence every move of their play.

At last the young man noticed that one of the players had fallen into a trap set by his opponent and was threatened with 'mate'. The hunter sighed in sympathy. The players gave a start at the sound, turned their heads and on seeing the youth, disappeared together with the board and the pieces. Only a large flat boulder covered with moss and two smaller boulders confronted the astonished young man.

He turned to his horse; but it had vanished. After searching among the undergrowth he found a horse's skull overgrown with lichen, a rusty bit between its teeth, and a greenish copper stirrup nearby where the saddle must have fallen.

Dismayed he hastened to the village, which he hardly recognised and which was full of strangers. Finally he found a very old woman who had heard from her grandfather a tale about how an uncle of his grandfather had been lost in the distant past while hunting up the valley.

Legend states that the hunter lived for many years, and was invincible at Chess, a legacy of watching a game played by immortals.

Chess is played on a chequer of eight by eight squares, first used in the Middle Ages. It is a battle game for two players who face each other across the board, placed so that each has a white square at the nearest right hand corner. The opening positions of the pieces are shown in figure A (see page 20). Each player starts with eight pawns, two bishops, two knights, two rooks, a queen and a king, in ascending order of importance. The pieces have different powers of movement.

# Chess II

**PLAYERS**
Two.

**PIECES**
Sixteen for each player. (See equipment sheet: king, queen, two bishops, two knights, two rooks and eight pawns.)

**AIM**
To immobilize (checkmate) the opposing king.

**ORIGIN**
India or Persia, 400–600 A.D.

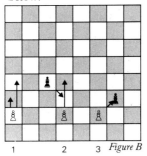

*Figure A*

## MOVES OF PIECES

### PAWNS
Move one square forward, except on their first move when they are permitted to move two squares forward if desired. They capture by moving one square diagonally forwards onto the square of the piece they capture. (See figure B.)

Even if a pawn moves forward two squares on its initial move, it is vulnerable to capture by any opposing pawn moving diagonally forward to occupy the square it would have occupied if it had initially advanced only one square. This is known as capture 'en passant' (in passing), shown in figure B below.

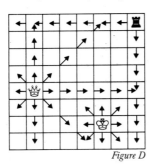

1        2        3   *Figure B*

When a pawn reaches the eighth *rank*, it can be promoted to any piece desired. This is usually a queen, but in special circumstances a knight, with its power of leaping, may be preferred.

### BISHOPS
Move diagonally in any direction any number of vacant squares, but always on the same colour, one of each player's bishops being confined to black squares, and the other to white. (See figure C.)

### KNIGHTS
Move two squares in any straight line except the

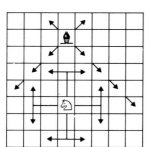

*Figure C*

diagonal, and then one square at right angles to the first half of the move, or one square in one direction and then two squares at right angles to it. During this L-shaped move, a knight is allowed to *jump* over intervening pieces of either colour without capturing them. (See figure C.)

### ROOKS
Move any number of vacant squares in any straight line except the diagonal. (See figure D.)

### QUEENS
Move diagonally like a bishop, or in any straight

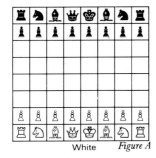

*Figure D*

line like a rook, backwards or forwards, and are the most powerful pieces on the board. (See figure D.)

### KINGS
Move one square in any direction (see figure D), and each may 'castle' once only in a game.

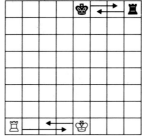

*Figure E*

'Castling' is a combined move of the king and one of the rooks. The king is moved two squares towards the rook, which is then placed on the other side of the king. 'Castling' is permitted only if:
a. There is no intervening piece between the king and the rook.
b. Neither piece has previously moved.
c. The king must not be 'in check', and must not cross or move onto a square under attack from an enemy piece. (See figure E.) If a king is under attack from an enemy piece the opposing player calls 'check'. If a player cannot protect his king from the attack by capturing the threatening piece, or moving the king, or by interposing one of his own pieces in the line of the attack, the king suffers 'checkmate', and the game is finished and lost.

### CAPTURING
Chess pieces capture by moving onto a square occupied by an opposing piece (the latter is removed from the board). Any piece can be captured by any other except for the king, who suffers 'checkmate' instead; then the game is over. Instead of one player winning by 'checkmating' the other's king, the game

may end in a draw. This occurs in the following two ways:

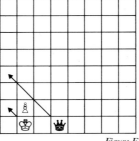

*Figure F*

(1) 'Perpetual check' when one king suffers a series of 'checks' from which he cannot escape. (See figure F.)

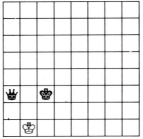

*Figure G*

(2) 'Stalemate' occurs when a player cannot make a legal move. (See figure G.)
The object of the game is to 'checkmate' the opposing king. The capture of enemy pieces may assist in this, but is not always necessary. It is possible to win a game without the loss of a single piece on the other side. (See figure H.)

*Figure H*

## RULES
1. White has first move. In a series of games each player retains his own colour and the advantage of having first move alternates. If a game is annulled, the same player makes the first move in the next game.

2. If a player is given a handicap he has choice of colour, and first move in every game unless otherwise agreed.

3. If a piece is misplaced at the beginning of a game, or is omitted except when a handicap is being given, the game must be restarted.

4. The players move their pieces alternately.

5. If a player touches a piece, he must move it if legally able to do so. If he cannot move it he must move his king.

6. If a player touches more than one piece his opponent may select which must be moved. If no touched piece can be moved, he must move his king.

7. If a player wishes to adjust a piece he must announce 'adjusting' before touching it.

8. If a player touches one of the opposing pieces he must capture it if he can, and if this is impossible he must move his king.

9. A move is finished when the player ceases touching his piece, but as long as his hand is in contact with it, he may move it onto any square that it commands that he has not previously touched in his deliberations. If a player touches all the squares which the piece commands, he must play it onto any one of them that his opponent may choose.

10. On reaching the eighth *rank* a pawn must be exchanged for another piece of the same colour. This completes the move. By these means a player may have two or more queens, three knights, and so on, in play at the same time.

11. Each player may 'castle' once in a game, obeying the criteria mentioned above.

12. The capture of a pawn 'en passant' (in passing) is obligatory if no other move is possible.

13. If an illegal move is made, the player must retract it, and either move the piece legally if it is his turn to play or move his king, at his opponent's choosing.

14. If a player captures a piece illegally, he must take it legally if this is possible, or move his own piece legally, or move his king, at his opponent's choosing.

15. Moves by a king in 'check' are illegal if they do not relieve the 'check'.

*Chessplayers, from a medieval manuscript.*

16. If a false move has been made, unless the move and all moves subsequent to it can be retracted and a proper move made, the game is annulled (for example a player's two bishops found on squares of the same colour).

17. A penalty cannot be imposed after the opponent has touched a piece in reply to an illegal move.

18. A player may claim a draw if:
a. The same move or the same series of moves has been played three times in succession.
b. The same position has occurred three times when it is the player's turn to move.
c. Fifty moves have been played without any piece being captured and with no pawn being moved.

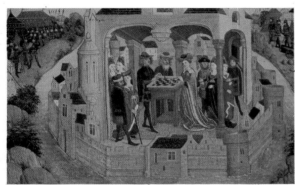

*Indian miniature of ladies playing chess.*

# Maharajah & the Sepoys

*This game is played with a chessboard and chessmen (see figure J).*

Maharajah and the Sepoys is an interesting game, although if the player with the sepoys never leaves a piece unsupported, he will finally hem in the maharajah and win the game. The great mobility of the Sepoys is always a danger and the king may be trapped behind his own pieces early in the game. Later when the board is clear, the sepoys may succeed in driving him into a corner with an inevitable 'checkmate'.

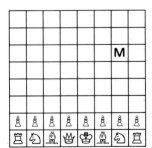

*Figure J*

**PLAYERS**
Two.

**PIECES**
Sixteen chessmen for one player; one maharajah (Chess king or queen of opposing colour) for the other.

**AIM**
Immobilization (checkmate) of the maharajah or the king.

**ORIGIN**
India.

## RULES

1. One player arranges his pieces, which represent sepoys, as for a game of chess.

2. The other has a single piece, the maharajah, which is placed on any vacant square on the board (see figure J).

3. The maharajah has the power of movement of a queen and a knight.

4. The other pieces have the same moves as in Chess.

5. The maharajah has the second move in every game.

*Chessplayers, detail from the 'Histoire du Grand Alexandre'.*

# Gala

This once popular game, also known as Farmer's Chess, survives only in the villages of Schleswig-Holstein, West Germany, where a few antique boards are found in remote farm houses. The checkered board of ten by ten squares is similar to that used for standard Draughts/Checkers with the addition of a central cross. Pieces moving over this central cross change direction, as explained in the rules.

Each player starts with twenty pieces consisting of two kings, five rooks, five bishops and eight pawns (see figure A). The pieces are made of light wood for one player and dark for the other and are all of the same shape, resembling small skittles, though the kings are a little larger than the others. The ranks are indicated by the colour of the upper half of the pieces: the bishops–red; the rooks–green; the kings–gold and the pawns unpainted.

The object of the game is to capture both opposing kings; all capture is by "replacement".

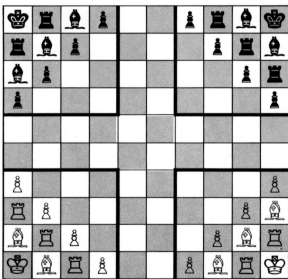

*Figure A*

*May-day Gala celebration in a German village.*

**PLAYERS**
Two.

**PIECES**
**Twenty for each side: two kings, five rooks, five bishops, eight pawns. (See equipment sheet.)**

**AIM**
**To capture both opposing kings.**

**ORIGIN**
**Europe, probably medieval.**

## MOVES OF PIECES

1. The pawns move diagonally up to the deflection-line, or onto the first square beyond it, remaining on the same colour. After crossing the line they can only move one square at a time in any direction, including backwards.

2. If a pawn returns to its original row of squares, its next move can only be diagonally forwards as on its first move.

3. The rooks move in any straight line except the diagonal and in any direction for any number of squares, but on crossing a deflection-line they move diagonally to the next deflection-line, that is, one square diagonally on. The whole movement can be completed as one turn of play, or the rook can stop on any square along the route. The next move after the diagonal-deflection in the deflection-zone continues in any straight line except diagonally, as far as desired, or until meeting another deflection-line. (See figure B.)

4. The bishops move diagonally any number of squares in any direction until crossing a deflection-line. After the first square behind the deflection-line within the deflection-zone, they travel in any straight line except the diagonal.

5. On crossing a second deflection-line the bishops resume their diagonal movement.

6. The kings move one square in any direction and are not affected by the deflection-lines.

7. If a king reaches one of the four central squares of the cross formed by the deflection-lines, at the next move he may be placed on any free square on the board, excluding the forty squares occupied by pieces at the beginning of the game. This can be a valuable privilege.

## RULES

1. Black has first move.

2. Kings, rooks, and bishops can capture when passing over a deflection-line.

3. If, however, a bishop is standing on a square next to a deflection-line, it cannot capture a piece standing on the adjacent square over the line (see figure B).

4. Pawns cannot capture when crossing over a deflection-line, but can on the next move.

5. If a player makes a move threatening a king he is obliged to call 'Gala', and the opponent must protect the piece or move it to safety.

6. If the threatened king cannot be protected it is removed from the board at the opponent's next move.

7. When one player has lost both his kings he has lost the game.

8. If only two opposing kings are left on the board the game is drawn.

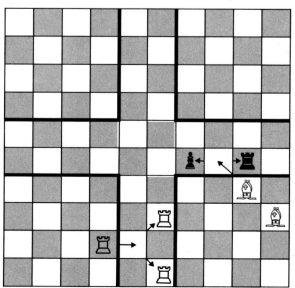

*Figure B*

# Chinese Chess

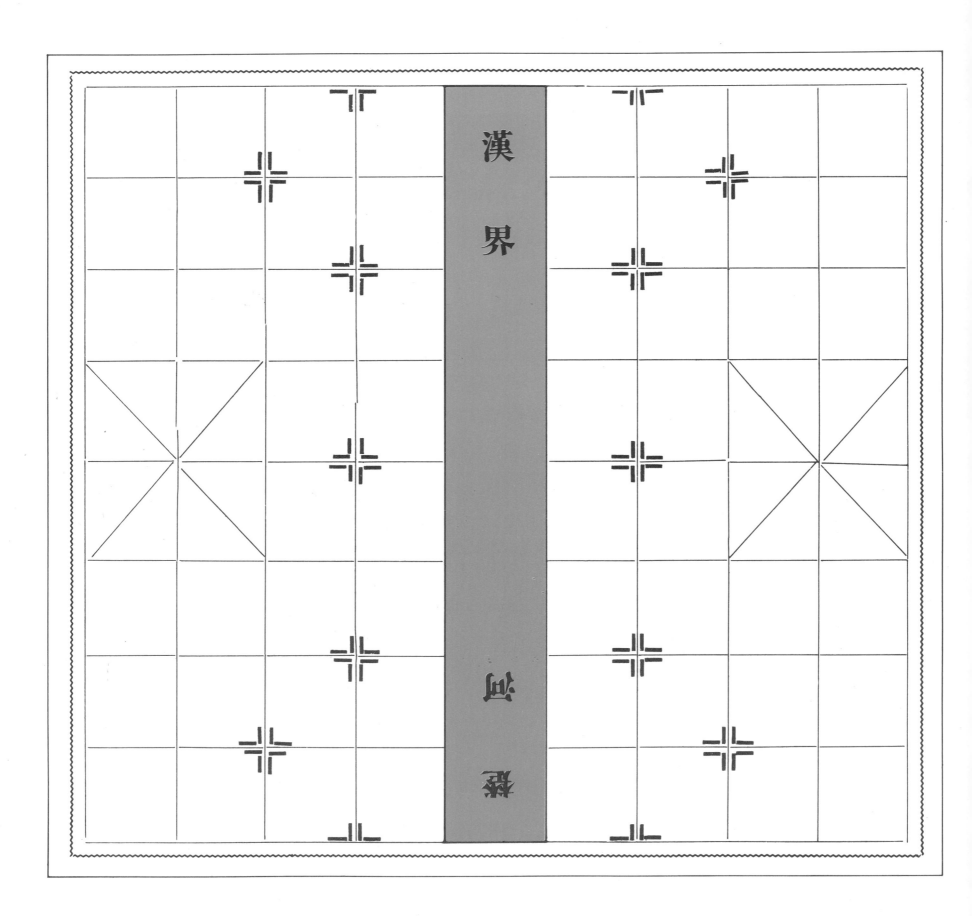

Siang K'i is the Chinese version of chess. The traditional game seems to have reached China from India about the middle of the eighth century A.D. by way of the caravan route through Kashmir and the Karakoram Pass to Hoang Ho. The game is mentioned in the 'Han Kwaihu' (Book of Marvels), written about the end of the eighth century and made public in 1088 A.D. At first the Chinese probably played the game in the Indian manner with similar pieces, but at an early date the Chinese altered the game by playing on the points instead of the squares, adding a river across the middle of the board and two fortresses at either end, reducing the number of pawns to five and adding new pieces in their stead. The chessmen or pieces became round discs inscribed with characters on the upper surface.

The reason for the change is explained in a story written by Ssu-Ma in 1084 A.D. The Emperor Wen-Ti was travelling through his kingdom and came upon some travellers playing the foreign game of Chess with carved ivory pieces. On sending one of his courtiers to enquire about the game, he was informed that the main piece was a Rajah, or in Chinese an Emperor. The discovery that his effigy was being moved to and fro at the command of a commoner so enraged the Emperor that he had the players decapitated and ordered the game to be played with inscribed discs and the Rajah (Emperor) to be replaced by a general, to preserve imperial dignity.

The river across the middle of the board represents the Hwang-ho, the Great Yellow River of China. Inside the fortresses the generals are supported by two mandarins who have the same power of movement as the viziers in the original Indian game. The generals and the mandarins are confined to the nine points within the fortress. (See the figure above.)

The aim in Siang-K'i is to checkmate the opposing general. If stalemate occurs and a general cannot move without entering into check, his player has lost and the game is over.

The game is played on a board of nine by ten lines, for the pieces are played on the points or intersections of the lines. The empty horizontal strip across the board representing the river is crossed by the pieces as if the vertical lines were continuous, except for the elephants which are not allowed to cross it.

At the beginning of the game each player has sixteen pieces, comprising one general, two mandarins, two elephants, two horses, two chariots, two cannons and five soldiers.

The Chinese were using high trajectory bombards some two thousand years ago. They were incapable of horizontal fire, so the Chess cannon was considered effective only when firing over the forward troops.

## PLAYERS
Two.

## PIECES
**Sixteen for each side: one general, two mandarins, two elephants, two horses, two chariots, two cannon, five soldiers. (See equipment sheet.)**

## AIM
**To immobilize the opposing general.**

## ORIGIN
**China, c.800 A.D.**

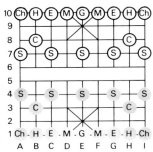

## MOVES OF PIECES
### GENERALS G
Move one *point* in a vertical or horizontal direction only and must remain within the nine *points* of the fortress. They may not stand on the same *file* as the other general unless another piece stands between them. A piece may become 'pinned' between them as it cannot move and expose its general to the other.

### MANDARINS M
Move one *point* diagonally forwards or backwards. They are confined to the fortress.

### ELEPHANTS E
Move two *points* diagonally. The intermediary *point* must be vacant. They are confined to their own side of the board, unable to cross the river.

### HORSES H
Move one *point* along any straight line followed by one *point* diagonally. The intermediary *point* must be unoccupied. This means that sometimes a horse can reach a *point*, but cannot return to the starting *point*.

### SOLDIERS S
Move one *point* forwards at a turn of play. After they have crossed the river they may also move sideways one *point*. They never move backwards or diagonally. A soldier may move several times sideways in different turns of play, capturing as it moves. If the opponent's back row is reached a soldier can only move sideways. There is no promotion.

### CHARIOTS C
Move any number of vacant *points* in a straight line forwards, backwards or sideways. They cannot move diagonally or *jump* over a piece.

### CANNONS C
Move like chariots, except that when capturing they must always *jump* over another piece of either colour which acts as a shield or 'screen'. They may land as many *points* beyond the 'screen' as desired. They cannot *jump* over two pieces, but can *jump* over one piece and capture the second. If there is no piece for a cannon to *jump* over, it cannot capture.

At the beginning of the game, the cannon on B3 can move backwards and sideways as far as G3 and A3, as if it were a chariot. It can also capture the horse on B10 and replace it with the cannon. Any piece, black or red, can act as a 'screen'.

## RULES
1. Black always has the first move.

2. Only one piece may occupy a *point*.

3. Only the cannon can *jump* over another piece.

4. Perpetual 'check' is not permitted. If the same position arises in two consecutive moves the attacking player must make some other move.

5. Every piece can capture every other piece which occupies a *point* to which it has access.

6. Capturing is not compulsory.

7. Captured pieces are removed from the board and cannot be re-entered during the game.

8. A general is placed in 'check' when threatened by a hostile piece, or by the opposing general on the same *file* without an intervening piece acting as a 'screen'. There are three possible replies to 'check':
a. The attacking piece may be captured and removed.
b. The general may move out of 'check'.
c. A piece may be interposed between the general and the attacking piece. If the attacking piece is a chariot, another piece may be interposed; if it is a horse a piece may be placed on the corner *point* of its path; if it is a cannon the interposing 'screen' may be removed, or another piece added. Capturing the 'screen' does not relieve the 'check' as one 'screen' has merely been exchanged for another.

9. If a 'check' cannot be lifted, the general suffers 'checkmate' and the game is lost. Games are also lost by stalemate.

# Draughts/Checkers

Draughts, known as Checkers in North America, was invented about 1000 A.D., probably in the south of France. The medieval game, called Fierges, used a Chess board, the 'tablemen' or pieces of Backgammon (see pages 88–91), and the moves of Alquerque (see pages 146–147). Each player had twelve pieces, which were known as 'fers', the name of the queen in medieval chess, or Fierges, and they also had her power of movement, namely one square diagonally in any direction. In Fierges, the pieces were allowed to capture by a diagonal "jump" over an enemy piece on an adjacent square landing on a vacant square immediately beyond. If the capturing piece could make more than one "short leap" in the same turn of play, multiple captures were permitted.

The 'Chronicle' of Philip Mouskat (1243 A.D.) refers to a king of Fierges, indicating that by the thirteenth century a 'fers' could be promoted to a king. Later when the chess queens were known as 'dames' (ladies) the game was called Jeu de Dames, as it is still called in France today. In Dames there was no compulsion to capture a piece at risk, another similarity to chess.

About 1535 A.D. compulsory capture of an enemy piece at risk was introduced and an attacking piece which missed this opportunity paid the penalty by being "huffed" or removed from the board. This new game was called Jeu Forcé to distinguish it from the older version without the compulsory capture rule which became known as Jeu Plaisant.

Modern standard Draughts/Checkers is based on the 16th century Jeu Forcé. The opening position of the pieces is shown in the figure to the right.

**PLAYERS**
Two.

**PIECES**
Twelve for each side.
(See equipment sheet.)

**AIM**
Capture or immobilization of all the opponent's pieces.

**ORIGIN**
Probably southern France, c.1000 A.D.

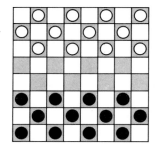

**RULES**

1. The pieces move only on the black squares.

2. The white corner square is always to the right of the players.

3. The players change colours at the end of each game.

4. The player with the black pieces moves first.

5. The pieces move diagonally forwards one square at a time. They cannot move backwards

6. When a piece reaches the opponent's back row it is 'crowned', becoming a king with the power of moving backwards or forwards. 'Crowning' ends a move. There may be several kings on the board at the same time.

7. 'Crowning' is indicated by placing two pieces on top of each other as shown in the figure below.

8. A capture is made by a *short leap* diagonally over an opposing piece onto a vacant square immediately beyond.

9. If the capturing piece can continue to leap over other enemy pieces in the same turn of play it is permitted to do so, and the captured pieces are removed from the board as they are captured. When a piece finally comes to rest the turn is finished.

10. If a player fails to capture an enemy piece at risk, his opponent has a choice of three penalties:
a. The piece must be returned to its position and the proper capturing move made.
b. The opponent may accept the move and let it stand. If this is done the piece must make the capture at the next move if this is still possible, or it

again becomes liable to a penalty.
c. The opponent may *huff* or remove the piece which should have made the capture and then continue his own move. *Huffing* does not constitute a move.

11. The first player to capture or immobilize the twelve opposing pieces is the winner.

*This seventeenth century French engraving shows a lady playing Draughts with her pet monkey; this animal had the reputation of winning the game as often as any human.*

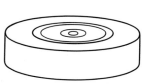

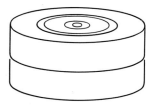

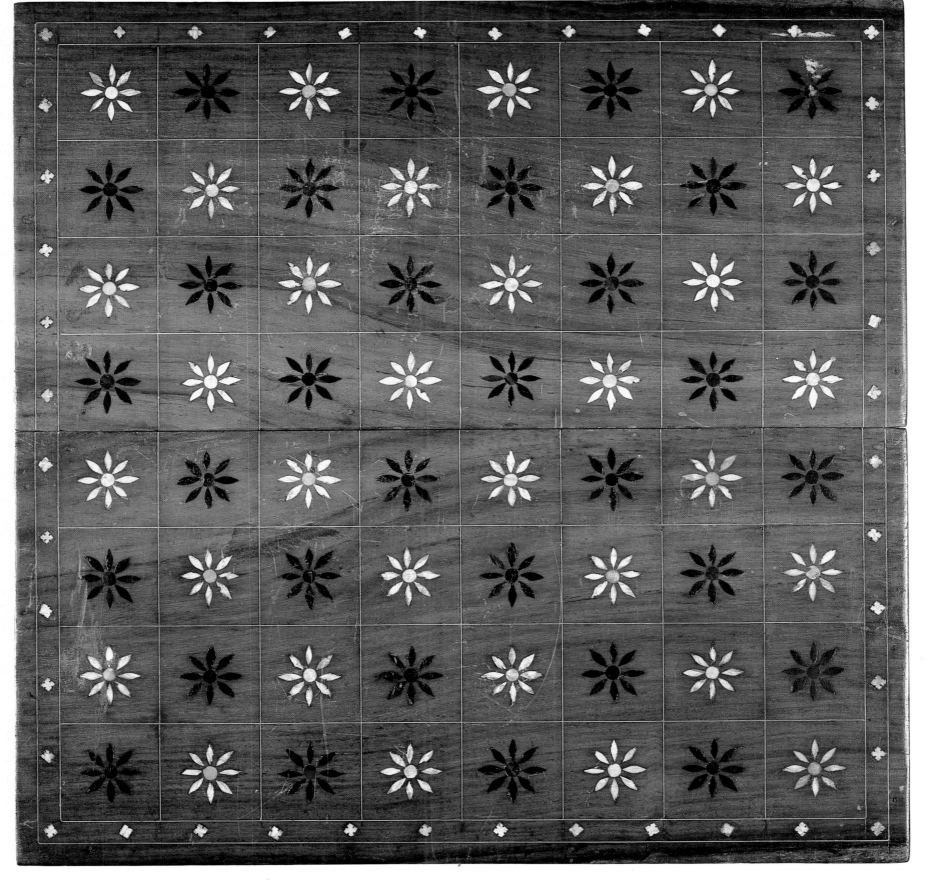

# Draughts/Checkers & variants

## Diagonal Draughts/Checkers

*The rules are the same as for the standard game, but that the pieces are arranged at the beginning of the game as in the figure below.*

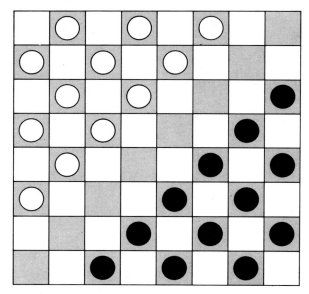

## The Losing Game

*The pieces begin in the same positions as in the standard game, but each player tries to lose his pieces as quickly as possible. Capturing when possible is compulsory, but there is no "huffing". If a player does not make a capture when this is possible, the piece is returned to its position and the capturing movement enforced.*

## Reversi

*Reversi was invented by Mr. Waterman in 1888 and published by Messrs. Jacques and Son. There were sixty-four pieces, blue on one side and yellow on the other, colours contrasting well with the standard nineteenth century black and white Draughts/Checkers boards. Reversi has recently enjoyed renewed popularity under the name Othello.*

**PLAYERS**
**Two.**

**PIECES**
**Sixty-four reversible: black on one side, white on the other. (See equipment sheet.)**

**AIM**
**To cover the board and have more pieces showing than one's opponent.**

**ORIGIN**
**England, 1888.**

RULES
1. A piece is tossed into the air and the other player calls out which side will land uppermost. If the call is correct the caller has the choice of starting or playing second.

2. The opening or *elder* player places a piece on any of the four central squares, his own colour uppermost.

3. The *younger* player then places a piece with his colour up on one side of the remaining three central squares.

4. The *elder* player then places a piece with his colour showing on one of the two remaining central squares.

5. The *younger* player completes the first stage of the game by occupying the last central square on his second turn.

6. After the central four squares are filled the players continue by alternate turns of play. Each piece is placed on a square adjacent to one

occupied by an enemy piece in an unbroken line with one of his own pieces, either in a straight line or diagonally. Any intervening enemy pieces between the player's pieces are captured and turned over or 'reversed'. Pieces in more than one direction may be 'reversed' in a single turn of play. A piece may change ownership many times during a game.

7. If a player cannot trap an enemy piece or pieces between two of his own he loses his turn and his opponent plays on until the baulked player can resume play. The players then place pieces alternately as before.

8. If there are no opposing pieces left, a player continues to play until he is also unable to make any 'reverses'.

9. The game finishes with all sixty-four pieces on the board and the player with the most pieces of his own colour uppermost is the winner.

10. If neither player can play, though both may have several pieces left, the game is blocked and finished. The player with most pieces of his own colour on the board wins.

11. Handicapping. The weaker player may be considered to have won if the game is drawn, or if he has only lost by one piece, two pieces, etc.

## Turkish Draughts/Checkers

*In Turkish Draughts/Checkers sixteen pieces are used instead of the familiar twelve, and they are arranged as in the figure A below.*

**PLAYERS**
**Two.**

**PIECES**
**Sixteen for each side.**

**AIM**
**To capture or immobilize all the opponent's pieces or to reduce them to a single piece against a piece elevated to king.**

**ORIGIN**
**Turkey.**

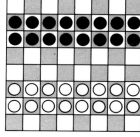

*Figure A*

RULES
1. Pieces move one square forwards or sideways but not diagonally or backwards.

2. Pieces capture by a *short leap* forwards or sideways and may take more than one piece in a turn of play. (See figure B.)

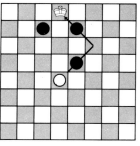

*Figure B*

3. Captured pieces are removed as they are *jumped* and a turn continues until the piece cannot make further captures.

4. When a piece reaches the opponent's back row it becomes a king.

5. A king can move in a straight line forwards, sideways or backwards (but not diagonally) any number of vacant squares and can land on any vacant square beyond the captured piece to make further captures. This is known as a *long leap*. (See figure C.)

6. The first player capturing or immobilizing all his opponent's pieces, or reducing the opposition to a single piece against a king wins the game.

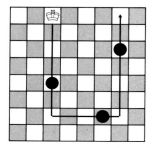

*Figure C*

*Left: Travelling games box, early nineteenth century, with ivory pieces arranged for Draughts/Checkers. The central drawer shows bone chess pieces of St. George pattern c.1850 and cards of the same period.*

## Pyramid

*In this game each player has only ten pieces on a Draughts/Checkers board and the opening position is shown in the figure below.*

**PLAYERS**
Two.

**PIECES**
Ten for each side.
(See equipment sheet.)

**AIM**
To occupy opponent's initial squares.

**ORIGIN**
Unknown.

**RULES**

1. The pieces move one square diagonally as in the standard game of Draughts/Checkers and *jump* over enemy pieces by a *short leap.*

2. A piece may make more than one *jump* in a single turn of play.

3. Pieces *jumped* over are not removed. At the end of the game each player has ten pieces still on the board.

4. Pieces may not *jump* over pieces of their own colour.

5. The player who is first to occupy his opponent's initial squares wins the game.

LA PARTIE DE DAMES DE LOUIS XIV

ALLÉGORIE POLITIQUE PROVENANT D'UN CALENDRIER DE LA SECONDE MOITIÉ DU XVIIᵉ SIÈCLE.

*Left: Louis XIV of France plays a vital game against Spain, Holland and Germany; a contemporary print.*

# Halma

*Halma was invented in England about 1880 and is played on a checkered board of sixteen by sixteen squares. The word Halma is based on the Greek for "jump". Two corners of the board are marked with camps of nineteen squares for two players with nineteen pieces of their own colour, and with camps of thirteen squares for the game to be played by four people with thirteen pieces each. The other two corners have camps of thirteen squares. The boundaries of the camps are marked with thicker lines.*

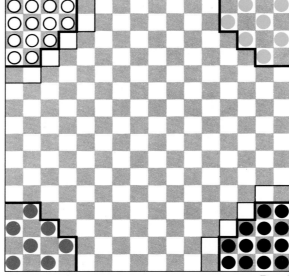

*Figure B*

**PLAYERS**
**Two or four.**

**PIECES**
**Nineteen each for two players; thirteen for four players. (See equipment sheet.)**

**AIM**
**A race to occupy all the squares of the diagonally opposite camp.**

**ORIGIN**
**England, c.1880.**

RULES
1. The game starts with the pieces arranged in their camps as shown in figure A for two players and figure B for four.

2. The players move one of their pieces to an adjoining empty square in any direction by alternate turns of play.

3. If the square next to a piece is occupied by another piece belonging either to the same player or to the opponent and the square immediately beyond in any straight line is empty, the piece can *jump* over the other. Further *jumps* if possible are permitted (but not obligatory) during one move.

4. No captures are made and no pieces are removed from the board.

5. The first player to occupy all the squares of the opposite camp is the winner.

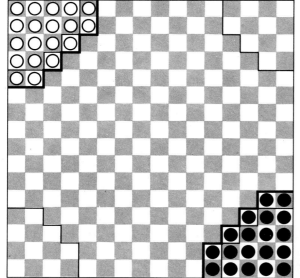

*Figure A*

# Nyout

*Nyout was probably being played by the inhabitants of the country before the kingdom of Korea was founded in 1122 B.C. It is still played by Koreans and is a very popular form of gambling. The game belongs to the group of Cross and Circle games. These are race games distinguished by a number of divisions arranged around a circular track with a central cross, the limbs of which form an alternative and shorter route to the finishing point.*

*If a piece lands on a cardinal "point" it travels along the particular arm of the cross leading to the centre from this "point", instead of continuing around the circle.*

*The Nyout board consists of twenty-nine marks which are often drawn on a piece of paper or even in the dust of a road. The marks at the four cardinal "points" and the centre are larger than the others. The mark at the north "point" is the 'ch'ut' or exit.*

*The moves of the 'mal' (horses) are controlled by the throws of four 'pam-nyout', casting-sticks about two and a half centimetres (one inch) long, white and flat on one side, convex and blackened by charring on the other. To prevent cheating they are thrown through a hoop of straw five centimetres (two inches) in diameter, fastened about thirty centimetres (one foot) from the ground to a stick. Other forms of double-sided dice, such as coins, may be used instead.*

**PLAYERS**
**Up to four.**

**PIECES**
**Two, three or four 'mal' or horses each. (See equipment sheet.)**

**SCORING**
**Four double-sided dice.**

**AIM**
**A race to get all one's horses round the course and off the board.**

**ORIGIN**
**Korea, c.1000 B.C.**

SCORING
Four curved sides or heads up scores five and another turn.
Four flat sides or tails up scores four and another turn.
Three flat sides or tails up scores three.
Two flat sides or tails up scores two.
One flat side or tail up scores one.

(If a block falls upright it counts as if it were convex side up.)

RULES
1. If two are playing, each player has four 'mal' or horses; if three, each has three 'mal'; if four, each has two 'mal'. The players sitting opposite each other act as partners.

2. All the players throw the 'pam-nyout' in turn, the highest scorer becoming the leader and the others arranging themselves in descending order counter-clockwise around the board.

3. The players enter their 'mal' on the mark at the left of the 'ch'ut' and travel counter-clockwise around the board according to their throws.

4. The object of the game is to move the agreed number of horses around the circle and out at the

'ch'ut' or exit. If a 'mal' lands on one side of the cardinal *points* it short-circuits along two limbs of the cross.

5. Throwing a five or a four allows the player another throw which is made before his piece is moved; it is moved on by the sum of the throws.

6. If one horse catches up with another belonging to the same side, both horses may double up as a team and move around as one piece.

7. A horse moving onto a *point* occupied by an opposing horse kicks it and sends it back to start again at the beginning. The player who sends an opponent's horse back wins an extra turn.

8. A player may move one of his partner's horses instead of his own.

*The Kyongbok Palace in Seoul, Korea.*

# Tablut

*Tablut originated among the Alpine Lapps. It appears to be related to Hnefatafl, mentioned in an Icelandic saga from the beginning of the fourteenth century; this was a similar game to Fox and Geese (see pages 50–51). Tablut was first described by the Swedish botanist Carolus Linnaeus (1707–1778) in the diary he kept when travelling through Lapland as a young student in 1732. This record of his journey was not published until the nineteenth century, long after his death. Linnaeus is now remembered as the first person to develop a coherent system for scientific classification of plants and animals, which is the basis of that still in use among scientists all over the world today.*

*The purpose of Linnaeus' journey was an 'investigation of the three Kingdoms of Nature'. He travelled almost four thousand miles in a hundred and fifty-three days, enduring appalling conditions and suffering every form of hardship from near starvation to shipwreck. It is astonishing that in such circumstances he should have had the necessary self-discipline to keep a meticulous, daily record of his impressions and observations. These were not confined to facts about plants and animals; he also made copious notes on the Laplanders themselves and their customs. His journal entries have many informative and beautiful illustrations and one of these is of a Tablut board made of embroidered reindeer skin.*

*Tablut, like all the Fox-and-Geese-type games played throughout medieval Europe and Asia, is an unequal contest between opposing sides which differ in number, appearance and movement. The original game represents a hunting situation in which one side has fewer pieces with greater freedom and the power to 'kill' or remove the opposition. These opposing pieces are more restricted in movement but compensate by being more numerous.*

*In Tablut, one player holds eight blond Swedish soldiers and their king, the largest piece on the board, while the opponent has sixteen dark Muscovites. The game is played on nine by nine squares and the central square is distinctly marked to represent the 'konakis' or throne. Only the Swedish king is allowed to occupy the 'konakis'.*

**PLAYERS**
Two.

**PIECES**
One player has eight blond Swedes and a king. The other player has sixteen dark Muscovites. (See equipment sheet.)

**AIM**
Either to get the king to the edge of the board, or to surround and immobilize the king.

**ORIGIN**
Lapland, possibly fourteenth century.

RULES
1. The pieces are placed on the board before beginning the game as in the figure right.

2. All the pieces move in any straight line except diagonally for any number of vacant squares.

3. A piece is captured and removed from the board when two enemy pieces move onto adjacent squares on a *row* or *column*. This is the *custodian* method of capture. A piece can move unharmed onto an empty square between two enemy pieces.

4. The king is captured if all four adjacent squares around him are occupied by enemy pieces, or if the fourth square is the throne. When the king is captured the game is won by the Muscovites.

5. If the king reaches any square on the edge of the board the Swedes are the winners.

6. When there is a clear route for the king to a square on the edge of the board the player warns his opponent by calling 'Raichi!' (the equivalent of 'Check!'). If there are two clear routes he calls 'Tuichi!' (Checkmate) and wins the game.

| | | | M | M | M | | | |
|---|---|---|---|---|---|---|---|---|
| | | | | M | | | | |
| | | | | S | | | | |
| M | | | | S | | | | M |
| M | M | S | S | K | S | S | M | M |
| M | | | | S | | | | M |
| | | | | S | | | | |
| | | | | M | | | | |
| | | | M | M | M | | | |

*Right: Carolus Linnaeus wearing Lapp costume.*

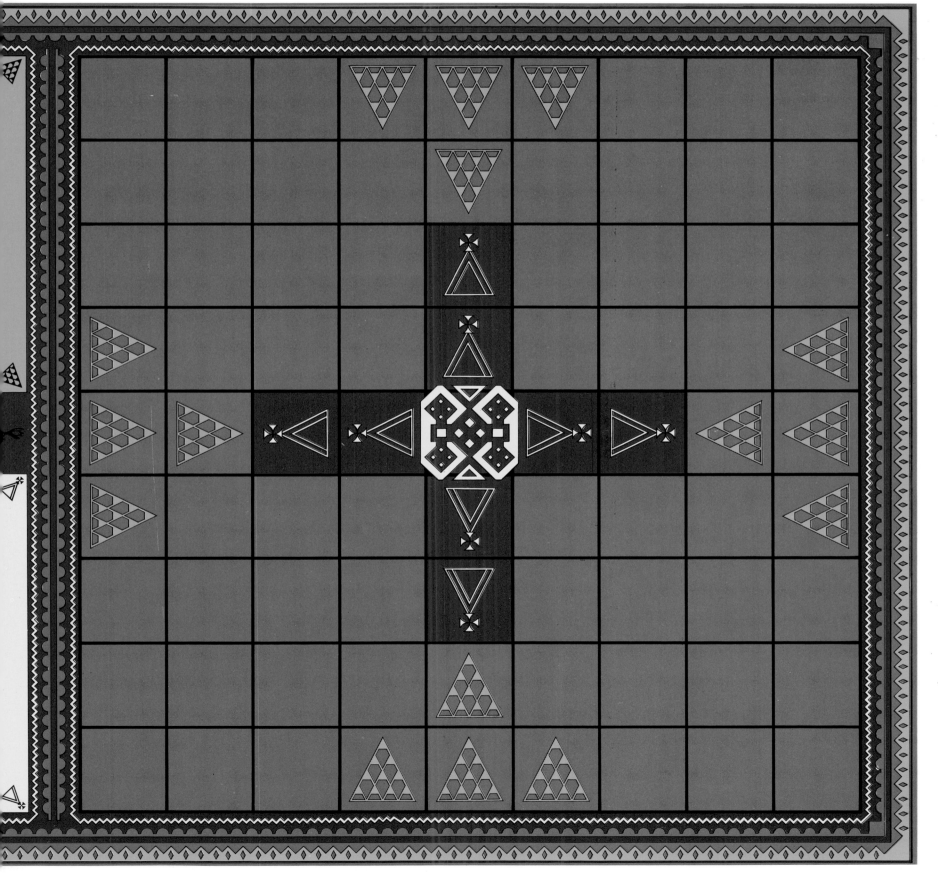

# Zohn Ahl

This is one of the Cross and Circle group of games which developed many variations among the North American Indians. This game is related to Sho-Li-We (Game of Canes), still used a century ago by the priests of an esoteric war society among the Zuni Indians of New Mexico to foretell the future. Zohn Ahl is now played purely for pleasure and only by the womenfolk of the Kiowa Indians, Oklahoma. The rapid changes of fortune during this game cause such great amusement that it is common for a party of women and girls to sit around a board for as long as half a day, laughing and joking as they follow the play.

A circle with the tips of a cross is scratched on the ground or embroidered on cloth or a skin. The illustration shows a Zohn Ahl board of hide embroidered with beads. Often the board is a blanket with the track marked out by forty small stones. There are always larger spaces at the four cardinal "points"; the north and south represent a river in flood and at the east and west are dry gullies. (See diagram.) Scoring is by means of casting sticks about eighteen centimetres (seven inches) long, flat on one side and convex on the other. Three sticks have a red stripe down the middle of the flat side and are therefore known as 'Guadal' (red). The fourth, known as 'Sahe' (green), usually has a green stripe on the flat side and an inscribed star on the convex side. These sticks are dropped against a flat stone, called an 'Ahl', placed in the centre of the board. Coins make a very suitable substitute for throwing sticks, using three of one kind and one of another.

**PLAYERS**
**Any number divided into two teams.**

**PIECES**
**Two markers; four counters for each team. (See equipment sheet.)**

**SCORING**
**Four casting sticks or coins.**

**AIM**
**A race to get the marker around the course and off the board.**

**ORIGIN**
**Kiowa Indian, North America.**

SCORING
One flat or head side up scores one point and if this is the 'Sahe', another turn. Two flat or head sides up scores two and if one of them is the 'Sahe', another turn.

Three flat or head sides up scores three and if the 'Sahe' is included, another turn.
Four flat or head sides up scores six and another turn.
Four convex or tail sides up scores ten and another turn.

RULES
1. Any number can play, divided into two teams, each having a marker representing a runner. These move in opposite directions around the board. Each team also has four white pebbles, shells or other small objects which are used as counters.

2. The casting sticks or coins are thrown by each team alternately, every member taking turns in advancing the team's runner according to the number scored.

3. If a runner lands in a river it must return to the start and forfeit a counter to the other team.

4. If a runner falls into a gully, its team loses a throw.

*Below: Kiowa Indians, 'Trailing-the-Enemy' and his wife, c.1890.*

5. If the two runners meet on a space, the last to arrive sends the other back to start again and also claims a counter from that team.

6. When the first runner arrives back at the start after completing the circuit the first lap is over and the opposing team has to pay a counter. The winner of each lap gains a counter.

7. If the throw is enough to carry the runner beyond the start, this surplus is used to begin the second lap.

8. The game ends when one team has lost all its counters; or if a time limit has been set, the team holding most counters at that moment is the winner.

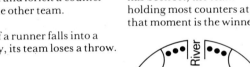

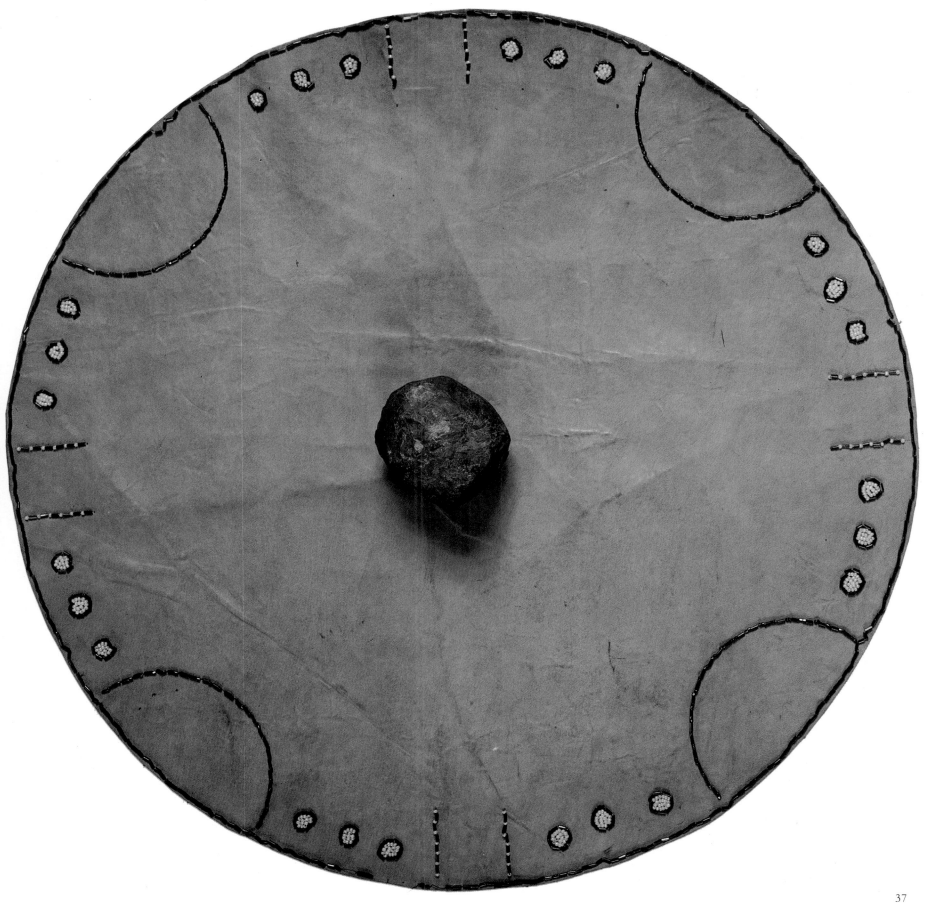

# Fighting Serpents

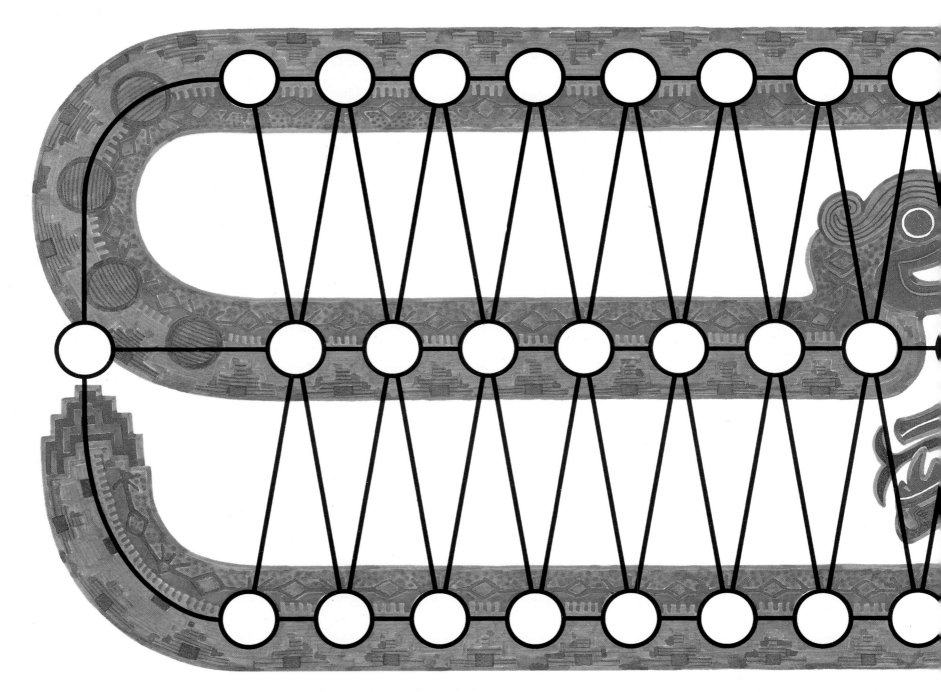

Fighting Serpents is a rough translation of 'Kolowis Awithlaknannai', as this game is called by the Zuni Indians of New Mexico. It is a modification of Alquerque, which was brought to the New World by the Spaniards during the sixteenth century. The Zuni adapted the abstract game of Alquerque to represent one of the dramas from their mythology, since Kolowis is the name of a mythical serpent.

The flat roofs of the Zuni houses were used as terraces and the game has been found cut into the roofing stones. Pebbles or pottery fragments were used as pieces. Each player starts the game with twenty-three pieces of his own colour set out as shown in the figure to the right.

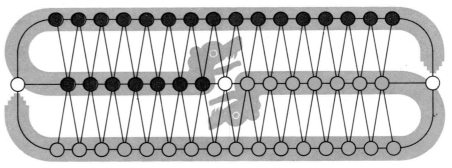

**PLAYERS**
Two.

**PIECES**
Twenty-three for each side. (See equipment sheet.)

**AIM**
Capture of all the opponent's pieces.

**ORIGIN**
Zuni Indian, New Mexico, sixteenth century.

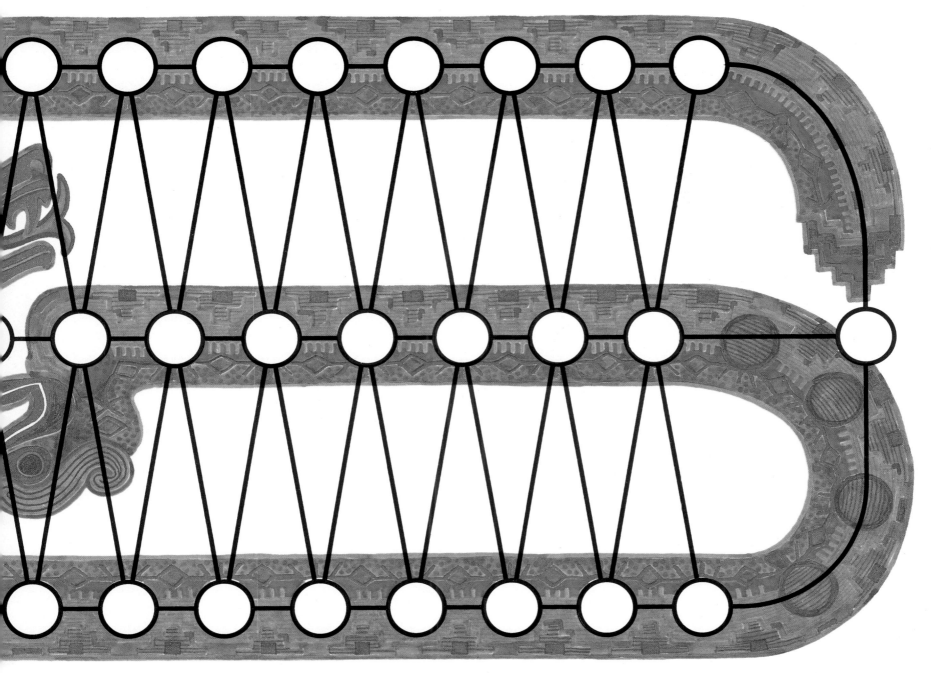

## RULES

1. Each player's pieces form 'serpents' which confront each other. The pieces are laid out on the row nearest each player and on half the middle row, except for the vacant central *point* and the two empty *points* at both ends of this row.

2. The pieces move one *point* along any line and capture by a *short leap*.

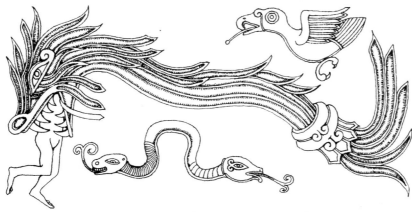

3. The opening player moves a piece onto the empty central *point*. This piece is captured by the second player with a *short leap*, and is taken off the board. Capturing is compulsory.

4. The players move alternately, and the pieces can move from one intersection to another in any direction along the lines.

5. More than one piece can be captured at a time.

6. The game ends when one player has lost all his pieces.

# Agon

*This game which dates from c.1890 is played by two on a hexagonal board formed of concentric rings. There is an outer ring of thirty hexagons, then twenty-four, eighteen, twelve, six and at the centre a single hexagon known as the throne. Each player has a queen and six guards of a distinctive colour. The initial position of the pieces is shown in figure A.*

**PLAYERS**
Two.

**PIECES**
Seven each side – one queen and six guards. (See equipment sheet.)

**SCORING**
One die.

**AIM**
A race to get the queen onto the central hexagon surrounded by her guards.

**ORIGIN**
Late nineteenth century.

RULES

1. The choice of first move is decided by the throw of a *die*.

2. The players move their pieces alternately, one space towards the centre, or sideways. They cannot move peripherally except in accordance with Rules three and four.

3. If a guard has enemy pieces on the contiguous spaces on either side of it, on the player's next move it must be lifted and placed on an empty space in the outermost ring.

4. If the queen is sandwiched between enemy pieces she also, at the next move, must be lifted, but can be placed on any vacant space on the board. This may be to her advantage.

5. If two or more pieces are compelled to move by being trapped at the same time, and one is the queen, she is moved first, and then the other pieces are placed in the outermost ring in successive turns of play, the order being optional (see figure B).

6. No piece can move onto a space which has enemy pieces on both adjacent sides.

7. Only a queen can move onto the central hexagon.

8. A piece must not be touched unless it can be moved.

9. The object of the game is to place the queen on the throne surrounded by her guards on the innermost ring. (See figure C.)

10. If a player's six guards occupy the inner circle surrounding an empty throne, the player loses the game as both queens are unable to fulfil their destinies.

11. A variant, designed to prevent monotony, starts by placing the queens on opposite corners of the board and then the guards are placed in alternate turns of play on any vacant space except on the throne. When all are on the board the game continues as already described.

*Figure A*

40

Figure B

Figure C

# Mu Torere

This game is played mainly by the Ngati Porou tribe living on the east coast of North Island, New Zealand, but it can be found among the other Maori tribes. It is the only Maori boardgame (though they have many action games); for this reason, and because the word 'mu' is thought to be taken from the English 'move', Mu Torere is sometimes held to be derived from Draughts/Checkers (pages 26–29). However, the form of the game is so different that this game is likely to be pure Maori, and dating to before the arrival of the Europeans. The first Maori settlers, known as the Moa Hunters, reached New Zealand about 800 A.D., but the main wave of immigration was that of about 1350, when the majority of the ancestors of the modern Maori arrived. Until the arrival of Europeans at the end of the eighteenth century, the Maori did not use metal or make pottery, but had reached a high standard in wood-carving, weaving and dyeing. Their social life was based on kinship groups: the tribe was made up of people with a common ancestry. Land was held by clans, not individuals, and was worked by extended families. However, the arrival of more and more British settlers from 1840 onwards put this system of communal land-holding under pressure. Faced by the loss of their lands, the Maoris fought the British in a series of wars between 1860 and 1872, but were defeated, and part of their lands came under European ownership. The impact of European civilization had a destructive effect on the Maori way of life, and their population fell from about a quarter of a million in 1840 to about fifty thousand at the end of the century. Today, however, they number almost two hundred thousand and make up eight per cent of the population of New Zealand.

The board consists of an eight-sided star and a 'putahi' or central circle. Each of the two players has four 'perepere' or pieces of distinctive shape or colour.

Usually the board was marked on the ground with a stick, or drawn on a stone slab with a piece of charcoal. More permanent boards, which could be carried around, were made by marking the design on the fresh green bark of a Totara tree. This is a spreading evergreen conifer that grows to a height of about thirty metres (ninety feet), and whose reddish wood, sometimes known as mahogany pine, is used in New Zealand today for house-building and for making furniture. The outlines of the game remained engraved when the bark dried and two straight sticks were tied at either end to prevent it curling.

**PLAYERS**
Two.

**PIECES**
Four for each side.
(See equipment sheet.)

**AIM**
Immobilization of opponent's pieces.

**ORIGIN**
Maori, New Zealand.

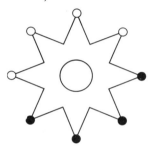

RULES
1. At the beginning of the game each player places his pieces on four adjacent *points* of the star. (See figure above.)

2. The players change colours at the end of every game.

3. Black always begins and the players move their pieces alternately.

4. There are three possible forms of move:
a. A piece may move from one of the *points* to the 'putahi', provided that one or both of the adjacent *points* are occupied by an enemy piece or pieces.
b. A piece may move from one of the *points* to an adjacent empty *point*.
c. A piece may move from the 'putahi' to a *point*.

5. Only one piece is allowed on each *point* or the 'putahi'.

6. *Jumping* over another piece is not allowed.

7. The player blocking his opponent so that the latter cannot move wins the game.

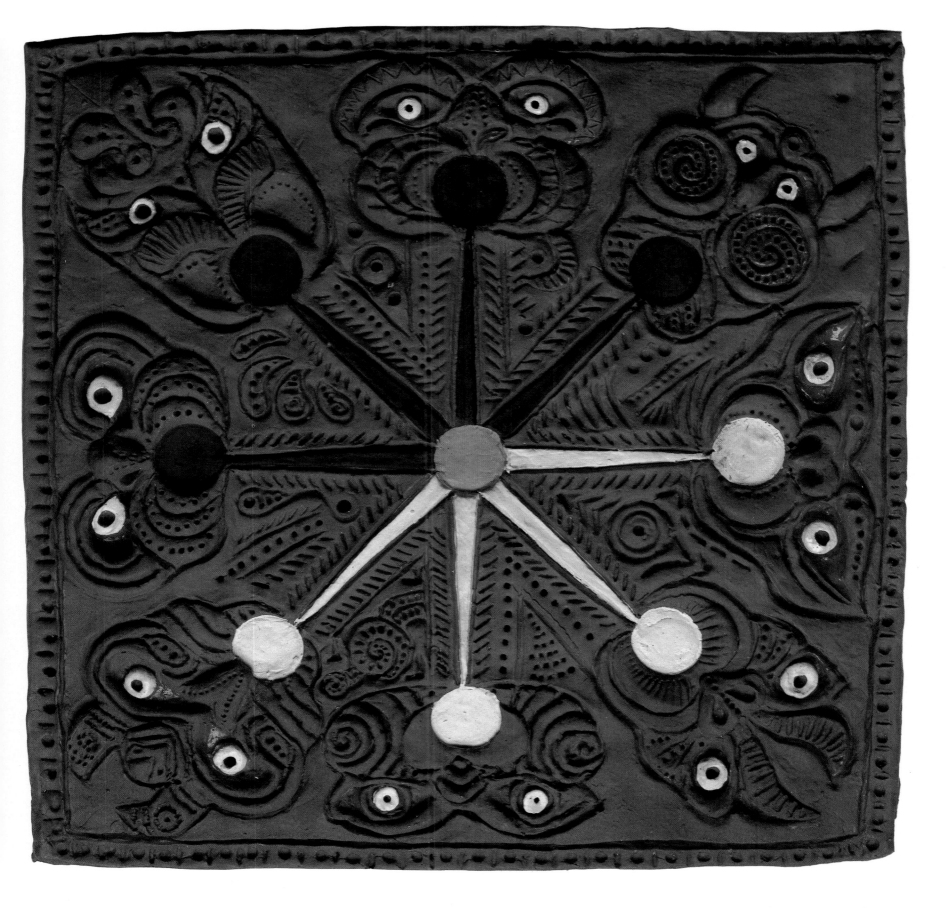

# Palm Tree

This game-board—now in the Metropolitan Museum of Art, New York—was one of the objects found in a tomb ascribed to Amenemhet IV (1801–1792 B.C.) during excavations in Thebes, Egypt, made by Lord Carnarvon from 1907 to 1912. The board is fifteen centimetres (six inches) long, ten centimetres (four inches) wide and seven centimetres (two and a half inches) high, and made of wood with an ivory top. A set of dog- or jackal-headed pegs was contained in a drawer in the board secured by copper staples and an ivory bolt.

A similar board found at Nippur in Mesopotamia was accompanied by three convex disks. Two had a simple cross engraved on one face and the third had a five-pointed star. These were probably used as dice. A board shaped like a Hittite shield, found at Megiddo, Israel—clearly made for a similar game—was accompanied by disks with either geometric or animal designs on one face and plain on the other. Other sites, in Egypt, have revealed similar disks and other boards—one in the shape of a tortoise decorated with red paste and blue glaze inlay, now in the Louvre Museum, Paris.

Interest in this simple game probably depended on gambling. Known to archaeologists either as the Game of Fifty-eight Holes, or the Game of Dogs and Jackals, it seems to have been the forerunner of a series of similar games distributed widely over the Near East.

Cribbage boards may have been derived from these ancient peg-boards—the holes are still grouped in fives, one half of the board belonging to one player and the other half to his opponent. For cribbage the number of holes has been increased to sixty-one for each player and cards rather than dice are used to control the movements of the pieces.

**PLAYERS**
Two.

**PIECES**
Five white dogs for one side and five black jackals for the other. (See equipment sheet.)

**SCORING**
Three double-sided dice or coins.

**AIM**
A race to reach the five top points on one side of the palm-tree and win the dates.

**ORIGIN**
Egypt, 2000–1788 B.C.

**SCORING**
One marked surface or heads uppermost scores one.
Two marked surfaces or heads uppermost score two.
Three marked surfaces or heads uppermost score three.
One unmarked surface or tail uppermost scores four.
Three unmarked surfaces or tails uppermost score five.
A throw of five wins another turn.

**RULES**
1. Both players contribute an agreed stake into a *pool*.

2. The right-hand side of the board belongs to White (dogs), and the left to Black (jackals). (See illustration to the far left.)

3. The rondel above the palm tree is the starting point and the pieces travel left or right around the edge of the board and up the tree to collect the dates. The players try to take up the five highest *points* on their side of the tree.

4. Exact throws are required to place the five pieces in their final positions, though the order in which this is done is unimportant.

5. The two players throw the three disks or coins alternately. Only by throwing a five can a piece be introduced onto the board at the starting rondel. The player then throws again and uses this extra turn to move his piece by the indicated amount.

6. A piece landing on a *point* marked with a horizontal sign earns the player an agreed stake.

7. A player cannot move a piece onto a *point* already occupied and if no other move is possible the score is lost and the turn ends. (See also Rule nine.)

8. If a piece lands on a *point* connected to another *point*, it moves along the line which acts as a ladder towards victory.

9. A player must move if he can and if he is unable to move any of his pieces his opponent may use the score in addition to his own.

10. The first player to marshal his five pieces on the uppermost five *points* of his side of the tree wins the game.

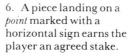
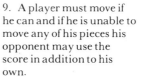

*Cribbage box with bone cards.*

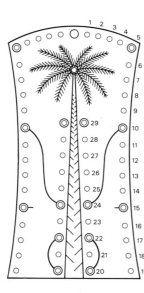

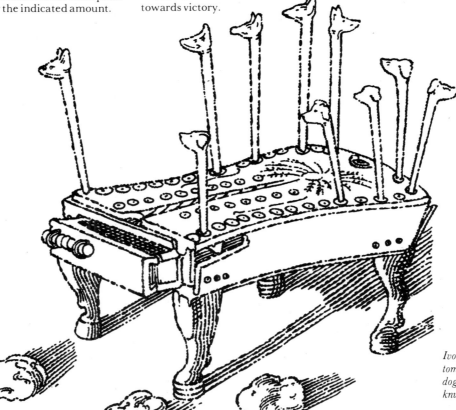

*Ivory Palm Tree game from the tomb of Amenemhet IV, with dog and jackal pieces and knuckle-bone dice.*

# Hyena

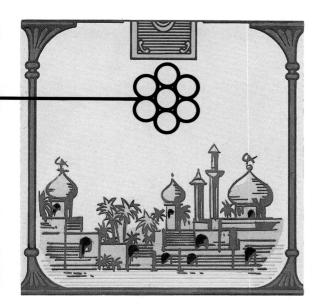

The Baggara are an Arab tribe who live in the flat lands to the east of the Nile in the Sudan. They were one of the beduin tribes who left Arabia and settled near the Nile after the seventh century conquest of Egypt. Later in the Middle Ages, some tribes, perhaps finding that the settled life in Egypt did not suit them, moved westward across the deserts of North Africa. From Tunisia the ancestors of the Baggara went south to Lake Chad, and then in the eighteenth and nineteenth centuries they turned eastward again to the Nile, where they live today. They live by herding cattle (their name means 'The Cattle People') and by the sturdy ponies that they breed, for the part of Africa that they inhabit will not support the camel. For the sake of their herds they lead a nomadic life, spending the rainy season of the year in the grasslands, and then moving south to the river when the weather is dry, so it is appropriate that this game should be based on one of the dangers that a wandering nomad can encounter.

This spiral game may be derived from the Coiled Snake Game of the Pharaonic period (see pages 120–121). The board is made by tracing a spiral in the sand and scooping out a random number of holes along its course. Each hole represents a camp at the end of a day's journey. A larger hole at the centre is the well of an oasis and at the start of the track is a village. Each player has a distinctively coloured marker, representing his mother.

The dice are three pieces of stick about fifteen centimetres (six inches) long, and are split so that one surface with the bark left on is rounded and green and the other is flat and white. If sticks are not available coins may be used instead.

**PLAYERS**
**Any number.**

**PIECES**
**A mother or marker for each player and one hyena. (See equipment sheet.)**

**SCORING**
**Three double-sided dice or coins.**

**AIM**
**To release the hyena or bring one's mother back to safety.**

**ORIGIN**
**Sudan.**

SCORING
The dice are tossed up into the air and on falling:
One white side or tail up scores a 'taba' (special mark).
Two white sides or tails up score two and the turn ceases.
Three white sides or tails up score three.
Three green sides or heads up score six.

RULES
1. Each player throws the sticks or dice in turn, moving his marker on at each throw according to his score, the turn finishing on a throw of two.

2. A player must throw a 'taba' before his mother can leave the village.

3. After throwing a 'taba' the player's mother moves along the spiral two, three or six camps as indicated by the throw. After the initial move, she does not move if a 'taba' is thrown, but 'tabas' are recorded on the sand or a piece of paper for later use. (See Rules five, six, eight and nine.)

4. Two or more mothers can share the same hole or camp.

5. A mother must reach the well by an exact throw. If the score is short, the mother may make up the missing camps by paying the equivalent number of 'tabas' from her son's store (which are crossed off the record).

6. At the well she spends two 'tabas' to wash her clothes, and two to start on the return journey. If the player hasn't acquired the necessary 'tabas', his mother must wait until he has collected them for her. While doing this the player may record any two, three

or six which he may score for use as soon as his mother is moving again.

7. The women return from the well to the village as on the outward journey.

8. The first mother to arrive back at the village (an exact throw is not required) releases the hyena which leaves the village on the payment of two 'tabas' by her son. The hyena travels at twice the speed of the other pieces, as its scores are doubled.

9. At the well the hyena is held up until it has paid ten 'tabas' for a drink.

10. On leaving the well it eats any mothers it overtakes. It cannot eat before drinking.

11. The player who releases the hyena is the winner, but there are degrees of losing. Any player whose mother is eaten by the hyena is teased unmercifully by those whose mothers reach safety.

*North African beduin with their camels.*

# Liar Dice

This improved variant of Poker Dice can be played with ordinary cubic dice, or five poker dice marked with an Ace, King, Queen, Jack, Ten and Nine (see equipment sheet). The board may be walled to make control of the dice easier, but this is not essential.

The board and dicing cup shown, made in Mexico where Poker and Dice are almost a national pastime, is of tooled leather and green baize. One side of the cup is decorated with the head of an Aztec warrior while the other shows a reproduction of the Sun Stone or Aztec Calendar. During repairs to the cathedral of Mexico City made at the end of the eighteenth century, this highly decorated stone was discovered below the foundations, which were built over the ancient temple site of Tenochtitlàn. The original—over three metres (three yards) in diameter—is carved from a single block of sandstone and represents the history of the world according to Aztec cosmology.

In the centre is the Sun, surrounded by various symbols, and the idea of movement is shown. Tiger, Water, Wind and Rain of Fire—signs of the four universes created before the Aztec era came into existence—are also represented. Around the centre is a band of hieroglyphs for the twenty days of the Aztec month. Other bands depict the sun's rays, precious stones, symbols of flowers and blood, elements of the solar cult and two fiery serpents signifying the chronological and cosmic orders.

**PLAYERS**
Any number.

**PIECES/SCORING**
Five poker dice or ordinary cubic dice. (See equipment sheet.)

**AIM**
Bluffing to remain the last player left in the game and win the contents of the *pool*.

**ORIGIN**
Mexico.

## RULES

1. The opening player casts the dice onto the board from a cup and hides them behind his left hand from the view of other players. He declares a score which may or may not be true.

2. This declaration may be accepted or challenged by the player on his left.

3. If it is challenged and the throw is shown to be at least as high or higher than stated, the challenger loses a life and pays a stake into the *pool*. If the score is below the declaration, the caster pays the fine and loses a life.

*Left: Modern Mexican board of leather and baize with liar dice and dicing cup on which the sun stone design is embossed.*

4. If the declaration is accepted, the dice – still concealed from view – are passed to the next player, who may retain all or throw any number of the dice in an attempt to improve the score.

5. The number of dice being re-thrown must be stated; for example, 'throwing two'.

6. The caster then makes his declaration, which must be higher than the one he accepted, and the player on the left may accept the new call or challenge it.

7. If a declaration of the highest possible call, 'five aces', is made, the next player may challenge or accept it.

8. If he accepts he is allowed five throws of the dice to achieve five aces and if he is successful the caller loses a life and stake, if not the acceptor loses.

9. Every player has three lives and when these are lost he is out of the game.

10. The first player to lose three lives is granted a fourth or extra life, a grace known as being 'on the parish'.

11. The last player left in the game is the winner and takes the contents of the *pool*.

12. If a challenge is made a new round starts.

## SCORING
Five of a kind. (Aces count high.)
A 'royal flush'. (The five dice in sequence, ace high.)
A 'low flush'. (The five dice in sequence, king high.)
Four of a kind.
Full house. (Three of a kind and a pair.)
Three of a kind.
Two pairs.
One pair.
'Pryle'. (Non-scoring hand.)

Except for the royal and low flushes, sequences do not count. A caster with a 'pryle' or non-scoring hand must make a scoring declaration and try to bluff the next player into acceptance.

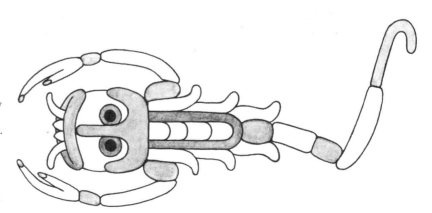

# Fox and Geese

Fox and Geese is one of a series of games originating in Northern Europe during the Viking Age. These were characterized by the number of pieces on the two sides being unequal and their objectives different. An early form of the game was played on a board of thirty-three holes arranged in the shape of a cross and joined together by a network of right-angled lines.

Fox and Geese, or a near variant called Halatafl (the Fox game), is mentioned in the 'Grettis Saga' (about 1300 A.D.) which was probably written by a priest living in northern Iceland. The earliest English reference to Fox and Geese occurs in the accounts of the royal household of Edward IV (1461–1483) when 'two foxes and twenty-six hounds of silver overgilt' were purchased to form two sets of 'Marelles'. References in medieval literature to 'Marelles' or 'Merels' may sometimes indicate Fox and Geese and not Nine Men's Morris. (See pages 142–145.)

In the late eighteenth century Fox and Geese boards were often round, with a groove at the periphery to hold captured geese. The lines were omitted on these boards and only moves in a straight line, except the diagonal, were permitted. The number of holes on boards varied: a form common in France had thirty-seven instead of the original thirty-three. A rustic English board exists which has sixty-five holes and all the diagonals drawn.

A weakness of Fox and Geese is that, properly played, the geese always win. To improve the fox's chances, in a later version seventeen geese were used, but they were not permitted to move backwards. On some boards diagonal lines were added allowing diagonal moves along them.

*An English eighteenth century version of a Fox and Geese board.*

**PLAYERS**
**Two.**

**PIECES**
**Eighteen geese on one side; one fox on the other. (See equipment sheet.)**

**AIM**
**Geese try to immobilize the fox; the fox, by catching enough geese, tries to prevent them.**

**ORIGIN**
**Iceland, c.1300 A.D.**

RULES
1. One player places eighteen geese on the board, filling one limb of the cross and also the whole lower line of *points* at right angles and adjoining this limb. The other player places the fox on any of the empty *points*.

2. The first move is made forwards, by a goose onto an adjacent empty *point* along any line. Diagonal moves are not permitted.

3. On subsequent turns of play the geese can move one *point* forwards or sideways but neither backwards nor diagonally.

4. The fox makes the next move one *point* in any direction along a line. Play continues by alternate moves.

5. The fox makes a capture by *jumping* over a goose on an adjacent *point* onto a vacant *point* beyond, and can continue to capture by similar *short leaps* in the same turn of play when this is possible. Captured geese are *borne off*.

6. Geese cannot capture the fox, but attempt to crowd him into a corner and deprive him of the power to move. If they succeed the geese win the game.

7. If the fox captures enough geese to make his own immobilization impossible, he has won.

# Asalto

Based on the medieval game of *Fox and Geese* (see pages 50–51), a later variant called *Asalto* was developed. During the mid-nineteenth century, influenced by the events of the Indian Mutiny, the game was revived and given a new name – *Officers and Sepoys*. The board represents a fort defended by three officers and besieged by fifty soldiers or sepoys.

*At the height of the battle of Lucknow during the Indian Mutiny.*

## PLAYERS
Two.

## PIECES
Fifty sepoys on one side; three officers on the other. (See equipment sheet.)

## AIM
Sepoys try to immobilize officers or occupy entire garrison; officers try to prevent the fort being occupied or themselves being immobilized by 'killing' enough sepoys.

## ORIGIN
India, nineteenth century.

## RULES
1. Two players control sides of unequal force – the fifty pieces of one side represent the besieging soldiers or sepoys and the other side is represented by three officers defending the besieged fort.

2. The fort is indicated by the area containing seventeen red *points*. One player places the three officers on any of these *points*.

3. The other player controlling the moves of the fifty soldiers places them on the white *points* at the intersections of the red and black lines on the remaining area of the board, which represents the countryside surrounding the fort.

4. Soldiers move one at a time along any red line but must always move towards the fort.

5. Officers, however, move in all directions on any lines, red or black.

6. By making a *short leap* and *jumping* over a soldier in a straight line to an adjacent and vacant position, an officer 'kills' the soldier who is then removed from the board.

7. If an officer fails to make a capture when this is possible, he is *huffed* and removed from the board.

8. The soldiers win if they immobilize the officers or occupy every *point* in the fort.

10. The officers win if they manage to 'kill' enough soldiers to prevent their being immobilized or the fort being occupied.

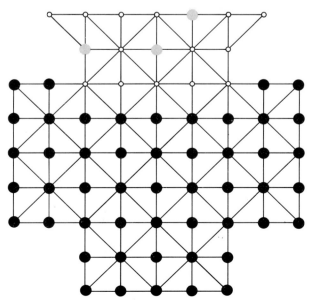

# Solitaire

This game is a form of Patience played by one person on a Fox and Geese board (see pages 50–51). It was reputedly invented by a French count to pass the time while imprisoned in solitary confinement during the French Revolution. However the German philosopher, Leibnitz, wrote in a letter dated January 17, 1716 that 'the game called Solitaire pleases me much'.

A later writer has compared it favourably to the crossword puzzle since players can even invent their own problems.

Solitaire is usually played on a board with thirty-seven positions or holes, thirty-six of which are occupied by counters or marbles at the start of play, while the central position is left vacant. If the variant thirty-three hole board is used, it is possible to finish with the last remaining piece in the central hole.

The object of the game is to reduce the thirty-six pieces to a solitary piece in the 'end' position. This is achieved by a series of moves consisting of "short leaps" to remove each piece 'leapfrogged'.

Above: Fox and Geese board set out for Solitaire.
Below: Victorian Asalto board.

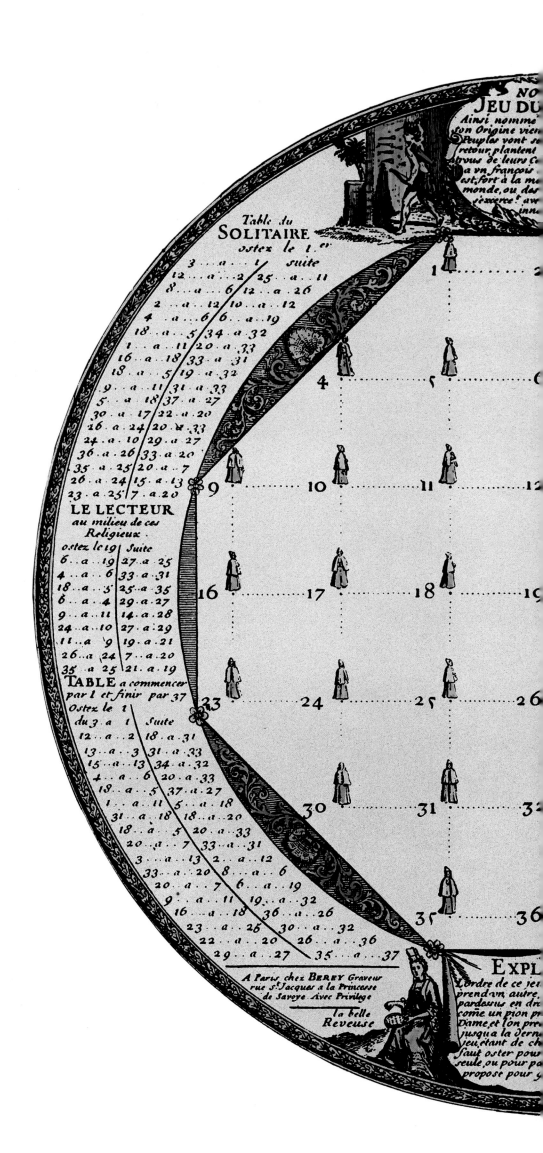

54

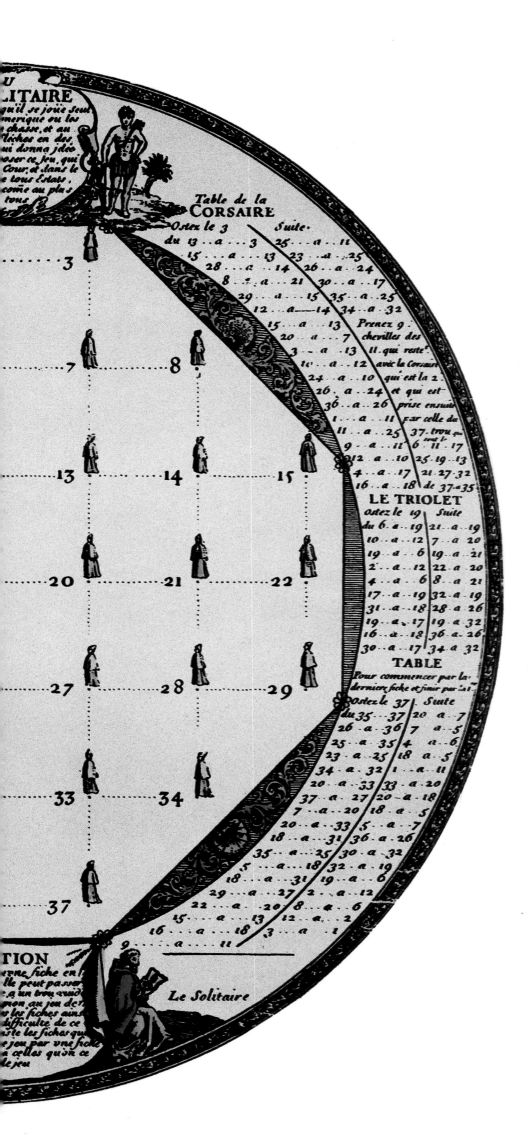

**PLAYERS**
One.

**PIECES**
Thirty-six.
(See equipment sheet.)

**AIM**
To remove the pieces –
leaving one or more as
pre-arranged.

**ORIGIN**
France, eighteenth
century.

RULES
1. One piece *jumps* over
another, landing in any
adjacent and empty space
in any straight line except
the diagonal.

2. The piece which has
been *jumped* is removed and
the 'leapfrogging' piece
remains in the position
where it landed, unless it
can continue *jumping* over
other pieces.

3. A move may be as long
or as short as the player
chooses, that is, there is no
need to continue *jumping*
suitable pieces unless he
wants to.

4. Any piece can *jump* any
other piece.

5. The solution to an
elegant problem is given
below in notation form. At
the start of play point
nineteen is vacant and the
game ends with pieces on
points four, eight,
nineteen, thirty and thirty-
four, in the form of St.
Andrew's Cross.

6 to 19; 14 to 12; 3 to 13; 20
to 7; 1 to 3; 3 to 13; 33 to 20;
29 to 27; 26 to 28; 15 to 29;
29 to 27; 24 to 26; 35 to 25;
18 to 31; 37 to 35; 35 to 25;
5 to 18; 9 to 11; 12 to 10; 23
to 9; 9 to 11; 26 to 12; 12 to
10; 10 to 24; 24 to 26; 26 to
28; 21 to 19; 18 to 20; 13 to
27; 28 to 26; 32 to 19.

6. Although any of the
thirty-seven positions
except the centre may be
left vacant at the start of the
game and the same one left
occupied as the 'end'
position, due to the
symmetry of the board
many of these games would
be equivalent. For
example, if 36 is the initial
vacant position, by turning
the board through quarter
turns, this becomes the
same as 19, 2 and 16.
Therefore, the vacant
positions can be reduced to
these seven – 35, 31, 25, 36,
32, 26, 19.

7. A greater variety of
games is possible if at the
start of play a different
'end' position is decided on
from the opening vacant
position.

8. There are twenty-one
basic games of Solitaire if
Rule seven is followed, as
indicated in the table
below.

Vacant – 'End' positions

| 35 | 35 | 18 | 21 | 1 |
|----|----|----|----|----|
| 36 | 36 | 16 | 2 | 19 |
| 31 | 31 | 11 | 14 | |
| 32 | 32 | 9 | 12 | |
| 25 | 25 | 28 | | |
| 26 | 26 | 23 | 6 | |
| 19 | 19 | 32 | | |
| 24 | 16 | 16 | 16 | |

9. In addition it is always
possible to end with a piece
in the original vacant
position, as described in
Rule six, providing another
seven possible games.

# To Bed with Venus

Excavations made during 1886 in Athens unearthed a silver gaming board with a scalloped circular design of twelve "points", together with an incomplete set of bone pieces shaped like Cycladian fertility goddesses (see illustration). Each piece was clearly numbered on one side only.

Two similar sets of carved bone pieces have been found in Italy at Pompeii—a Greek colonial city. These pieces were also clearly numbered one to fourteen, although again some pieces were missing. A comparable set of numbered pieces shaped like little boars was discovered in 1937. These were found in a wooden box inside a house at Herculaneum, another south Italian city, buried during the same volcanic eruption as Pompeii in 79 A.D.

These four finds suggest that perhaps a complete set consisted of fourteen pieces and that the game in some way involved the twelve "points" of the board.

To Bed with Venus has been devised especially for this book. The design, based on the Athenian board, is inspired by the myth of Venus, Goddess of Love, emerging from the sea on a shell.

The suggestive pieces found at Pompeii have been utilized for a game appropriate to the gambling passions and ribald humour known to have existed in that ancient city. It is easy to imagine some form of To Bed with Venus being played by Pompeians in their luxurious villas sometimes decorated with the erotic frescoes and figurines still visible today.

Any number may play (although it is better limited to six) and there are fourteen goddesses or pieces, numbered one to fourteen on one side, blank on the other. Stakes other than money may have been at risk, similar to those in strip poker.

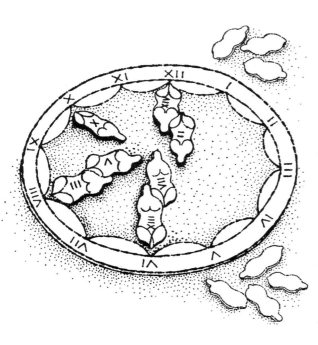

**PLAYERS**
Any number.

**PIECES**
Fourteen goddesses or pieces.
(See equipment sheet.)

**AIM**
To accumulate a score of one hundred before the other players.

**ORIGIN**
Athens and Pompeii (newly devised rules).

RULES

1. The pieces are placed beside the board, number side down, and the order of play is decided by each player turning over one piece. The player who uncovers the highest number has the advantage of starting. The other players take their turn in a clockwise direction around the board.

2. The opening player picks up all the pieces, shakes them in his cupped hands and casts them onto the table. Those with a number showing are placed on the board according to the following rules.

3. The number of the piece or goddess must correspond with the number on the board. For example, piece VI is placed pointing towards *point* six if used as a singleton.

4. Two pieces may also be 'coupled' to form the *point* number – by addition or subtraction. For example, *point* twelve could be occupied by a 'coupling' of VIII and IV (addition), or XIV and II (subtraction).

5. The player tries to use up all his numbered pieces either by making 'couples', which help his score (see Rule nine) or as *singletons* at any particular *point*.

6. If all the numbered pieces are utilized, the player picks up the

remaining blank pieces, shakes them in his hands and casts again.

7. Again the blank pieces are ignored and the numbered ones played onto the board as before.

8. Play continues in this way until either all the pieces have been used, or one or more cannot be played as their *point* is already occupied. The turn then ceases and the player counts his score.

9. All couples score both numbers; for example, fourteen minus two at the twelve *point* scores fourteen plus two, equals sixteen; while six plus four at the ten *point* on the board would score ten. All *singletons* occupying *points* are neutral, while any vacant *point* together with any unused pieces with their numbers showing count against the player. In the figure, left, the player scores five plus three, thirteen plus seven and fourteen plus two, equals forty-four; but empty *points* on the board cost him one plus two, plus three, plus four, plus five, plus seven, plus nine, plus eleven equals forty-two. The concealed pieces, I, IV, VI, VIII, IX, XI and XII are neutral. Thus the player's final score on this turn is forty-four minus forty-two, which equals two.

10. Each player in turn picks up all the pieces, shakes them in his hands and casts them onto the table. His turn continues until either he has used up all the pieces, or has one or more which cannot be placed. When this occurs he calculates his score and the next player's turn then begins.

11. The first player to reach a hundred wins the game.

# Tablan

The board consists of four rows of twelve squares and each of two players has twelve pieces of his own colour. At the beginning of the game a piece stands on each square of the player's back row. (See figure B.) Four dicing sticks, plain on one side and painted on the other, are thrown up two or three times before they are allowed to fall to the ground. Four coins may be substituted and used in the same manner.

| l | k | j | i | h | g | f | e | d | c | b | a |
|---|---|---|---|---|---|---|---|---|---|---|---|
| m | n | o | p | q | r | s | t | u | v | w | x |
| X | W | V | U | T | S | R | Q | P | O | N | M |
| A | B | C | D | E | F | G | H | I | J | K | L |

*Figure A*

**PLAYERS**
Two.

**PIECES**
**Twelve for each side**
**(See equipment sheet.)**

**AIM**
**Occupation of the most home squares.**

**ORIGIN**
**Mysore, India.**

**SCORING**
One plain or tail side up scores two points and another throw. Four plain or tails sides up score eight points and another throw. Four painted sides up score twelve points and another throw. No other throw scores, and the sticks or coins are passed to the other player.

**RULES**
1. The first move of a piece can only be made on a throw of two.

2. A throw of two can be split into two ones if required, two pieces being moved one square each.

3. Throws of eight and twelve can be split similarly into two fours or two sixes.

4. The pieces move in the direction shown in figure A. Black pieces move A to L, L to M, M to X, X to m,

58

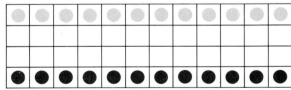

*Figure B*

m to x, x to a and a to l. White pieces move in the opposite direction.

5. Pieces can only capture opposing pieces when they are on the two central rows, or when displacing them on the opponent's back row. Captured pieces are removed from the board.

6. Once a piece reaches a square on the opponent's back row it is immobilized

and does not move again during the game. It cannot be captured.

7. The opponent's home row is occupied square by square starting from a to l (or L to A). (This is an optional rule.)

8. More than one piece can be moved in a turn of play, and more than one capture made if Rules four, five and six are obeyed.

9. There is no doubling up of pieces.

10. Players have to use throws whether convenient or not. The only exception is if the caster has only one piece left near the end of the middle row next to the opponent's back row and the throw does not allow him to occupy one of the squares A to L or a to l. These squares are occupied one after another according to the alphabetical order. (This is optional. Note Rule seven.)

11. The player occupying the most opposing home squares wins the game.

*South Indian compendium of games containing Tablan, reproduced above; Pentalpha (pages 60–61); Cows and Leopards and Lau Kati Kata (pages 62–63).*

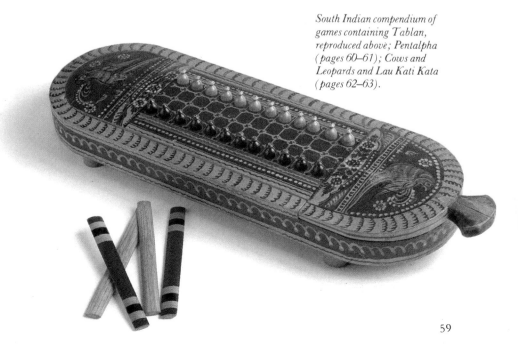

59

# Pentalpha & variants

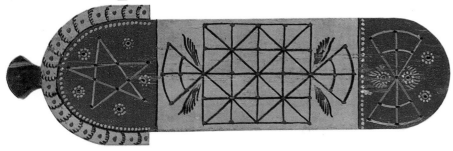

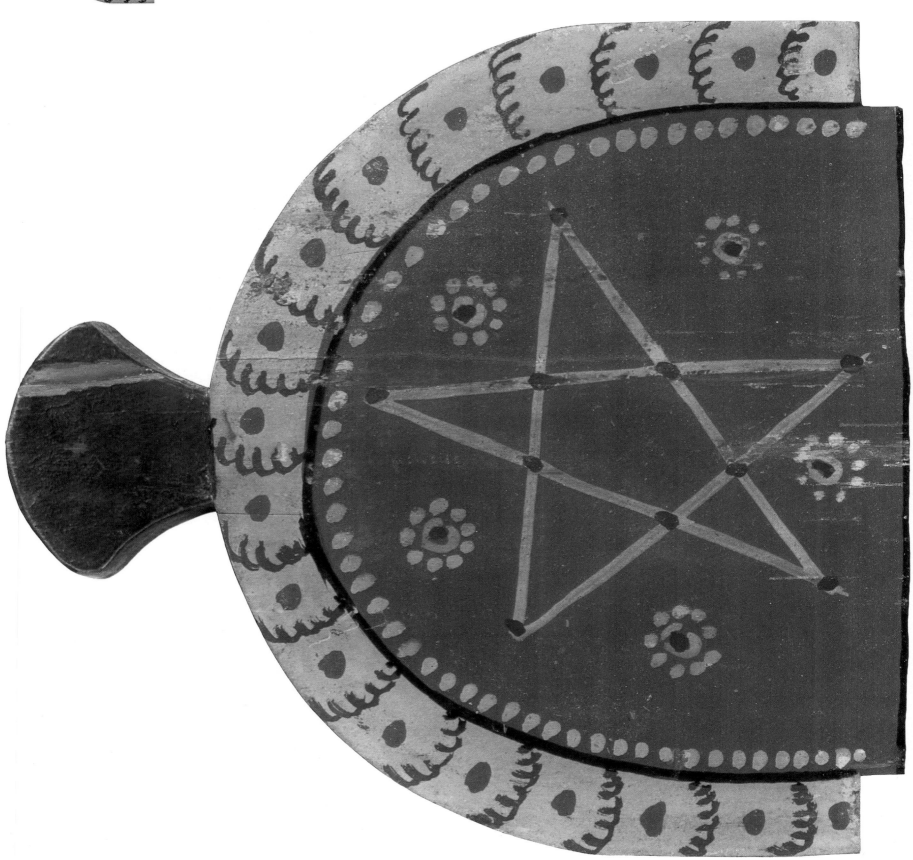

A pentagram is among the several diagrams of games cut into the roofing slabs of a temple at Thebes which stands on the west bank of the Nile in Egypt. The temple was begun by Rameses I, who was the founder of a new royal line, the Nineteenth Dynasty. He was a successful soldier, and was adopted by the last Pharaoh of the previous dynasty, Horemheb, who had no sons of his own. After he became king, Rameses turned his attention to a programme of temple-building, leaving his son, Seti, the task of reconquering Palestine and Syria, which the Egyptian Empire had lost due to the neglect of previous rulers. When Seti in turn became Pharoah, he continued work on the temples his father had begun. The gaming boards appear to have been made by the masons who were shaping the slabs in the quarries before they were placed in the roof, for three of the diagrams were partly cut away when the stones were trimmed to be fitted into their final position.

Almost as soon as the Greeks started navigating the Mediterranean at the beginning of the seventh century, they were attracted to Egypt, tales of whose wealth and power had come down to them from the time before the invasions and chaotic political changes of the previous centuries throughout the Middle East. In the middle of the seventh century the Egyptian ruler Psamtik began hiring Greek mercenary soldiers, and by about 620 B.C. there was a Greek settlement at Naucratis on a western branch of the Nile Delta, where traders from the Aegean imported wine, oil and silver and exported papyrus, manufactured goods and later corn. They found the Egyptian state enfeebled by comparison with the glorious past, but still wealthy by the standards of the small Greek cities they came from and they were much impressed by the long continuity of Egyptian civilization.

The Greeks played a form of Senat (pages 82–83) called Kubeia, and another game called Petteia that seems to have come from Egypt, so it is possible that they took the pentagram game from Egypt too. However, as we do not know the rules of the Egyptian game this is only a supposition, though Sophocles in the fifth century B.C. refers to a game called Pente Grammai, played on five lines.

Pentalpha, still played in Crete today, is probably a derivation of this classical game. In northern India, a variant of the game is known as Lam Turki and after the nine pieces have been introduced onto the board they are removed as in Solitaire. (See Rules three and four.) Pentalpha is a game for one player who starts with nine pieces and tries to introduce all onto nine of the ten points of the board in a particular manner. Unless the secret is discovered, this game is quite difficult.

**PLAYERS**
One.

**PIECES**
Nine pebbles or pieces. (See equipment sheet.)

**AIM**
Introduction of pieces onto the board in a certain order.

**ORIGIN**
Greece, 5th century B.C.

RULES
1. A piece is placed on any unoccupied point, while the player calls 'one'. Then it is moved through another point, 'two', and onto a third point, 'three'. The three points must be in a straight line.

2. This one-two-three sequence is followed for each of the pieces; the first and third points must be empty, but it is not necessary for the second point to be empty.

## Lam Turki

Rules one and two are the same as for Pentalpha, whereas Rules three and four apply only to Lam Turki, the Indian version.

3. A piece is lifted over another onto an empty point beyond, the intervening piece being removed from the board.

4. In a series of similar short leaps all the pieces but one are removed.

*Columns of a temple at Thebes, Egypt.*

# Vultures & Crows (Kaooa)

In Madhya Pradesh, central India, the same board is used for 'Kaooa', which is the game for two players using pieces representing a vulture for one and seven crows for the other. The crows try to hem in the vulture.

**PLAYERS**
Two.

**PIECES**
One vulture for one side; seven crows for the other. (See equipment sheet.)

**AIM**
The vulture tries to destroy four crows; or the crows try to trap the vulture before being reduced to three.

**ORIGIN**
India.

RULES
1. A crow is entered on any point on the board.

2. The vulture is placed on another point.

3. Another crow is entered and the vulture then moves to an adjacent point from his first position.

4. The vulture captures by a short leap over a crow, but is not permitted to capture more than one in any turn of play.

5. The crows are unable to move until all seven have been entered on the board. Then one crow can move to an adjacent point at each turn of play.

6. If the crows trap the vulture and deprive him of the power to move they win the game.

7. If the vulture destroys four crows they become too weak to trap him and he is the winner.

# Cows and Leopards & Lau Kati Kata

Cows and Leopards, under different names and with minor variations in the method of play, is found throughout southern Asia. One player controls two leopards and the other has twenty-four cows with which to try and immobilize the leopards.

**PLAYERS**
Two.

**PIECES**
Two leopards on one side and twenty-four cows on the other.
(See equipment sheet.)

**AIM**
Leopards try to reduce the number of cows until they are too few to immobilize the leopards; cows try to hem in the leopards.

**ORIGIN**
Southern Asia.

RULES
1. The leopard player places a leopard at any *point* on the empty board.

2. A cow is then put on any chosen *point* on the board.

3. The second leopard is introduced onto any *point* on the board.

4. Another cow follows and then a cow is added to the board after each move of a leopard onto an adjacent *point* in any direction.

5. Only when all the cows are on the board can they begin to move.

6. The leopards win if they manage to kill enough cows to make it impossible for the cows to immobilize them.

7. All pieces move one *point* in a turn of play, except for a leopard who makes a capture by a *short leap*. When possible more than one capture may be made in a single turn of play.

8. If the cows completely hem in the leopards, they win the game.

9. The capture of a cow at risk is compulsory.

## Lau Kati Kata

*In this game from Lower Bengal the rules are the same as for Alquerque (see pages 146–147) except that each player has six pieces of his own colour. These are placed on the intersections and the central "point" is left empty at the start of play.*

# Sixteen Soldiers

Sixteen Soldiers

Sixteen Soldiers, played in Sri Lanka (Ceylon) and southern India, is one of a large group of war-games similar to Alquerque (pages 146–147). Both sides are of equal strength. Each player has sixteen pieces of his own colour and the board is similar to the one used for Cows and Leopards (see pages 62–63). The initial position of the pieces is shown below.

In a variant of Sixteen Soldiers, the two players use an additional seven pieces each.

# Tiger

In the Tiger game, only two opposing triangles are used in addition to the main square. This is unlike Sixteen Soldiers (Rule five) and Cows and Leopards (see pages 62–63) in which all four external triangles are used. One player controls a tiger which is placed on the apex of either of the triangles in play and the other player has twenty-four men, nine of which are placed on the central "points" of the square.

**PLAYERS**
Two.

**PIECES**
Sixteen for each side.
Additional seven pieces for each side in variant. (See equipment sheet.)

**AIM**
To capture all the opposing pieces.

**ORIGIN**
Ceylon; southern India.

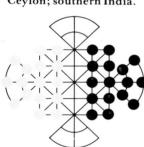

**RULES**
1. The players move their pieces alternately and all pieces can move in any direction along the lines of the board, in a straight line or diagonally, to the next point of intersection.

2. A capture is made by *jumping* over an enemy piece onto a vacant *point* beyond.

3. Any number of enemy pieces may be captured in one turn of play by a piece making a series of *short leaps*.

4. When a player loses all his pieces he loses the game.

5. As a variant, each player has seven additional pieces placed on the *points* of the triangles on his left, leaving only three empty *points* along the central transverse line.

**PLAYERS**
Two.

**PIECES**
One tiger for one side and twenty-four men for the other.

**OBJECT**
The tiger tries to reduce the men to ten; the men try to immobilize the tiger.

**ORIGIN**
India.

RULES
1. In a turn of play any piece may be moved to an adjacent *point* along a marked line.

2. Only the tiger has the power to capture, but capturing is not compulsory.

3. If a tiger has a man, or an uninterrupted succession of an odd number of men adjacent to it along a marked line, and if the *point* immediately beyond the man or odd number of men is vacant, the tiger can leap over the enemy pieces onto the vacant point beyond, removing them from the board.

4. The game begins by the tiger-player removing any three men from the board, whether they form a row or not. He then places the tiger on any vacant *point*.

5. For the next fifteen moves the other player places his remaining men on the board on any vacant *point*, the tiger moving and capturing as opportunity arises in his turn of play.

6. When all the men have been entered on the board, movement of one piece is permitted to an adjacent *point* along a line.

7. The player of the men usually resigns if he is reduced to ten 'men'.

8. If the tiger is hemmed in and cannot move he loses the game.

*Woodcut from the sixteenth century 'Historia Animalium' by Konrad Gesner.*

*Rebels*

*Rebels is known in China as 'Shap luk kon tsu tseung kwan', and is played by labourers and children, the boards often being marked out in the dust of country roads. One player controls the pieces representing sixteen rebel soldiers and the other commands their loyalist general.*

**PLAYERS**
Two.

**PIECES**
Sixteen rebels on one side, one general on the other.
(See equipment sheet.)

**AIM**
Rebels try to capture the general; the general must capture enough rebels to make further play impossible.

**ORIGIN**
China.

RULES
1. At the beginning of the game the pieces are placed as in the figure below.

2. The rebels make the first move.

3. All the pieces move one *point*, along any marked line, but only the general can enter the triangular

sanctuary. If he is trapped within it and cannot move out, his player loses the game.

4. The general captures by *intervention*. He occupies a *point* immediately between two rebels on the same marked line and removes both from the board.

5. The rebels make a *custodian capture* of the general by occupying the *points* on both sides of him, all three pieces being on the same marked line.

6. For example: Black begins by moving A4 to B4. White replies C3 to D4, capturing the rebels on C5 and E3, but makes a fatal mistake, for Black moves B4 to C4, capturing the general and winning the game.

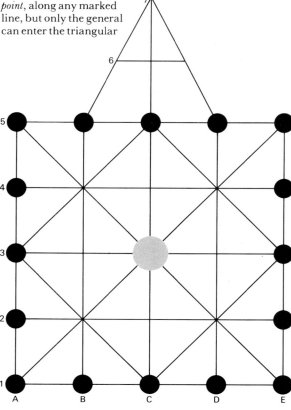

67

# Faro I

# Faro II

Faro is one of the oldest banking games and is thought to have originated in Italy, belonging to the same family of games as Lansquenet, Florentine and Monte Bank. It was very popular in France during the reign of Louis XIV and was introduced into the United States via New Orleans.

The Bourbon whiskey poster illustrated here shows a scene at the old Orient Saloon in Bishee, Arizona, about 1890. Such scenes, liable to erupt into sudden gun-play, were common in this meeting-place for stock promoters, road agents and con men (tricksters). During the 1880's the 'Orient' was a favourite haunt of 'Nifty' Doyle, the singer; 'Dutch Kid' with 'Sleepy Dick' at his side; Murphy the dealer in a black fedora, and close to him 'Smiley Lewis'—a Beau Brummel with a pocket full of mining stock for sale. Meanwhile, in the background, Tony the proprietor kept a watchful eye for possible trouble.

Faro is a game of pure chance. There are many esoteric methods of staking bets, but they add little to the game and tend to confuse the inexperienced, so they are omitted here. The betting units are decided before play begins. These may be units of currency—from the smallest to the highest; or may represent any other commodity; or the game may be played simply with gaming chips as token units without actual value.

A full pack of 52 cards is used and as it is essential for the dealer and players to know which cards remain in the pack, 'cue sheets' may be used. (See next page.) A 'winner' is indicated by a stroke (1). A 'loser' is indicated by a zero (0). 'Soda' is indicated by a dot (.). 'Hock' is indicated by a dash (–). A 'split' is indicated by a cross (x). (See Rules eleven, fourteen and fifteen.)

In gaming saloons, a record of the game was also kept on a 'case-keeper' managed by an employee of the banker. The 'case-keeper' is like an abacus in the form of a miniature board with four beads on a wire opposite each card, as illustrated on the next page. When the deal begins all the beads are pushed against the cards, but as soon as 'soda' is discarded the corresponding bead is moved to the far end of the wire. With every 'turn' (see Rule thirteen) the two beads opposite the cards involved are moved away. When all four cards of a denominator have been played the denomination is dead. If anyone places a stake on a dead denomination it becomes the property of the first player, including the dealer, to notice it and declare the error.

The 'Suicide Table' of Virginia City's Delta Saloon in Nevada, United States of America, was infamous even by standards of the mining West. Three of the table's owners suffered such heavy losses that they committed suicide, giving the table its bad reputation. Originally a Faro bank table, it was brought to Virginia City in the early 1860's. The first owner, said to have been one Black Jake, lost $70,000 in one evening and shot himself.

Bucking the Tiger

CYRUS NOBLE WHISKEY
old goods

The second owner, whose name has been lost, ran the table for a single night's play. Unable to meet his losses, it is said that he committed suicide, although another version of the story claims that one of the punters saved him the trouble.

The table was then stored for several years because no one would deal on it. However, in the late 1890's it was converted for playing another gambling game known as Blackjack or Twenty-one. Its evil reputation seems to have been forgotten until one night during a snowstorm a miner, who had been cleaned out in another gambling house, stumbled half-drunk into the 'Delta'. According to the story, he gambled a gold ring against a $5 gold piece and won. He played all night and by morning had won $86,000 in cash, a team of horses and an interest in a gold mine; everything the owner of the table possessed. A third suicide followed and the table has never been used again. It can still be seen in the old Delta Saloon in Virginia City and evokes memories of a past era. Perhaps the ghosts of its dealers still lean on its green cloth watching for the turn of a card. . .

Whiskey advertisement, c.1890.

**PLAYERS**
Any number.

**PIECES**
Gaming chips. (See equipment sheet: various colours, denoting units of graded value – fifty of the lowest unit, twenty-five of a higher unit and twenty-five of the highest.) One fifty-two pack of cards.

**AIM**
Gambling game of pure chance.

**ORIGIN**
Italy.

**RULES**
1. The dealer acts as the banker, and the stakes involved may be limited at his discretion.

2. Players purchase chips from the banker to facilitate making bets. These were made of ivory or bone but are now usually made of plastic. Their value is denoted by different colours or numerals are stamped on them.

3. The limits imposed by the banker on the size of bets are of two kinds, either a 'plain' or a 'running limit'.

4. The 'plain limit' is the greatest amount to be staked on a card as an initial bet.

5. The 'running limit' is the 'plain limit' multiplied by four. For example, if the 'plain limit' is five, the 'running limit' would be twenty. When the player bets five units and wins he can leave the original stake and its increase, amounting to ten units, where it was, or move it to another card, where he may win another ten units, thus making his stake twenty units, which is the 'running limit' imposed by the particular dealer. If he wins again he can only stake twenty units on the next turn.

6. Allowing a bet to run on in this way is known as 'parleeing' a bet. If the first bet was five units, the second would be ten units, the third twenty units, the fourth forty units, the fifth eighty units, etc. Most bankers allow players to 'parlee' indefinitely as the percentage is in their favour.

7. The banker has a board about one metre long and half a metre wide (three feet by one and a half feet), covered with a green or a grey cloth on which are painted the thirteen cards of one suit, usually spades. The board is placed on a table about one and a quarter metres by three quarter metres (four feet by two and a half feet).

8. Having decided which cards on the Faro board they wish to bet on, the players lay their chips down on the cards selected.

9. When all the bets are placed, the dealer shuffles and cuts the pack, then places the cards face up beside the board, to his right on the table. Traditionally a metal box is used to avoid cheating. This has an opening at the top, large enough for the full face of the uppermost card to be seen. At one end of the box, near the top, is a horizontal slit, wide enough to permit the passage of a single card. The top card is always kept opposite the slit by four springs in the bottom of the box forcing the pack upwards.

10. The first top card is known as 'soda' and is not used, but 'discarded' to the left of the board. The next card is the first 'loser', and is placed between the unplayed pack and 'soda' (discard pile) in front of the dealer. The card left face up on the pack is the 'winner' for that turn.

There is a 'winner' and a 'loser' for every turn, the 'loser' being placed to the left of the pack and the winner left on top of it. On the next and following turns, the winning card of the previous turn is 'discarded' onto the same pile as 'soda'.

11. 'Loser' cards win for the banker and he takes all stakes resting on the corresponding card on the board unless the stake has been 'coppered'. (See Rule fourteen.)

*Above: case-keeper.*

12. 'Winning' cards win for the players, the amount of any bet placed on the corresponding card on the board being paid by the banker.

13. Each pair of cards is known as a 'turn'. There are twenty-five 'turns' to a game; the 'soda' and 'hock' (the last card turned up) making up the fifty-two cards of the pack.

14. A player may bet that a card will be a 'loser' by placing a 'copper' on the top of his stake. This is called 'coppering' as originally copper coins or copper washers were used for this purpose.

15. Whenever the 'winning' and 'losing' cards in a 'turn' are the same, (two kings, two sixes, etc.), this is known as a 'split' and the dealer takes half the chips staked on them. In an honest game this is the bank's percentage and can be expected to occur about three times in two deals.

16. At the end of each 'turn' bets are settled and new ones made for the next 'turn'.

17. When the pack is exhausted (note, the last card or 'hock' is not used), a fresh deal is made and the playing continues as before. Originally the 'hock' card belonged to the dealer and increased the banker's percentage.

18. A player may avoid risking his stake on any particular turn by declaring to the dealer: 'I bar this bet for a turn.'

19. A player may reduce his stake by half if he declares to the dealer: 'one-half this bet goes,' and unless the order is revoked, it remains in force until the end of the deal.

20. When there is only one turn left in the pack (two cards plus 'hock'), players may 'call the last turn', that is, guess the order in which the last three cards will appear. If the three cards are different and a player guesses correctly he wins four times his stake. If there are two cards the same, he wins twice his stake.

*The coins in this and the previous page are house-tokens and an 'Eisenhower dollar' used in Nevada casinos.*

| A | 0 | 0 | 0 | 1 |
| 2 | 0 | 1 | 1 | 1 |
| 3 | 1 | 1 | 0 | 0 |
| 4 | 1 | 0 | 0 | 0 |
| 5 | 0 | 0 | X | |
| 6 | 1 | 1 | 1 | 1 |
| 7 | 1 | 0 | 0 | 1 |
| 8 | 1 | 1 | 0 | 1 |
| 9 | 0 | 1 | 0 | - |
| 10 | 0 | 0 | 0 | 1 |
| J | 1 | 1 | 1 | 0 |
| Q | 1 | 0 | 1 | 0 |
| K | . | 0 | 0 | 1 |

*Left: an example of a Faro cue sheet. The dot ( . ) indicates 'soda'. The dash ( − ) indicates 'hock'. A stroke ( / ) indicates a 'winner'. A cypher ( 0 ) indicates a 'loser'. Here, a king is 'soda', the five split out, a nine is 'hock'.*

# Gold Rush

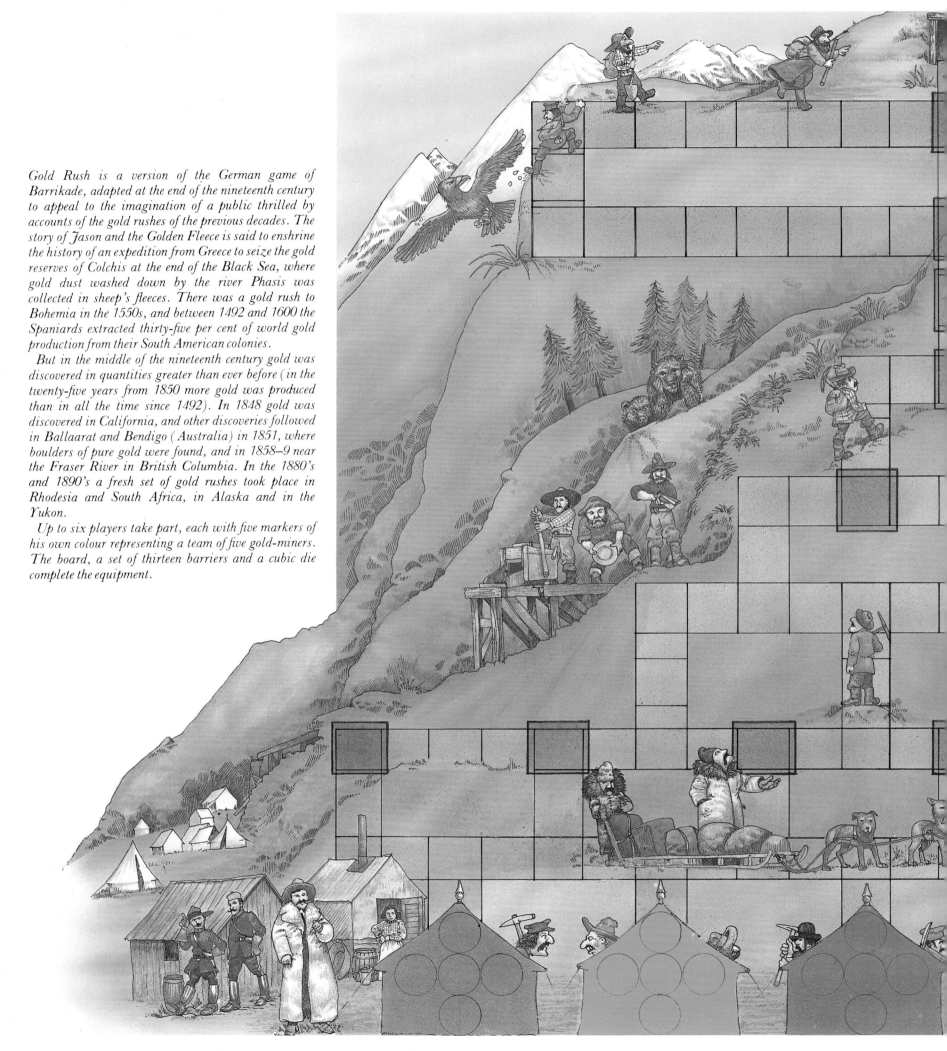

Gold Rush is a version of the German game of Barrikade, adapted at the end of the nineteenth century to appeal to the imagination of a public thrilled by accounts of the gold rushes of the previous decades. The story of Jason and the Golden Fleece is said to enshrine the history of an expedition from Greece to seize the gold reserves of Colchis at the end of the Black Sea, where gold dust washed down by the river Phasis was collected in sheep's fleeces. There was a gold rush to Bohemia in the 1550s, and between 1492 and 1600 the Spaniards extracted thirty-five per cent of world gold production from their South American colonies.

But in the middle of the nineteenth century gold was discovered in quantities greater than ever before (in the twenty-five years from 1850 more gold was produced than in all the time since 1492). In 1848 gold was discovered in California, and other discoveries followed in Ballaarat and Bendigo (Australia) in 1851, where boulders of pure gold were found, and in 1858–9 near the Fraser River in British Columbia. In the 1880's and 1890's a fresh set of gold rushes took place in Rhodesia and South Africa, in Alaska and in the Yukon.

Up to six players take part, each with five markers of his own colour representing a team of five gold-miners. The board, a set of thirteen barriers and a cubic die complete the equipment.

## PLAYERS
Two to six.

## PIECES
**Five markers for each player and one set of thirteen barriers. (See equipment sheet.)**

## SCORING
**One cubic die.**

## AIM
**A race to manoeuvre all the miners of one team into the Gold Mine.**

## ORIGIN
**Germany, 1890's.**

## RULES
1. The players place their five miners outside their tents and put the little square barriers on the *points* indicated on the board.

2. The players throw the cubic *die* in turn, the player with the highest score casting again to start the game. Players with equal scores throw again to decide seniority. The player with the lowest score moves last.

3. A miner leaves his tent and moves the number of *points* the player has scored, counting from the *point* nearest to his tent.

4. He may move forwards or sideways according to his score, but not sideways in both directions in the same throw.

5. If a player throws a six, he moves one of his miners by six *points*, and then throws again, to move the same piece according to his new score.

6. A miner can pass over another miner of any colour.

7. Only one miner can rest on any *point*.

8. If a miner lands on a *point* occupied by a miner of another colour, the latter is sent back to his tent to begin his journey again.

9. All five miners of a team may be on the trail at the same time.

10. A miner cannot pass a barrier. To get beyond it he must land on it with an exact throw.

11. When a miner lands on a barrier he rests there until the next throw. On moving off, the player has the choice of leaving the barrier where it is, or of moving it to some other unoccupied *point*, either to protect his own miners, or to hinder those of his opponents. Barriers cannot be placed on the starting line, which must remain clear.

12. If a miner is resting on a barrier, and a miner from a rival tent lands on it, the first miner is sent back to the start again and loses the privilege of moving the barrier.

13. If all the miners belonging to one player are blocked and he cannot use a throw, the throw is lost.

14. If a miner is one *point* from the Gold Mine, and the player scores any number other than a one and cannot move his other miners, the number scored must be used to move the miner away from the Gold Mine. If this is not possible because he is blocked by a barrier, or the *point* is occupied by one of his own pieces, the throw is lost.

15. The first player to manoeuvre all his miners into the Gold Mine wins the game.

**PLAYERS**
Two or more.

**PIECES**
One marker for each player. (See equipment sheet.)

**SCORING**
One six-sided die.

**AIM**
A race round the board to reach square one hundred.

**ORIGIN**
Probably United States of America, 1898 or 1899.

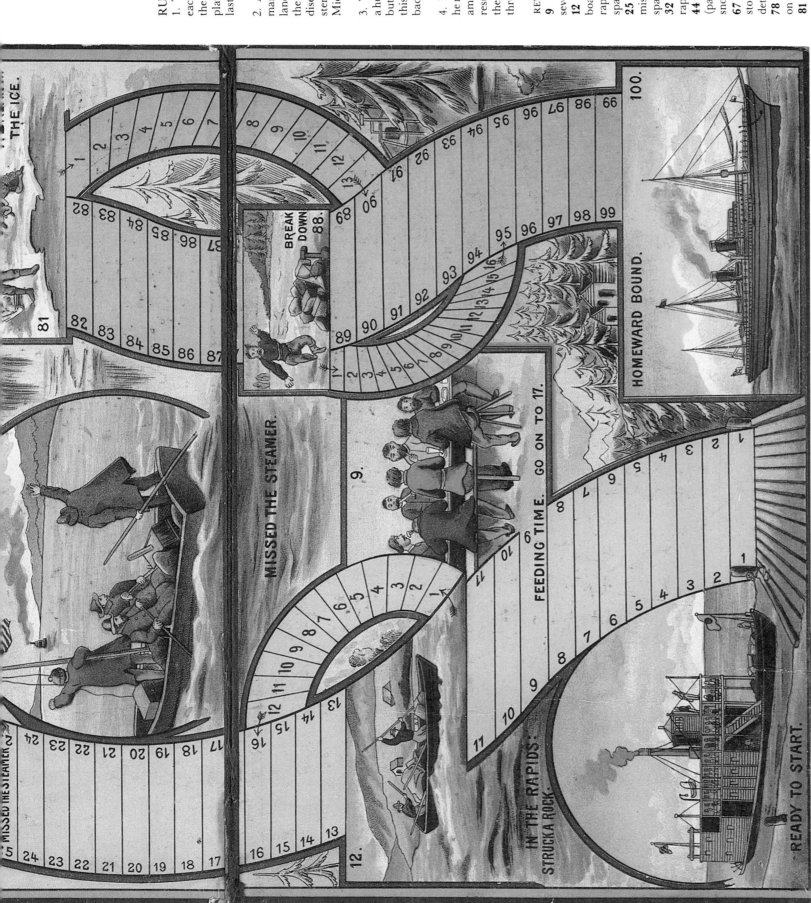

## RULES

1. The *die* is thrown by each player to determine the order of play: highest playing first and lowest last.

2. At the start of play, the markers are placed on the landing-stage, to represent the players' disembarkation from the sternwheeler at St. Michael's.

3. The first player to reach a hundred wins the game, but if a player overshoots this number he counts backwards by the excess.

4. If a player throws a six he moves his piece by this amount and obeys any resulting instructions, but then casts again. Every six thrown earns another turn.

## REWARDS AND PENALTIES

**9** Feeding time. Go to seventeen.

**12** The 'scow' (rowing boat) strikes a rock in rapids. Portage along red spaces to sixteen.

**25** The river steamer is missed. Detour along red spaces to thirty-six.

**32** Man overboard in rapids. Miss a turn.

**44** The 'komatik' (packsled) is stuck in a snowdrift. Miss a turn.

**67** Arrive at Dawson City stoney broke. Take red detour to seventy-nine.

**78** A nugget is found. Go on to eighty-nine.

**81** Blocked by thawing and broken ice. Take red detour to ninety-five.

**100** The winner: board a sail-and-steamship, probably representing the 'Portland' bound for 'Up to Klondyke' (note the quaint spelling) was probably published in 1898 or 1899 when the gold fever was at its height. A game for two or more players, each with a distinctive marker and using a six-sided 'die'.

*Gold dust was discovered in 1896 on Rabbit Creek off the Yukon River, near a small place called Dawson in the Klondike. The creek was soon renamed Bonanza Creek and rapidly became the centre of a mining camp. After a ship had called in at Seattle from Alaska in the spring of 1897, news of the Klondike was flashed round the world by telegraph and caused a sensation. During the next few months thousands of men and several women struggled to the Klondike area. The longest, slowest, most expensive but also the safest route was by ship from Seattle to St. Michael, a port a few miles north of the Yukon Delta, and then up the river by sternwheeler to Dawson. In two years Dawson had grown from a few shacks into a city.*

'Seattle or the 'Excelsior', for San Francisco.

75

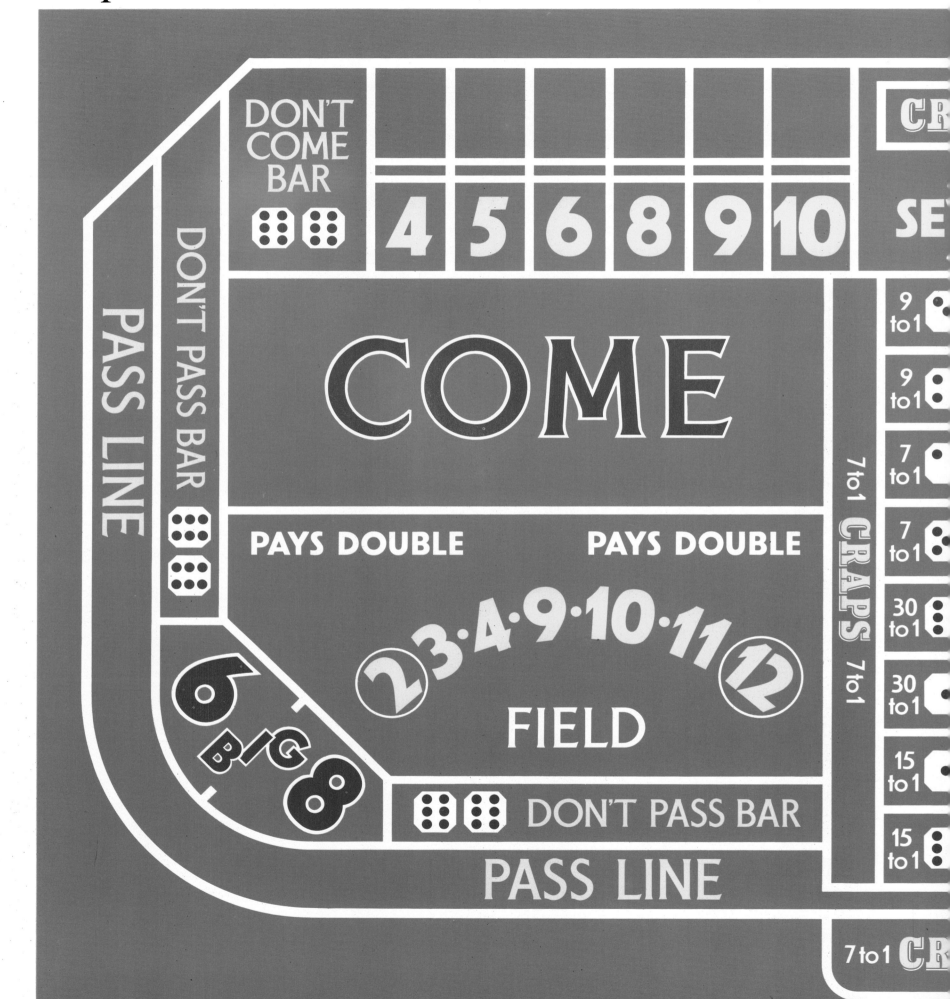

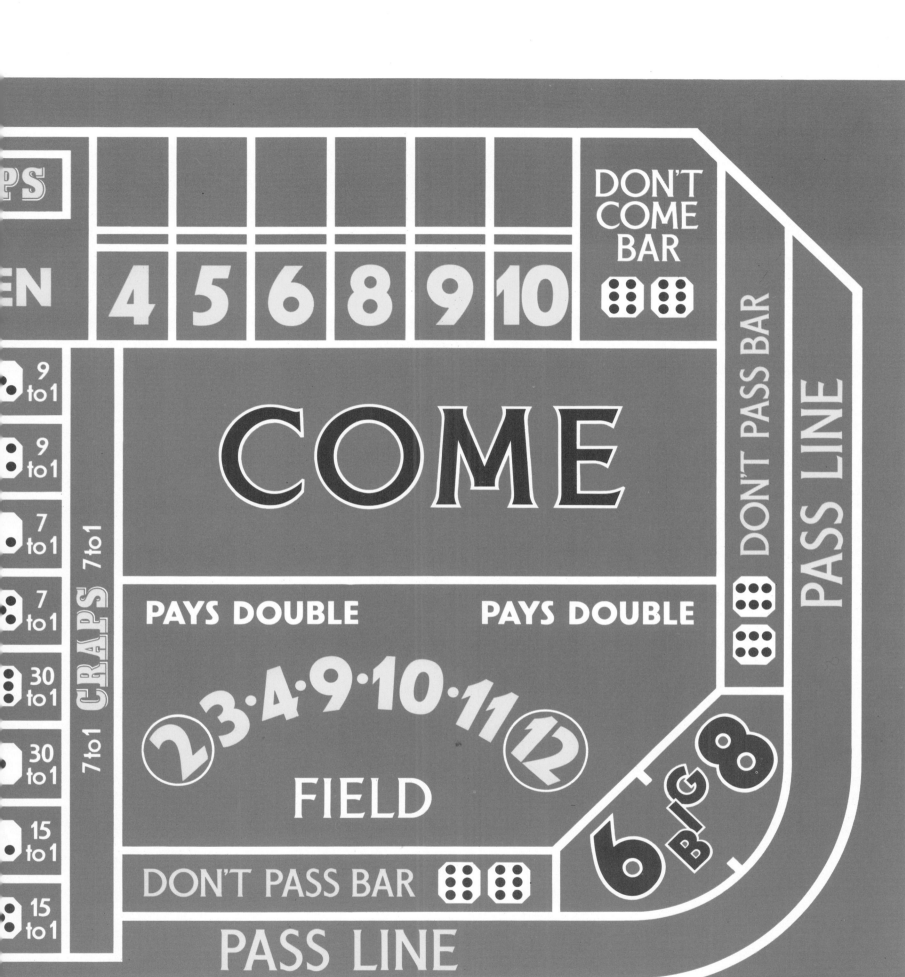

# Craps II

Craps developed from Hazard, which was a very similar gambling game popular from the time of the Middle Ages. The young men in Chaucer's 'The Pardoner's Tale' (fourteenth century), who set out to 'deal with' Death after one of their comrades died and met him in circumstances they did not expect, were, we are told, given up to 'such folly as riotous living, Hazard, brothels and taverns'. Hazard continued to be very popular with gamblers throughout the seventeenth and eighteenth centuries, and it was through Hazard that William Crockford made his fortune and founded the gaming club that still bears his name in London, England. Born in 1775, he was the son of a London fishmonger, and at first followed his father's trade. But he soon abandoned fish for gambling, became a partner in a gaming house (he is reported to have won one hundred thousand pounds in twenty-four hours), a bookmaker and a race-horse owner. In 1827 he opened his new gaming house, whose splendour dazzled contemporaries, and where the highest and most fashionable of London society gathered to take supper and pass the night with wit and Hazard. Hazard was also common in New Orleans around 1800, where the rules were simplified to produce Craps as it is played today.

Craps is still the most popular casino game in Nevada, United States of America, and is increasingly played at home. To cater to this demand, modern miniature Craps tables manufactured in plastic by the Japanese are sold in many Nevada resorts. The small circular compartment into which the two dice are dropped is so constructed that their weight triggers an electrical contact with a small motor powered by three torch batteries. The base of the compartment revolves rapidly and the dice are thrown out against the side of the table. Bets are not placed on the table as in the full-sized casino game, but on a separate board, to prevent the chips being scattered by the dice. The rules given here for family Craps have been adapted from those used in casinos.

In a casino, all bets are against the house and the craps table is usually operated by four employees: the Boxman, who sits at the centre of one side of the board, drops all currency into the money box and watches all transactions; two Dealers, who stand one at either side of the Boxman, collect the losing wagers and pay off the winning wagers on their own side of the table; and the Stickman, who stands in the middle of the players' side of the table, is responsible for the handling of the dice and the Proposition bets located in the centre of the layout.

Craps is played with two six-sided dice and chips are used for stakes, each player starting with twenty of his own colour. The illustration shows chips of White, Blue, Yellow, Red and Green.

**PLAYERS**
Any number.

**PIECES**
Twenty gaming chips of distinct colour for each player. (See equipment sheet.)

**SCORING**
Two cubic dice.

**AIM**
Gambling to beat the odds.

**ORIGIN**
Medieval Europe.

**RULES**
1. Each player casts the two dice in turn, the highest caster becoming the 'shooter' and the other players arranging themselves around the board with the next highest scorer on the left of the 'shooter' and the lowest on his right.

2. The 'shooter' places a number of chips in front of himself as his bet. He is betting that he will win and the other players are invited to put up collectively an equal amount as a bet that he will lose. The bets can be won or lost on the first roll or throw of the dice.

3. 'Natural'. If the 'shooter' throws seven or eleven (the sum of the numbers shown on the top faces of the two dice) he wins and collects his opponents' bets. These two numbers are known as a 'natural'.

4. 'Shooter's point'. If the 'shooter' throws two, three, or twelve, he loses; these numbers being known as 'craps'. Any other number – four, five, six, eight, nine, or ten – is neutral, but becomes the 'shooter's point'. He continues to cast the dice until he throws either his 'point', (the same number again) when he wins, or a seven when he loses.

5. A seven on the first roll is a win for the 'shooter', but in later rolls it loses. All bets are settled either way on a throw of seven.

6. When the 'shooter' wins he 'passes', retains the dice and is the 'shooter' for the next roll. When he loses, he 'misses' and the dice are passed clockwise to the player on his left, who becomes the new 'shooter'.

7. The game ends when every player has been the 'shooter', but a new game may carry straight on.

8. Players may also bet among themselves. They might bet that the 'shooter' 'passes', or 'misses'. A bet that the 'shooter' will win is called a 'right bet', and that he will lose a 'wrong bet'.

9. At any stage in the 'shooter's' series of rolls, players may bet that he 'comes' or 'don't come'. A 'come' bets that the 'shooter' will win; 'don't come' bets that he will lose.

10. Further side bets may be made after the 'shooter' has made his 'point', when players can bet either that he makes it or that he does not.

11. Many other side bets can be made, the most popular being the 'hardway bets' which are usually made after a count has been established to increase the amount wagered on that 'point'. These 'hardway bets' are the four 'point' totals with even numbers – four, six, eight and ten – which are valid only if a pair of the same number appear. For example, a 'hard' four is made up of a pair of two's. The player loses if either seven, or an 'easy' combination of one-and-three is cast. The wager is only settled by a roll of a 'hard' or 'soft' combination, or a seven.

**BETTING**
Craps boards vary in details; the one shown here is like those used in the United States of America, such as in the Nevada casinos.

a. A bet on the 'pass line' pays even money, winning on seven or eleven, and losing on two, three, or twelve on the first roll, known as the 'come-out' roll. If any other number comes up, this is the 'shooter's point'. If the same number comes up again before a seven is thrown the 'punter' (betting player) wins, in all other cases, he loses.

b. 'Don't pass bar'. This is the opposite of (a.), the 'punter' losing on seven or eleven, and winning on two or three on the first roll. (Twelve is a 'stand-off' and no one wins.) The 'punter' also loses if the 'point' comes up before seven.

c. 'Come'. A 'come' bet may be made at any time after the first roll, the 'punter' winning on seven and eleven, and losing on two, three or twelve. Any other number is the 'punter's point', and if it comes up again before a seven appears he wins.

d. 'Don't come'. This is the reverse of (c.), the 'punter' losing on a seven or eleven, and winning on two or three. (Twelve is a 'stand-off'.) The 'punter' wins if seven comes up before his 'point'.

e. 'Field'. This is a bet for one roll only. The 'punter' bets on two, three, four, nine, ten, eleven and twelve. If any of these numbers is thrown on the next roll, he wins even money except on two or twelve when he wins two to one.

f. 'Big six and eight'. The 'punter' wins even money if a six or an eight is rolled before a seven.

g. 'Any seven'. If a seven is thrown on the first roll after the 'punter' bets, he wins four for one.

h. 'Hardways'. The 'punter' wins at the odds quoted on the board if the exact combination of numbers comes up on which the bet is laid. The 'punter' loses if the same number is rolled in any other way, or if a 'seven' comes up.

i. 'Any craps'. The 'punter' wins seven for one if two, three, or twelve is thrown on the first roll after he places his bet.

j. 'Eleven'. The 'punter' wins fifteen for one if eleven is thrown on the first roll after placing his bet.

k. 'The odds'. Once a 'point' is established, either a 'shooter's point' on the first roll, or a 'come point' on a succeeding roll, the 'punter' can get odds with the dice, or give odds against the dice. Two to one is given on ten and four, three to two on five and nine, six to five on eight and six. The 'punter' lays the same odds when betting against the 'point'. The pay-off is made on whether or not the 'point' shows before the seven.

l. 'Place bets'. The 'punter' may make a 'place bet' on the following numbers: four, five, six, eight, nine or ten. The number placed must be made by the 'shooter' before a seven is thrown. The pay-off is as follows: nine to five on four or ten; seven to five on five or nine; seven to seven on six or eight. 'Place bets' may be removed at any time before a roll.

*A group of players leaning over a Craps table intent on placing their bets.*

# Seega & High Jump

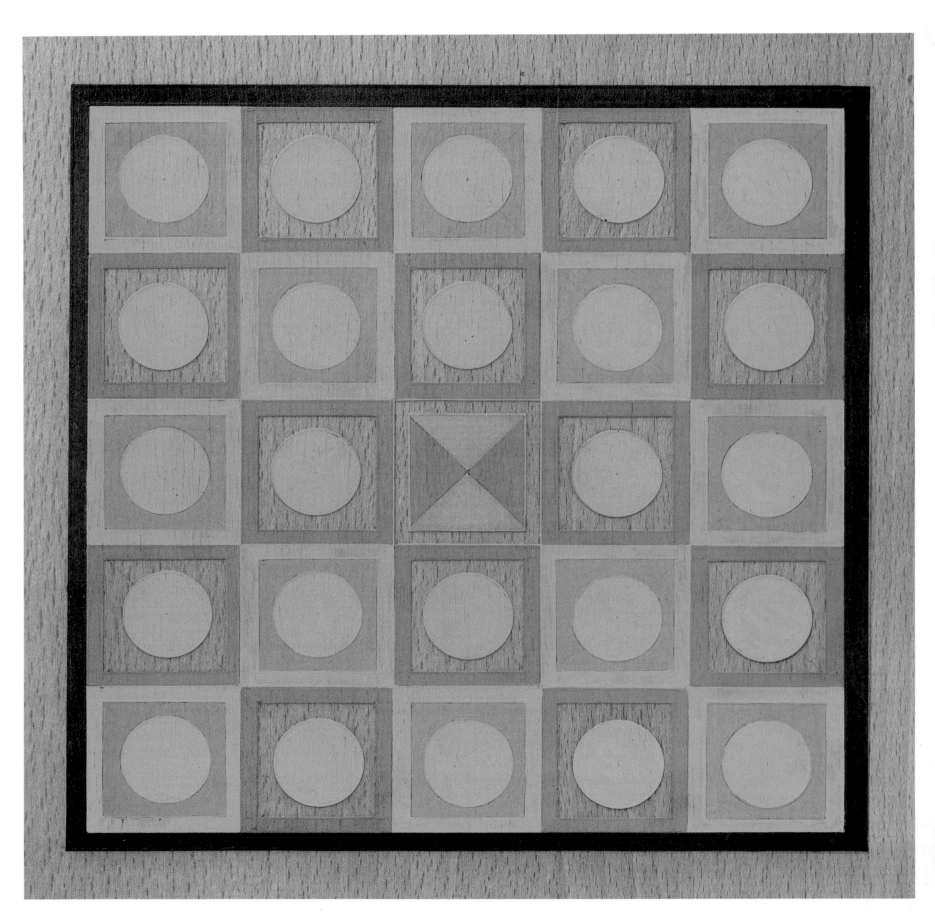

# Seega

*In the early part of the last century Seega was popular with Egyptian peasants and it is still played by the Somalis. A board of five by five squares is marked out on the ground with the central square differentiated in some way. The two players start with twelve stones each of their own colour, although any suitable pieces may be used. There are two phases in the game.*

*Seega may also be played on a board of seven by seven squares with each player having twenty-four pieces, or on a nine by nine board with forty pieces for each player.*

**PLAYERS**
Two.

**PIECES**
Twelve for each side.
(See equipment sheet.)

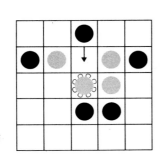

**AIM**
Major win: to capture the most opposing pieces.
Minor win: to retain more pieces than the opponent in a 'barrier' position.

**ORIGIN**
Egypt, late eighteenth century or earlier.

RULES

PHASE ONE
1. The players have alternate turns, each placing two pieces at a time on any vacant squares, except for the central square which is left uncovered in the first phase.

2. When all the pieces are in position, the player placing the last two begins the second phase.

PHASE TWO
3. A piece can move to any adjacent vacant square, including the central one, in any straight line except the diagonal.

4. Capture is made by the *custodian* method: a piece is removed from the board if it can be trapped between two hostile pieces, all three occupying *points* on a straight line. The player continues to move his piece

as long as it can capture. (See figure above.)

5. Although the capture of offered pieces is compulsory, a player has the right to choose a lesser in preference to a greater number if there is an alternative.

6. A player can move a piece between two hostile pieces without it being taken, but if one of the pieces is moved and then returned it makes a *custodian* capture.

7. A piece on the central square is safe from attack, even though it is trapped between two hostile pieces.

8. If a player cannot make a move, the opponent must take an extra turn and make an opening for the player who is blocked.

9. A player achieves a major win if he captures all his opponent's pieces.

10. If a 'barrier' position arises, as shown in the figure below, the player with the most pieces on the board achieves a minor win.

11. If both players have the same number of pieces in a 'barrier' position, the game is drawn.

12. The frequency of draws is a weakness in the game. Each player can make a 'barrier' with only

his own pieces behind it and these can be moved without the possibility of attack. The initial placing of the pieces in the first phase is important in preventing these 'barriers'.

*Somalis with their cattle at a watering-hole.*

# High Jump

*The Somalis also use the Seega board for another game called High Jump. The opening position of the stones or pieces is shown in the figure below.*

**PLAYERS**
Two.

**PIECES**
Twelve for each side.
(See equipment sheet.)

**AIM**
Capture or blockage of opponent's pieces.

**ORIGIN**
Somalia.

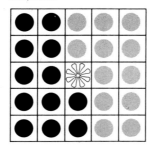

RULES
1. The stones or pieces move as in Seega: one square in a straight line, in any direction except the diagonal.

2. Pieces capture opposing pieces by *jumping* over them in any straight line except diagonally, onto a vacant square immediately beyond. Several pieces can be taken in a succession of *short leaps* by one piece in one turn of play.

3. Making a capture is not compulsory.

4. The player who captures or blocks all his opponent's pieces wins the game.

# Senat

Senat is the Egyptian forerunner of all the Backgammon family of race-games. Later developments include the Greek game called Kubeia, otherwise known as Grammai. The Roman game of Ludus Duodecim Scriptorum (see pages 84–85) was probably a derivation of this game. The Senat pieces illustrated below right were found by Sir Flinders Petrie. He first came to Egypt in 1880, and spent several decades excavating there. He was the first archaeologist to use the pains-taking methods of modern excavation: the trowel, the camel-hair brush and the record-book; it is because of his work that archaeology, the attempt to gain evidence about the past through its physical remains, distinguished itself from mere treasure-hunting.

The game of Senat illustrated here, is based on a board, now in the Louvre Museum, Paris, France, thought to have once belonged to Queen Hatshepsut (c.1500 B.C.). It forms the upper surface of a shallow box divided into thirty squares by strips of ivory. The underside of the box is marked out into twenty squares for another game called Tau (Robbers) as shown in the

figure below. This gaming box held twenty little carved pieces, each in the shape of a lion's head, which were presumably used for both games.

Another Tau board was found in Cyprus dated about 1580 B.C. (figure A); it seems to be a link with earlier forms of the game found in the Royal cemetery at the ancient Sumerian city of Ur, in modern Iraq. Three

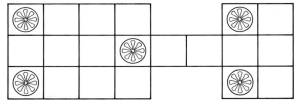

Figure B

complete boards and three fragments were found by Sir Leonard Woolley during excavations conducted between 1922 and 1934. The intact examples show a twelve-square rectangle arranged in four rows of three, joined by two squares to a smaller rectangle of six squares arranged in two rows of three. (See figure B.)

If the smaller rectangle is straightened out into a tail this board is obviously similar to that found in Cyprus.

Three of the Ur boards were accompanied by casting

sticks used like dice to control the moves of the pieces. Dice in the shape of a pyramid with four triangular sides, two corners tipped and two plain, were found with two of the other boards.

No rules of the game have survived, but this reconstruction is based on a study of the available material and comparison with other games of the same group.

The earliest record of Senat is a wall-painting on the tomb of Hesy of the Third Dynasty, about 2686 to 2613 B.C. (see figure C). As the game was probably a race-game, it is likely that the pieces entered at the I-square at the left hand end of the top row and travelled along it. The C-sign represented ten; so throws totalling ten would bring them to the C-square of the same row, and ten more to the star. At this early date it seems that the players had seven pieces each and used four casting sticks to control their movement. These casting sticks were either rounded or painted on one side while the other contrasting side was either flat or plain respectively. Any suitable double-sided dice, such as coins, may be substituted.

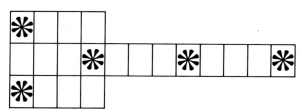

Figure A

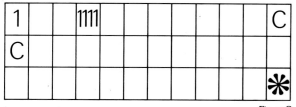

Figure C

## PLAYERS
Two.

## PIECES
Ten lions for one side and ten dogs for the other. (See equipment sheet.)

## SCORING
Four casting sticks or four double-sided dice or coins.

## AIM
A race to marshal all one's pieces in position on the board.

## ORIGIN
Egypt, c.2686–2613 B.C.

## SCORING
One painted side or head up scores one.
Two painted sides or heads up scores two.
Three painted sides or heads up scores three.
Four painted sides or heads up scores four.
Four plain sides or tails up scores five.

## RULES
1. At the beginning of the game all the pieces are off the board.

2. The players throw the four double-sided dice alternately, and enter their pieces onto the marked squares I, II, III, X, and ♀ according to their scoring. Only a single piece can rest on any of these squares at a time and if the square of the number thrown is already occupied, the turn is lost.

3. A player may move a piece onwards from a marked square, or introduce another of his pieces onto the board if this is possible, with any throw.

4. Pieces on marked squares are safe.

5. There is no 'piling' of pieces (one on top of another). After passing the fifth square, marked with the sign of a gateway (♀), any piece 'hit' by an opposing piece (the piece already occupying a square when a hostile piece lands on it) is removed and starts again.

6. The first piece to arrive on the thirtieth square (marked with a star on Hesy's board—see figure C), wins a bonus of five points, setting the pattern of play – the player's other pieces land on even squares while his opponent moves his pieces onto odd squares. At the end of the game the pieces of both players are distributed alternately along the lower and middle rows.

7. Once a piece is on its final square it is safe from attack.

8. The first player to marshal all his pieces on his own squares wins the game and ten points, scoring an extra point for each additional throw required by his opponent to complete his final formation.

*Right: Herihot, the High Priest of Amun in Egypt, playing Senat, c.1080 B.C.*

*Right: Senat pieces found by Sir Flinders Petrie in the Nile Valley, Egypt*

83

# *Ludus Duodecim Scriptorum*

Ludus Duodecim Scriptorum, which in Latin means 'Game of the Twelve Letters', is played on a board of three rows of "points", usually in the form of letters. The letters make short sentences as on the board reproduced here, which is a copy of one found at Timgad, a Roman town in north Africa. The English version shown in figure A is adapted to give the spirit of the Latin, rather than its exact meaning: 'to swim' has been substituted for the original 'to wash'.

Another board found at Ostia, the ancient port of Rome, Italy, was meant for beginners and indicated the direction in which the pieces could move (see figure B).

| | |
|---|---|
| TO HUNT | TO SWIM |
| TO PLAY | TO GRIN |
| THIS IS | TO LIVE |

Figure A

No rules for Duodecim Scriptorum have survived, but literary references exist relating it to a later version called Tabula which flourished in the Roman Empire from the first to the seventh centuries A.D.

The rules for Tabula still exist and are similar to Sugoroku (see pages 92–93). The game was played on a board with two rows of twelve spaces or points, using three cubic dice. The rules given here have been derived from these sources and are probably very close to those originally used.

| | |
|---|---|
| CCCCCC | BBBBB |
| AAAAAA | AAAAAA |
| DDDDDD | EEEEE |

Figure B

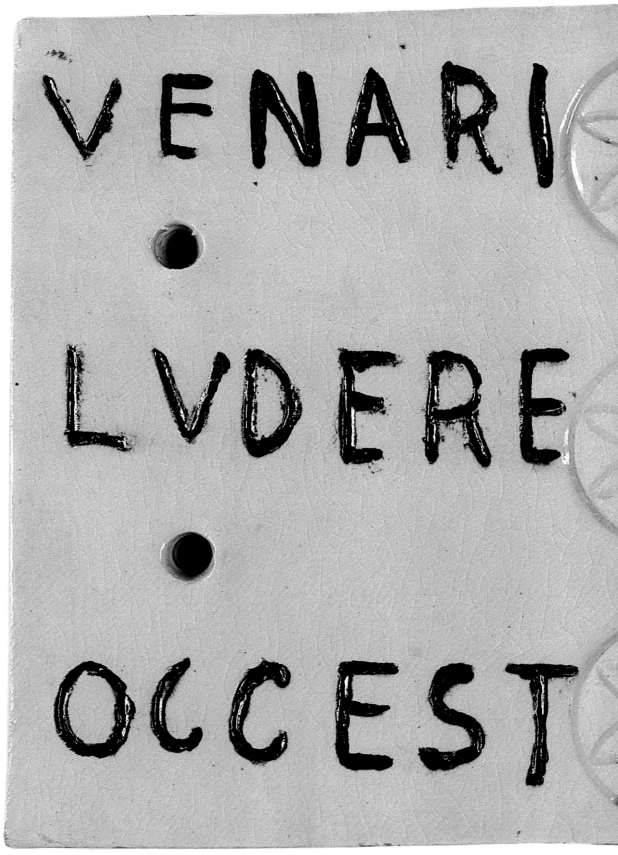

VENARI
LVDERE
OCCEST

**PLAYERS**
Two.

**PIECES**
**Fifteen for each side.**
**(See equipment sheet.)**

**SCORING**
**Three cubic dice.**

**AIM**
**A race to get one's pieces**
**off the board in an anti-**
**clockwise direction.**

**ORIGIN**
**Roman Empire.**

**RULES**
1. Each player has fifteen
flat discs or counters which
are off the board at the start
of play. They are
introduced onto their own
set of six 'A' *points*
according to the throws of
three cubic dice – marked
on their six faces with the
numerals from one to six.

2. When all a player's
pieces are on the six 'A'
*points*, (any number may
occupy the same *point*),
they begin to move anti-
clockwise around the
board in the direction A-B-
C-D-E and off the board.
(See figure B.)

3. Once off the 'A' *points*,
*singletons* known as 'vagi'
(wanderers) are sent off the
board when hit by an
opponent's piece, and have
to be re-entered at the
player's next throw.

4. A player can pile any
number of pieces on a
space; piled men called
'ordinarii' (orderlies) are
immune from attack and
hold the *point* against the
opponent's pieces.

5. Pieces that are blocked
and cannot move on any
throw of the dice are known
as 'inciti' (immovables).

6. The three dice are
thrown alternately by the
players and the numbers
scored can be used singly
or in combination, but
cannot be divided.

7. *Doublet* and *triplet*
throws do not give a second
turn.

8. Every throw of the dice
has to be used, even if this is
to the player's disadvantage.

9. The first player to *bear
off* all his pieces is the
winner.

# Chasing the Girls

Iceland (which means island in Icelandic) lies roughly mid-way between Greenland and the European mainland in the northern Atlantic. It was probably from here that the early Vikings launched their forays into Greenland and 'Vinland', or America. The island was first discovered by Norsemen around 870 A.D. and was quickly settled. The Althing, the Icelandic parliament (claimed to be the oldest in Europe), dates back to 930 A.D. The warring and dissension among the island's leading families over the next few centuries became one of the main themes of the Icelandic sagas, which are often held to be one of the finest European literary achievements of the Middle Ages. From the thirteenth century, Iceland was linked with Norway, then with Denmark, achieving indepedence in 1944.

Today, Iceland is the most sparsely populated country in Europe. Its inhabitants, nearly all direct descendants of the Vikings, live along the coastal plains and river valleys, with sheep farming, and more especially the prosperous fishing industry, as their chief means of support. The interior of the country is a huge barren plateau offering a rich contrast between enormous glaciers and the biggest collection of hot springs and solfarätas (which emit hot gas) to be found anywhere in the world.

In isolated parts of Iceland, table-boards of a Backgammon type (see pages 88–91) are still found with "points" made of strips of wood tacked onto a plank, similar to the Tabula boards of the Late Roman period. A popular game played in these outlying districts is 'Ad Elta Stelpur', or Chasing the Girls.

The opening position of the pieces is shown in the figure to the right.

*Below: an Icelandic farmstead.*

## PLAYERS
Two.

## PIECES
Six white girls for one side and six red for the other.
(See equipment sheet.)

## SCORING
Two cubic dice.

## AIM
Either to force all the opponent's pieces off the board, or if only two opposing girls remain – a chase to capture each other.

## ORIGIN
Iceland.

## RULES

1. To establish the order of play a single cubic *die* is thrown by the players and the lower scorer starts the game.

2. Thereafter two cubic dice are thrown, but only scores of six, one and any *doublet* are used.

3. A throw of any *doublet* (other than sixes) allows two pieces to move the indicated number and the player has another turn.

4. A throw of six-and-six counts as a double *doublet* and the player may move four of his girls by six *points* each.

5. A throw of six, one or a *doublet* may be used to move one girl the combined number of *points*.

6. A throw of six or of one allows one girl to move this number of *points*.

7. All girls move in an anti-clockwise direction, and continue to circulate around the board until one player has lost all his girls.

8. If a girl lands on a *point* already occupied by an opposing girl the latter is removed from the board and is out of the game.

9. Doubling up on a *point* is not allowed. If a girl lands at a *point* on which there is another girl from the same team, the second girl to arrive is placed on the first vacant *point* beyond.

10. The method of play changes when a player has only one girl left, called a 'Hornaskella', or 'Corner-Rattler'. In Iceland a letter re-addressed several times and carried about in a postman's bag without reaching its owner is sometimes referred to as a 'Hornaskella'.

11. The 'Corner-Rattler' can only land on the corner *points* of the four quarters of the board, for example, A, F, G, L, M, R, S and X. (See figure below.)

12. A throw of one moves the 'Corner-Rattler' on to the next corner *point*.

13. A throw of six moves the 'Corner-Rattler' on two corner *points*.

14. Throws of one-and-one and six-and-six count double a single throw of these numbers. No other *doublet* permits a 'Corner-Rattler' to move, but the player has another turn. If a girl becomes a 'Corner-Rattler' on P and the player threw six-and-one, then she would move to point R by virtue of the one and on to point A by virtue of the throw of six. A throw of two-and-two entitles the player to another throw. If this were five-and-one, the 'Corner-Rattler' would move to A, etc.

15. The 'Corner-Rattler' can only capture a girl standing on a corner *point* and is herself vulnerable to attack on these *points*. She is also safe from capture if she stands on a *point* between two hostile girls, for example, if White throws four-and-one when red girls are on Q, R and S, and there is a white 'Corner-Rattler' on M, then the 'Corner-Rattler' moves to R and captures the red girl on this *point*. If Red next threw one-and-two, the red girl cannot move onto R and capture the 'Corner-Rattler' because she is between two opposing girls. So only the red girl on S can move to T, or the red girl on Q to T, the next vacant *point*.

16. If Red threw one-and-six, however, the red girl on S could move to A, using the six, and then the red girl on Q could move to R and capture White's 'Corner-Rattler' and win the game.

17. If both players are reduced to 'Corner-Rattlers' the game may develop into a long chase before one is captured.

| L | K | J | I | H | G | F | E | D | C | B | A |
|---|---|---|---|---|---|---|---|---|---|---|---|
|   |   |   |   |   |   | ● | ● | ● | ● | ● | ● |
|   |   |   |   |   |   |   |   |   |   |   |   |
| ○ | ○ | ○ | ○ | ○ | ○ |   |   |   |   |   |   |
| M | N | O | P | Q | R | S | T | U | V | W | X |

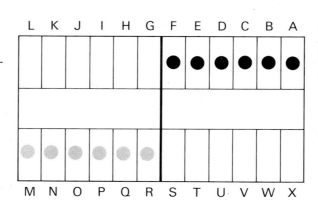

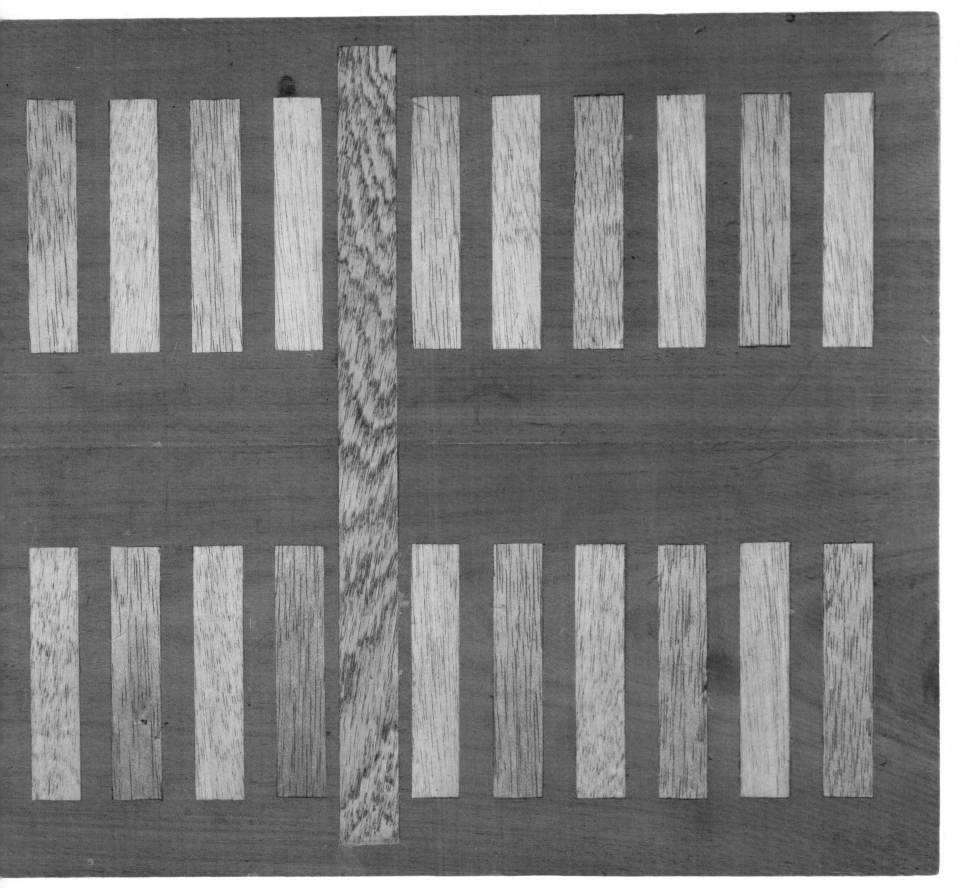

# Backgammon I

# Backgammon & Doublets

The origin of Backgammon has been lost, but among those credited with its invention is Ardshir, the first of the Sassanian kings who reigned in Persia from 226 to 241 A.D. The first mention of Nardshir, the Persian name for Backgammon, is in the Babylonian Talmud written between 300 and 500 A.D. This game has been known throughout its long history by a great variety of names in the many different countries where it has been adopted as a popular pastime.

Chinese works record the introduction of Nard (a later abbreviation of the Persian name) from India into China in the third century A.D. In Chinese the name is 't'shu-p'u', according to Sung dynasty manuscripts (960–1279 A.D.). The Greeks knew the game as Tabla or Taula in the sixth century A.D.

Tabula (the Latin for Tables) was played avidly by both the Emperor Claudius (41–54 A.D.), who wrote a book on the subject, and the Emperor Zeno four centuries later. One of the Emperor Zeno's dice throws at this game—which ruined a very favourable position—has been recorded in an epigram written by Agathias (527–567 A.D.). This and other literary references have enabled scholars to reconstruct the rules and method of play for Tabula with considerable certainty.

By the sixth century Tabula was known as Alea and the four parts of the board were referred to as Tables, a survival of the old name. During the Middle Ages, Tables became the name both for the board and the game played on it.

The first English reference to Tables occurs in a collection of Anglo-Saxon verse given to Exeter Cathedral about 1025 A.D. By the eighteenth century the game most commonly played within the Tables was called Backgammon in England and the United States, and Trictrac in France and the Middle East. These are the names still in use.

The variety of Backgammon boards is endless: simple slats of wood nailed to a plank found in Icelandic farmhouses; magnificent inlaid tables of ivory and rare woods from the Middle East; or the ornate ebony and mother-of-pearl travelling boxes made for European nobility in the seventeenth century. One shown on the dust-cover of this book has Backgammon on the outside, Nine Men's Morris and Chess on the inside. During the nineteenth century, game-boards were disguised as learned volumes, bound in leather with gilt lettering on the spine. Two halves of a Chess board were on the front while a Backgammon board was on the inside.

The Backgammon board consists of twenty-four "points", twelve light coloured and twelve dark, arranged alternately. Each player has twelve "points" on his side of the board divided into two groups of six "points"—the 'inner' and 'outer table' – by the 'bar' or ridge running from one side of the board to the other (see figure A). A dicing cup and two dice are used and each

player has fifteen pieces of his own colour. Gaming counters and a doubling cube are optional. At the beginning of the game the board and pieces are arranged as in figure B.

Stakes are not essential to enjoy this game but many prefer to play for small sums. Players may agree to 'voluntary doubling'. This means that either player may then double the stake before he makes his first throw of the dice. Thereafter the right to 'double' alternates. A 'double' may only be offered when it is the player's turn to play, and before he has cast his dice. When a player calls, 'I double', the other must either accept and play on for double the stake, or resign and lose the value of the game at the moment of resignation (see Rule 19a). The double for a 'gammon' (see Rule 19b) and the triple for a 'backgammon' (see Rule 19c) apply in addition to any existing 'voluntary doubles'; so it is a wise precaution to agree a limit on the number of 'voluntary doubles'.

Some players permit 'automatic doubling' each time the throw for start of play results in the same numbers falling uppermost. The number of 'automatic doubles' is usually limited to one or two. Most modern Backgammon sets include a 'doubling cube' with two, four, eight, sixteen, thirty-two and sixty-four on the respective faces; each time a double is accepted the cube is turned to serve as a reminder to both players of the bets involved.

## PLAYERS
Two.

## PIECES
Fifteen for each side. (See equipment sheet.)

## SCORING
Two cubic dice and one doubling cube.

## AIM
To race one's pieces round and off the board.

## ORIGIN
Persia, 226–241 A.D.

## RULES
1. Each player throws one die and the player with the higher number has the choice of colour and side of the board and the first throw of the game. If the initial throws are the same the players throw again.

2. The opening player casts his dice and moves his pieces corresponding to the two numbers scored. He may move two pieces, each by one throw; or one piece by one throw; or one piece

by the two throws, in either order. A throw of four-and-two may move one piece four points and two points, or two points and four points, or else two pieces, one by four points and the other by two points.

3. Each point played onto must be 'open', that is, not containing two or more hostile pieces.

4. If a player can play both numbers thrown, he must do so, even if it is to his disadvantage. If only one number can be played and there is a choice, it must be the higher.

5. If a player throws a doublet he scores twice the number thrown and a throw of three-and-three scores as three plus three, plus three, plus three. The player may move one piece by this amount; or two pieces by three plus three each; or one piece by three, and the other by three times three; or two pieces

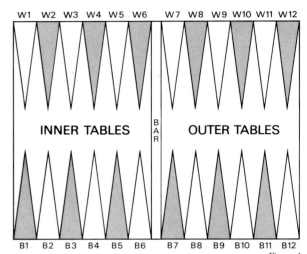

*Figure A*

by three and one by three plus three; or four pieces each by three. When two or more scores are used to advance one piece, each separate move must be onto an open point.

6. A point occupied by two or more pieces is 'closed' to the opponent's pieces and the latter are not permitted to land on it.

7. Pieces can jump over hostile pieces, but cannot land on a point held by two pieces or more as such a point is 'closed'.

8. A point occupied by one piece is 'open', and the piece is vulnerable to attack. A piece of the opposite colour landing on the point sends the singleton known as a 'blot' off the board to rest on the 'bar', and the opponent is said to have scored a 'hit'.

9. A player with a piece on the 'bar' cannot move any of his pieces until the piece on the 'bar' has returned to the game by re-entering the opponent's 'inner table'. If the 'blot' cannot re-enter, the throw is lost.

10. If Black had a piece on the 'bar' and threw four-and-two, he could enter on W4 or W2 if either were 'open', but not on W1, W3, W5 or W6, even if they were 'open'. (See figure A.)

11. If there is an opposing 'blot' on the point of entry this is 'hit' by the re-entering piece and is in turn sent to the 'bar'.

12. If the opponent's 'inner table' is completely 'closed', the player with a piece on the 'bar' does not throw the dice, but must wait until a point is 'open'.

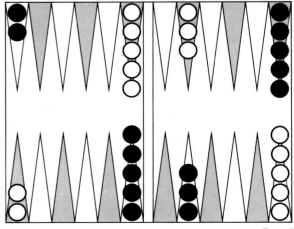

*Figure B*

13. On re-entry the player may use the throw of the other die to move the re-entered piece, or any other piece, at his discretion.

14. Players must use both numbers of a throw, or all four of a *doublet*, if this is possible, even if it is to the player's disadvantage.

15. When all a player's pieces are in his 'inner table' he may *bear off* pieces, or remove them from the board and out of the game. If White threw three-and-two he could *bear off* a piece from W3 and another from W2, or he might use the numbers to move a piece inside the 'inner table' towards his I-point.

16. If a higher number is thrown than any of the pieces in the 'inner table' this throw is used to *bear off* the highest piece. A number thrown may not be used to *bear off* a piece lower than itself if it is possible to move a higher piece. For example: if a player threw five- and-four he would have to move a piece or pieces on the six-point, or five-point, or four-point, before he could *bear off* a 'blot' on the three-point.

17. When a number is thrown which is higher than the highest point on which the player has pieces, he must *bear off* a piece from the outermost occupied *point*. He may, however, use the numbers in either order, and this may enable him to avoid leaving a 'blot'.

18. If a piece is 'hit' after the player has started *bearing off*, it is placed on the 'bar'. Until the piece is once more in the player's 'inner table', *bearing off* cannot continue.

19. The game ends when one player has *borne off* all his pieces. There are degrees of losing:
a. If the loser has *borne off* a piece he loses by a single game and loses his stake.
b. If he has not *borne off* a piece he loses by a 'gammon' and has to pay double the stake.
c. If he has not *borne off* any piece and has a piece on the 'bar' or in the opponent's 'inner table' he loses by a 'backgammon' and has to pay triple the stake.

## Doublets

*Many games can be played on a Backgammon board. Doublets, from Iceland, is considered to be one of the oldest forms of Tables still existing.*

*Doublets gives beginners an opportunity of learning how to handle dice, move pieces, "bear off" and become generally familiar with the mechanics of play before they start the more complex assessment of probabilities in a game of Backgammon.*

*This simple game depends entirely on luck and a beginner has the same chance of winning as an expert.*

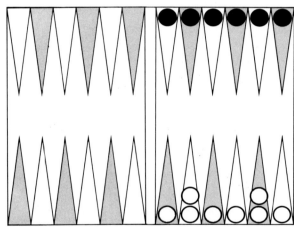

*Figure C*

**PLAYERS**
Two.

**PIECES**
**Twelve for each side (see equipment sheet).**

**SCORING**
**Two cubic dice.**

**AIM**
**Making *doublets* with the pieces and being first to remove them from the board.**

**ORIGIN**
**Iceland.**

RULES
1. Each player stacks two pieces on every *point* in the opposite right hand 'table'.

2. The players then each throw a die and the winner throws two dice to begin the game. The top pieces are moved – according to the number cast – beside the lower pieces on the same point and nearer to its tip. For example, if White threw five-and-two, the top pieces on the two- and five-points would be placed nearer the tip of their respective *points*. (See figure C.)

3. If a *doublet* is thrown the player can only move one piece but has a second throw. This is repeated as long as a *doublet* is thrown.

4. The other player then throws the dice and moves his upper pieces in the same way. If a number is thrown corresponding to a *point* whose upper piece has already been lowered, this part of the throw is lost.

5. When a player has moved all his pieces down he begins to stack them up again. When all the points are once more doubled up, the player begins to *bear off* as in Backgammon.

*Noblemen playing Backgammon, from a medieval manuscript.*

*Nineteenth century Chinese lacquered Backgammon board laid out for play.*

# Sugoroku

A Sugoroku board (see Backgammon pages 88–91), belonging to the Emperor Shomu (reigned 724–749 A.D.), is now kept in a warehouse annexe to a very old temple in Nara City, which was the capital of Japan from 10 to 784 A.D. The Emperor's board, made of rosewood inlaid with ivory and mother-of-pearl, was built as an oblong box with the sides fretted out. This gives a lightness and grace absent from boards of later periods, which were made of thick slabs of wood with four stumpy legs.

In the nineteenth century, the Tokugawa government introduced severe penalties for gambling and Sugoroku fell into disrepute. A Tokyo club of about forty members tried to revive the game at the beginning of this century, but today the rules and even its existence have been forgotten by most Japanese. Sugoroku is now only played by nuns in the Buddhist temples of Kyoto City.

On a recent visit to Japan, Mr. K. Whittle obtained the modern Sugoroku board reproduced here, but a game of the same name which he was shown had little similarity to the ancient Sugoroku. This modern version uses only the right half of the board and depends on chance as in Doublets (see page 91).

**PLAYERS**
Two.

**PIECES**
Fifteen for each side.
(See equipment sheet.)

**SCORING**
Two cubic dice.

**AIM**
Capture of the most opposing pieces.

**ORIGIN**
Japan.

**RULES**
1. At the start of the game the board is empty.

2. The players alternately throw two dice and move pieces onto the board according to their throws.

3. A *doublet* gives another throw.

4. When all the pieces are on the board in the player's 'home table', *bearing off* begins.

5. When a player's *point* corresponding to a throw is empty, but the opposite enemy *point* contains one or more pieces, these are captured and removed from the board and held by the captor.

6. If a player throws a *doublet* and his corresponding *point* is either empty or contains only one piece and the opponent's matching *point* is empty, he takes one or two of the opposing player's pieces which have been *borne off* and puts them back on the opponent's empty *point*.

7. When one player has all his pieces off the board the game is over and the winner is the player who has captured most of the opposing pieces.

*Left: nineteenth century Japanese games table.*

93

# Puluc

*Puluc is played by the Ketchi Indians, who live in the highlands of Guatamala in Central America. They are descendants of the Mayas, who at the peak of their civilization built elaborate stone cities, used writing and developed a system of numbers for use with their complicated calendar. Why their civilization fell is unknown, but their descendants reverted to simple peasant communities. To play, ten ears of corn are laid on the ground like rungs of a ladder. The two players sit at opposite ends of this maize trail, each having five counters of his own colour representing tribal warriors. Traditionally these are made of cross sections of a small stick and four flat corn ears with one surface blackened are used as dice. Coins make good substitute dice.*

**PLAYERS**
Two or more.

**PIECES**
Five warriors or markers for each player. (See equipment sheet.)

**SCORING**
Four double-sided dice or coins.

**AIM**
To retain most warriors.

**ORIGIN**
Ketchi Indian, Central America.

SCORING
Two yellow surfaces or heads up score two.

Three yellow surfaces or heads up score three.

Four yellow surfaces or heads up score five.

Four black surfaces or tails up score four.

RULES
1. At the beginning of the game each player throws the dice; the one with the highest score throws again to start the game.

2. The players take turns to throw the dice.

3. At a player's first throw he enters one of his warriors onto the trail.

4. At his next throw the player may enter another warrior onto the trail, or move on his first the indicated number of spaces.

5. A player cannot move a warrior onto a space occupied by another of the same colour – there is no doubling up.

6. A player may move a warrior forwards onto a space occupied by an enemy. The latter is taken prisoner by being placed under the victor and is moved backwards along

the trail by the victor in his journey towards the far end of the trail.

7. If the victor and his captive reach the end of the trail, the victor returns to his village ready to re-enter the trail for another

journey, while the captive is out of the game. An exact throw is not required to leave the trail.

8. If a warrior moves onto a space occupied by an enemy in charge of a prisoner, the warrior is placed on top of the whole stack and reverses its direction towards his own goal.

9. Possession of a stack may change several times, and with it the direction of its progress. On its arrival at the end of the trail, the top counter and all others

of the same colour are returned to the player's village to make new journeys, while the captives are out of the game.

10. If a warrior reaches the end of the trail without incident he returns to the village, ready to start again.

11. A stack may capture a single piece, or another stack.

12. When a player has lost all his warriors he has lost the game.

# Surakarta

This Javanese game is named after the ancient town of Surakarta on the river Solo in central Java. The unusual board shape is inscribed in the sand or volcanic ash whenever the game is played.

Java is the most important of the Indonesian islands. It is also by far the most densely populated. The French writer Raynal (1713–1796) described it as 'a land prodigal of delicious fruit . . . sweet penetrating odours exhaled from every plant in a perfumed land . . .' Appropriately, the Javanese are an exceptionally beautiful race, the predominating strains being Indian, Chinese and Mongoloid. Added to such natural wealth, central Java is rich in magnificent architecture. The most notable examples are the Hindu shrine of Borobodur and the restored group of temples at Prambanan. Many of the sculptured reliefs on these buildings illustrate the legends of Rama and Krishna, Hindu myths which continue to live in the imaginations of the Javanese although Hinduism was displaced by the Islamic faith in the sixteenth century. The famous 'wajang', or shadow puppet plays, are still based on the lives of Rama and Krishna.

Surakarta, which used to be the principal city of the island, is now a smaller, quieter place than Jakarta, the modern capital of Java. Its broad, central streets are tree-lined and in the many open courtyards attached to the larger buildings, women sit cross-legged on the ground making the 'batik' cloth which is the main industry of the region.

The game of Surakarta is played by two players, each having twelve pieces, one player using stones, the other shells, though more conventional playing pieces of two distinct colours would be equally suitable. The winner of the game may be decided by one of two methods: either play continues until a previously determined score is arrived at, or a particular number of contests is decided on and the player with the highest score at the end is the victor, having lost the fewest pieces throughout the play. The method of capture, whereby the capturing piece must first travel around one of the circles at the corners of the board, is not known to exist in any other recorded board game.

**PLAYERS**
Two.

**PIECES**
Twelve for each side.
(See equipment sheet.)

**AIM**
Capture of opposing pieces.

**ORIGIN**
Java.

RULES

1. The players decide on either the set number of contests to be played; or what score must be achieved to win.

2. The initial position and movements of the pieces are shown in figure A.

3. The players draw lots for the advantage of moving first.

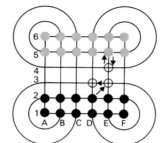

*Figure A*

4. The pieces move one *point* at a time in any direction, forwards, backwards, or diagonally, except when capturing a piece. *Jumping* over another piece is not permitted, nor is landing on an occupied *point*, except when making a capture. (See Rule six.)

5. Examples of the movements of pieces are shown in the figure above. The piece on D2 could move to E3. (Diagonal.)

The piece on E5 to E4. (Forward.)
The piece on E3 to D3. (Sideways.)
The opposing piece on E4 to E5. (Backwards.)

6. Capture is only permitted after the piece has travelled along one of the circular lines and it must enter and leave the three-quarters of a circle along a line at a tangent.

7. Examples of captures are shown in figure B.

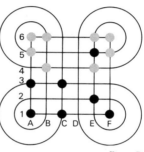

*Figure B*

A piece on C3 moves to C6, circles to A4 and takes the opposing piece on B4; or a piece on C3 moves to F3, circles to D1, moves to D6, circles to F4 and takes the opposing piece on E4; or a piece on E2 moves to F2, circles to E1 and takes the opposing piece on E4. The opponent can capture if he moves from B4 to A4, circles to C6 and takes the piece on C3; or from E4 to F4, circles to D6, moves to D1, circles to F3 and takes the piece on C3; or from B4 to B1, circles to A2 and takes the piece on E2. Note that the circles are only used when making a capture.

8. At the end of each contest the remaining pieces on the board are counted and recorded towards the winning total agreed at the beginning of the game.

*Sculptured figures from Hindu myths on the temple walls of Borobodur in central Java.*

# Siege of Paris I

**PLAYERS**
Two or three.

**PIECES**
Thirty-six attackers
divided into two equal
groups – one white, the
other black – each
comprising one general,
one colonel, two
captains, two lieutenants
and twelve soldiers.
Eight defenders – all
brown – one general, one
colonel and six soldiers.
(See equipment sheet.)

**AIM**
Either immobilization of
garrison force by
besiegers, or capture of
all besieging soldiers and
six besieging officers by
defenders.

**ORIGIN**
France, 1870's.

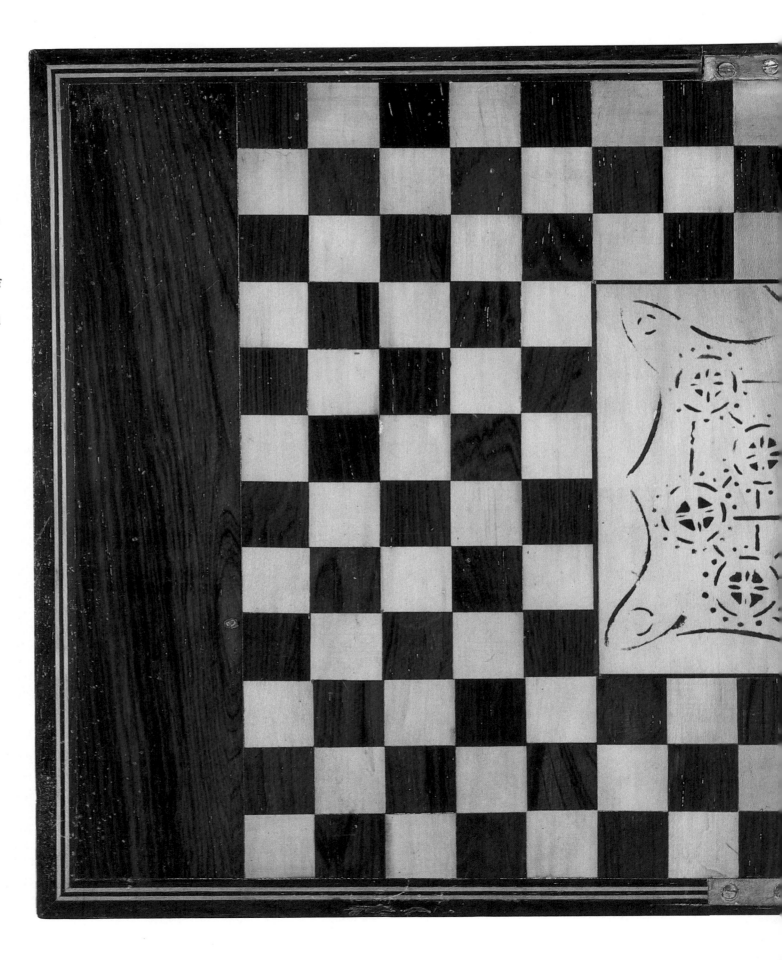

# Siege of Paris II

Siege of Paris, like Asalto (see pages 52–53) is a game associated with a specific event. On July 19, 1870, France declared war against Prussia and was involved in a series of disastrous battles. The Prussians completed their encirclement of Paris by September 18, 1870. This was the start of the Siege which lasted for a hundred and thirty two days, causing deprivation, hunger and lack of communication with the rest of the world for the Parisians. As so often, necessity provoked invention and the first air-mail occurred during this period. Letters of a limited weight were air-lifted by balloon across the Siege Lines and then forwarded by overland transport to their destinations. By December 27, the German general Moltke was in position to attack Paris. On January 19, 1871, the defenders launched an abortive sortie of ninety thousand men against the German lines near Versailles. Although Paris was not occupied, she suffered the humiliation of a German triumphal march down the Champs-Elysées on March 1, 1871.

Siege of Paris appeared early in 1871 and after a brief craze disappeared, failing even to be mentioned in most popular games books of the period. Boards, however, still occasionally appear in antique shops.

The board reproduced here is made of two hinged pieces of mahogany-covered plywood. When closed, one surface forms a board for the Snail game (see pages 122–123) and the other is a board for Asalto.

The central six-by-six squares represent a fortress marked with eight circles joined together with lines and connected by lines to two squares at either side of the fortress. The dark squares of the board are of rosewood and the light of a fruit-wood, probably pear. The fortress, also of fruit-wood, has the design blocked in ink and the whole board is French polished.

Siege of Paris is a curious hybrid. The concept of sides of unequal strength and different objectives is derived from the Norse games of Tablut (see pages 34–35), Fox and Geese (see pages 50–51), and the derivative Asalto; while the varying power of movement of the pieces, the restriction of some pieces to certain squares, and the method of capture by direct replacement is taken from Chess (see pages 18–21).

## RULES

1. Siege of Paris can be played by three players, with one commanding the garrison, and the other two in charge of allied troops. Usually it is played only by two players.

2. Opening positions (see figure A):
a. All attacking pieces begin on squares of their own colour: the general on the right of the back row, the colonel on the left, the captain next to them, the lieutenant in the centre. The garrison force begins anywhere within the fortress.

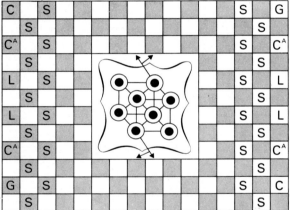

**Black**         **White**
*Figure A*

b. The besieging soldiers always remain on squares of their own colour, but the officers move onto squares of either colour.

3. Moves of the besiegers:
a. The generals move on white or black squares by one, two or three squares at a time, forwards, sideways, or diagonally forwards. They may not change direction during the turn of play.
b. The colonels move on white or black squares, one or two squares at a time, forwards or sideways.
c. The captains move on white or black squares, one square at a time, forwards or sideways.
d. The lieutenants move one or two squares diagonally, and always remain on squares of their own colour.
e. The soldiers move one square diagonally at a time and cannot be captured once they enter the fort.

4. The besiegers win the game by placing two soldiers and one officer within the fort or by blocking the garrison forces and depriving them of the power of movement.

5. Moves of the garrison pieces:
a. The general can move one square in any direction, forwards, backwards, sideways or diagonally. He may capture by displacement either on black or white squares.
b. The colonel moves on black or white squares, backwards, forwards, or sideways one square in any direction and captures in the same way. (Note that he cannot move diagonally.)
c. The soldiers move diagonally only, backwards or forwards one square at a time, and capture in the same way. Not more than three garrison soldiers may be on squares of the same colour (three on black and three on white) and they do not change the colour of their square on moving or capturing.

6. The garrison pieces are of a different colour from both groups of besiegers.

7. The fortress is occupied by one general, one colonel and six soldiers. The arrangement of the garrison forces within the fortress is optional.

8. The officers and soldiers of the garrison cannot be captured, but the pieces can be hemmed in by the besiegers, and if they are unable to move the game is lost.

9. The garrison player is compelled to capture an unsupported piece when requested to do so by the besieging player.

10. The garrison forces win by capturing all the enemy soldiers and six of the officers. If an attacking soldier gains entrance to the fortress the game is only drawn.

11. There are two exits from the fortress along the marks onto two white squares and two black.

12. The garrison player has the first move.

13. The White player then moves one of his pieces.

14. The garrison replies with a move.

15. Then the Black player moves a piece. (That is, the Black and White players move alternately with the garrison player, interspersing his moves between theirs.)

The coins shown on these pages commemorate the arrival of pigeon mail into Paris during the long siege.

*Left and facing: letters sent by balloon during the siege of Paris are known by philatelists as 'ballons montés'.*

18. It is possible for the officers of the garrison to remain within the fortress guarding the entrances, but if their soldiers on the board are immobilized one of them must venture outside to maintain movement on the board.

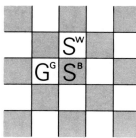

16. Only garrison pieces can capture, and this is achieved by a piece moving onto the square occupied by a besieging piece which is not supported by another of its own pieces (similar to the rule governing the king in Chess, which can only capture a piece if it is unsupported).
In figure B the garrison piece Sg could not capture the besieging piece Sb as it is supported by Sw2.
In figure C the garrison general Gg could take either of the besieging men Sb or Sw as they are not supporting each other nor are they supported by any other piece.

17. Inside the garrison the pieces can only move along marked lines from one circle to another.

*Figure C*

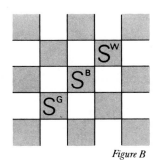

*Figure B*

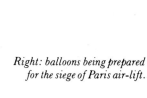
*Right: balloons being prepared for the siege of Paris air-lift.*

*Right: Service medal awarded to members of the Garde Nationale who defended Paris.*

The GAME of the RACE

This game simulates a steeplechase. The board represents an oval race-track, numbered from one to a hundred. Every tenth line is marked and there are also two fences, a gate and two water-jumps which may be placed anywhere along the track at the discretion of the players.

Each player has a horse-and-jockey wearing distinctive colours. (These were originally made of lead.) They move according to throws of two dice from a cup. A set of gaming counters is shared out equally among the players before the game begins.

**PLAYERS**
Any number.

**PIECES**
Horse-and-jockey or marker for each player; one set of obstacles – two fences, two water-jumps and a gate; one set of gaming chips. (See equipment sheet.)

**SCORING**
Two cubic dice.

**AIM**
A race to reach the winning post and gain the major part of the stake.

**ORIGIN**
England, probably nineteenth century.

**RULES**
1. Each player puts an agreed stake into a *pool* for the winner.

2. The players throw the two dice in turn to establish the order of starting, the highest scorer casting first and the lowest last. (When the horses are nearing the finishing post there is a slight advantage in casting early in the round.)

3. The players select their horses and place them in order from the inside rail, with their forefeet resting on the first line.

4. The players cast the dice in turn, moving their horses to the line indicated by the throw.

5. If a horse lands on one of the marked lines (every tenth line), or on any number where the mobile barriers have been placed, he must return to his former number and loses a turn as penalty.

6. Rule five does not apply to the hundred line, which is the winning-post.

7. After a horse passes the ninety line its owner uses only one *die*.

8. The owner of the first horse to reach a hundred and the winning-post takes three-quarters of the stake in the *pool*, leaving the rest for the owner of the horse placed second.

9. After the first horse has won the major part of the *pool*, the others continue to race for second place.

10. The owners of horses not reaching the eighty line by the time the second horse has passed the post are 'distanced'. They owe the winner of the race half the amount of the stake and must also put the same amount towards the *pool* for the next race.

11. Onlookers may take part in the game by placing side bets against each other or against any of the owners of the horses.

# Bizingo

This game is played on a checkered board in the shape of an equilateral triangle with eleven units to each side. Every unit is joined by lines to the corresponding units on the other two sides, dividing the board into a hundred and fifty-seven small triangles and three larger ones. The Castle Museum in York, England holds an example of Bizingo and this account is reproduced by courtesy of the Museum trustees.

Bizingo is a game for two players and each has a contrasting set of eighteen pieces. These consist of sixteen smaller pieces and two slightly larger which represent captains with special powers. The board illustrated here is marked to indicate the opening position of the pieces.

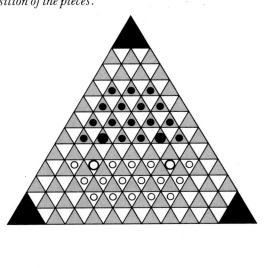

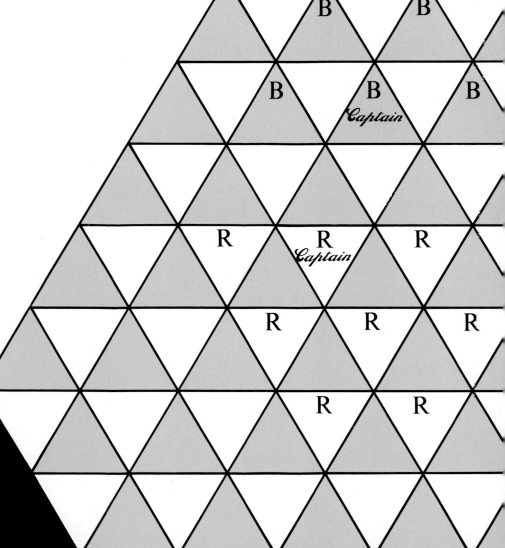

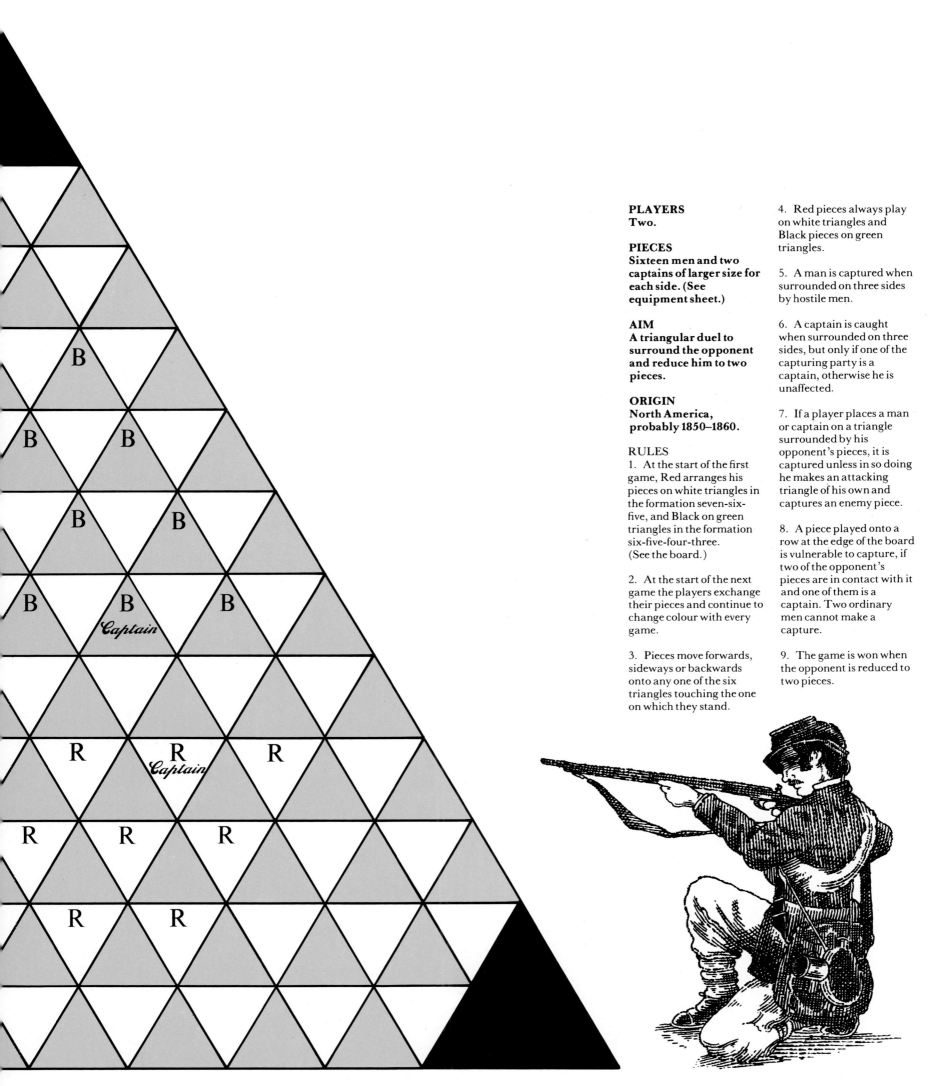

**PLAYERS**
Two.

**PIECES**
**Sixteen men and two captains of larger size for each side. (See equipment sheet.)**

**AIM**
**A triangular duel to surround the opponent and reduce him to two pieces.**

**ORIGIN**
**North America, probably 1850–1860.**

RULES
1. At the start of the first game, Red arranges his pieces on white triangles in the formation seven-six-five, and Black on green triangles in the formation six-five-four-three. (See the board.)

2. At the start of the next game the players exchange their pieces and continue to change colour with every game.

3. Pieces move forwards, sideways or backwards onto any one of the six triangles touching the one on which they stand.

4. Red pieces always play on white triangles and Black pieces on green triangles.

5. A man is captured when surrounded on three sides by hostile men.

6. A captain is caught when surrounded on three sides, but only if one of the capturing party is a captain, otherwise he is unaffected.

7. If a player places a man or captain on a triangle surrounded by his opponent's pieces, it is captured unless in so doing he makes an attacking triangle of his own and captures an enemy piece.

8. A piece played onto a row at the edge of the board is vulnerable to capture, if two of the opponent's pieces are in contact with it and one of them is a captain. Two ordinary men cannot make a capture.

9. The game is won when the opponent is reduced to two pieces.

# Shut the Box

*This game, popular among sailors and fishermen, is played in pubs around the English coast and the Channel Islands. Illustrated below is a variant of the game, carved in East Africa. Where or when the game originated is, however, unknown. The equipment for this game consists of nine coins and two cubic dice. Any number can play, each in turn trying to shut the boxes with their coins.*

**PLAYERS**
Any number.

**PIECES**
Nine counters or coins.

**SCORING**
Two cubic dice.

**AIM**
To cover the most boxes and achieve the lowest possible score.

**ORIGIN**
Probably Channel Islands, eighteenth century.

RULES
1. Each player in turn throws the dice and uses his score to cover or shut the numbers on the boxes or squares of the board with coins. With a throw of six-and-two, he may use each score separately and place a coin on the numbers six and two, or use the sum of the throw and place a coin on eight.

2. The player continues his turn by throwing again, but if he cannot shut a box his turn ceases. The sum of the numbers remaining exposed is counted against him. The board is cleared and the dice are passed to the next player.

3. If the sum of the numbers left on the board is six or less, one *die* is discarded, and play continues with the other until all the boxes are shut, or a score is cast which the player cannot use, when his turn ceases.

4. If all the boxes are shut the player has no points registered against him, and he passes the dice to the next player.

5. When a player has accumulated forty-five points or more he is out of the game.

6. The last player left in the game is the winner.

*Above: nineteenth century engraving of two fishermen exchanging yarns.*

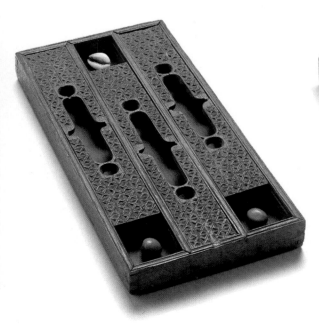

*Far left: Zambian version of Shut the Box carved in the nineteenth century, and here set out for play with a cowrie shell as the die and stones as counters.*

*Left: modern version manufactured in Jersey and until recently used in Jerry's Club, London.*

# Patolli

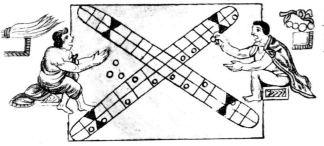

*Left: two men playing Patolli from a history of the Indians by Spanish priest Durand, and published in Mexico, 1880.*

Patolli takes its name from the Aztec word for beans, which are used as dice in this, their favourite gambling game. It is one of the cross and circle type games with the circle omitted and the spaces on the cross doubled.

The board is a straw mat with a large diagonal cross marked out in liquid rubber. Each limb of the cross is divided into fourteen compartments. Some mats are decorated with lucky devices, such as the figure of fortune or two clubs, its symbol.

Twelve small coloured stones are used as markers. Two players use six each, three players have four each and four players have three each. According to throws of the dice, these pieces are moved along the divisions of the the cross. The dice consist of five large black beans or 'patolli' with a hole drilled in one side making a white pip.

Father Diego Duran, writing about 1560 A.D., described Mexican gamesters walking about with a 'patollizitli' mat rolled up under one arm and carrying a little basket containing the dicing beans and coloured markers.

The 'patolli' were rubbed between the hands of the gamblers while they shouted out the name 'Macuilxochitl' (God of the Five Roses) to the Mexican god of gambling. Then the beans were thrown onto the mat. Coins may be substituted for dice.

**PLAYERS**
Two or more.

**PIECES**
Twelve markers.
(See equipment sheet.)

**SCORING**
Five 'patolli' or coins.
(See equipment sheet.)

**AIM**
To remove all one's pieces from the board and win the stakes and forfeits.

**ORIGIN**
Aztec (before the Spanish Conquest of Mexico in 1521).

SCORING
One pip or heads up scores one point.
Two pips or heads up score two points.
Three pips or heads up score three points.
Four pips or heads up score four points.
Five pips or heads up score ten points.
Little more is known about the game and as this is inadequate for playing, the additional rules have been devised by comparison with other Amerindian games.

RULES
1. The players put an agreed sum into a *pool* and decide upon the size of the forfeits.

2. The players choose their set of coloured markers.

3. Each player casts the 'patolli'. The highest scorer starts the game by introducing one of his pieces onto the nearest central square. He then moves the piece according to his score along the divisions in either direction around the board. (His other pieces must then travel in the same direction.)

4. The second player then throws the 'patolli' again and he also has free choice of direction of movement, but all his pieces must continue to travel in the same way.

5. The players' pieces may be travelling in the same or opposite directions.

6. After the entry of the first piece, the others can only enter with a throw of one.

7. No piece may enter a compartment occupied by another piece.

8. A player may move two or more of his pieces to satisfy a throw; but if only one piece can move this must be moved even if it is to the player's disadvantage.

9. If a player cannot move any piece he pays a forfeit into the *pool*.

10. A player landing on a marked compartment misses a turn.

11. A piece moving onto one of the rounded compartments at the end of the limbs wins another throw.

12. Pieces travel around the track and are *borne off* the board from the square next to the starting square.

13. The first player to remove all his pieces from the board wins the stakes and forfeits in the *pool*.

14. If there are four players, they can either play solo or arrange themselves into two teams, the two partners sitting opposite each other. Each team throws alternately and each partner has every fourth throw.

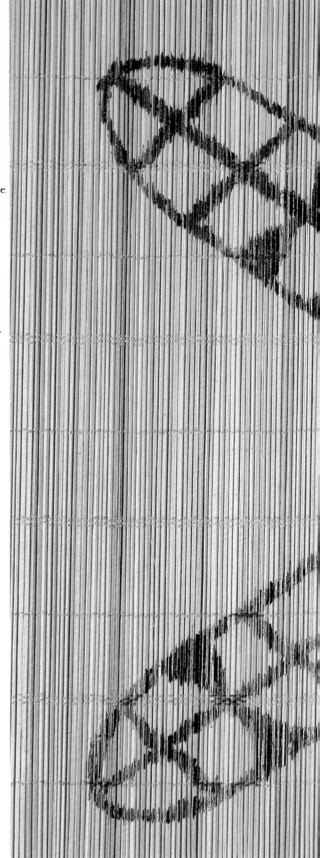

*Figure of Macuilxochitl copied from a Oaxaca ceremonial vase.*

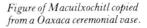

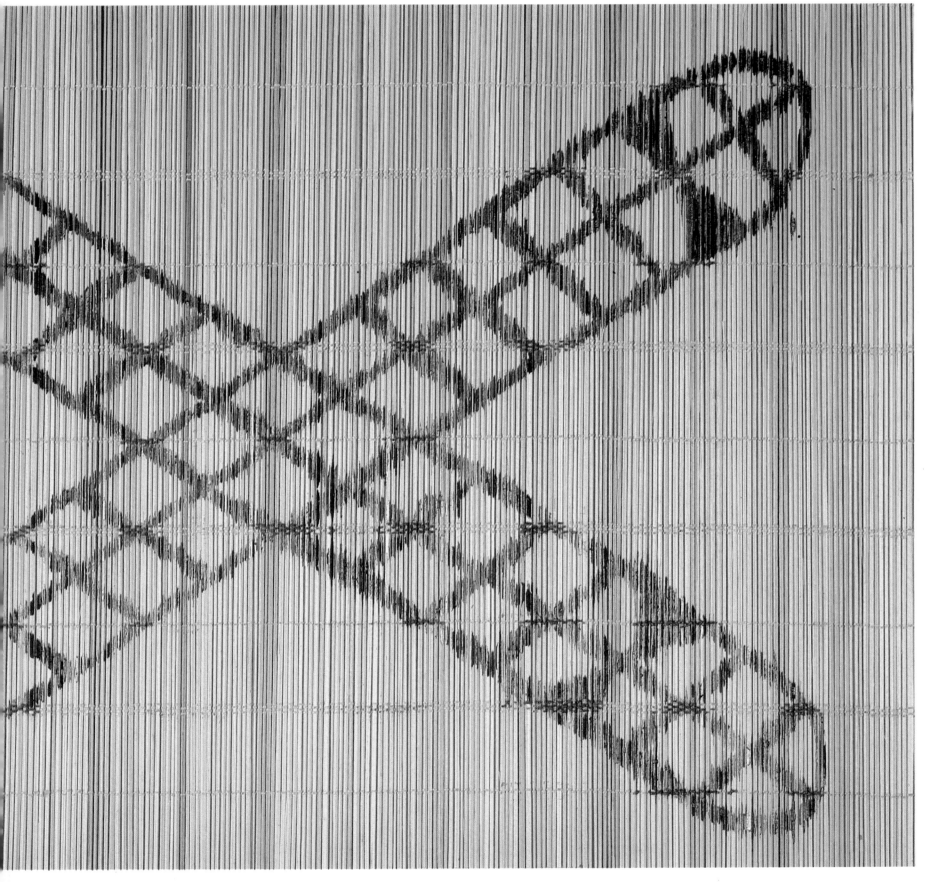

# Pachisi

Pachisi, which means 'Twenty-five', is played throughout the Indian sub-continent by people in every walk of life, from princes in their palaces and inmates of the zenanas (women's quarters), to the regulars of tea houses and bargain hunters in the market-place. The standard board is a piece of cloth cut into the shape of a cross, with embroidered divisions forming squares. It is a modified form of Nyout which travelled westwards to India in the distant past.

During the sixteenth century the Mogul Emperors played Pachisi in their palaces on marble courtyards laid out as boards, the pieces being slave girls dressed in yellow, black, red or green saris and moving around the marble squares as instructed by the players seated on a central dais. Traces of these boards remain at the palaces of Agra, Allahabad and Fatehpur Sikri.

The marked squares represent castles in which the pieces are free from attack and capture. A castle occupied by a player's piece is open to his partner's pieces but barred to the opposition. Each player has four markers of one colour. Traditionally these are painted pieces of wood, shaped like bee-hives. These pieces are controlled by the throws of six cowrie shells, although six small coins may be substituted. It is possible to play this game like the modern variant, Ludo, using any four distinctly coloured pieces for each player.

*Women playing Pachisi in a small village near Madras, south India.*

## SCORING

Two cowries with their mouths up, or two coins heads up score two.
Three cowries with their mouths up, or three coins heads up score three.
Four cowries with their mouths up, or four coins heads up score four.
Five cowries with their mouths up, or five coins heads up score five.
Six cowries with their mouths up, or six coins heads up score six and a 'grace' or another turn.
One cowrie with its mouth up, or one coin head up scores ten and a 'grace'.
No cowries with their mouths up, or all coins tails up score twenty-five and a 'grace'.

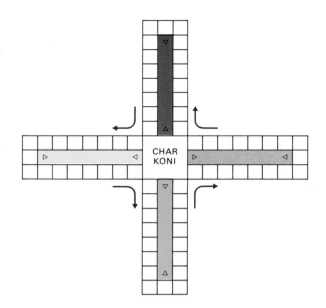

**PLAYERS**
Two or four.

**PIECES**
One set of four for each player.
(See equipment sheet.)

**SCORING**
Six shells or coins.

**AIM**
A race to get the pieces round and off the board.

**ORIGIN**
India.

RULES

1. Four players arrange themselves around the board; those sitting opposite each other are partners, yellow and black playing against red and green.

2. At the beginning of the game all the pieces are placed on the central space, known in Hindustani as the 'char-koni' (throne).

3. The cowries or dicing coins are thrown from the hands. When six, ten or twenty-five is scored the player wins a 'grace' and continues to throw until he casts a two, three, four or five, when his turn ceases.

4. At the beginning of the game each player's first piece may leave the 'char-koni' and enter the track on any throw, but the other pieces can only be entered on a throw of six, ten or twenty-five.

5. Each piece leaves the 'char-koni' down the middle of the player's own limb of the cross, and travels anti-clockwise around the board, returning up the middle of his own limb back to the 'char-koni' (see figure above)

6. On finishing a turn the player moves his piece before the next player begins. Each throw permits a player to move his piece the indicated number of spaces. If he throws more than once in a turn, the different scores may be used to move the same piece, or different ones, but a single throw cannot be split between two pieces. For example, on a throw of five, a piece is moved five spaces, not one piece by two and another by three.

7. If a player moves a piece onto any square (except a castle square) occupied by an enemy piece, the latter is removed from the board and must re-enter the game at the 'char-koni' by a throw of six, ten or twenty-five. A player making a capture throws again. Any number of pieces of paired colours may occupy a castle square at the same time.

8. A player need not cast when it is his turn, or he may make a throw and then decline to use it. This may be to avoid risk of capture, or to help his partner.

9. On reaching the castle at the end of the third limb, a piece may wait there in safety until a throw of twenty-five permits its transfer to the 'char-koni'.

10. Pieces may double up on any square but doubled men can be sent off the board if they are hit by an equal or larger number of men belonging to an opponent, unless they are resting on a castle square.

11. If a single piece reaches a square occupied by two or more of the opposition's pieces the square is barred to it and some other move must be made. If this is impossible, the turn is lost.

12. As each piece completes the circuit of the track by arriving back at the middle row of its own limb of the cross, it is taken off the board.

13. Pieces can only re-enter the 'char-koni' by an exact throw.

14. Both partners win or lose together. If one rushes ahead and out of the game, the partner has only one throw to the opponents' two. This makes it easier for the opponents to keep just behind the remaining piece or pieces and then with a capturing throw send a piece off the board to begin all over again.

# Ludo

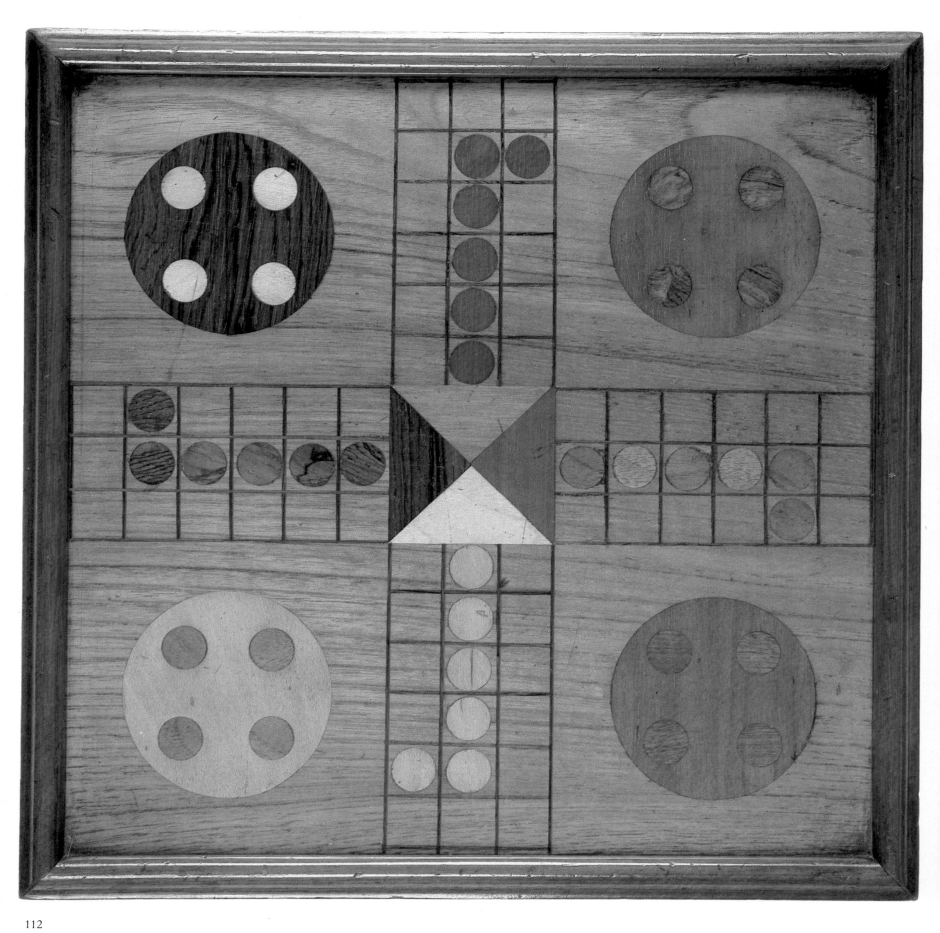

*Ludo was introduced into England as a modification of Pachisi in 1896. The six cowries originally used as dice were replaced by a cubic "die" with a dicing cup. Flat bone disks were used as markers instead of the wooden bee-hive pieces. Several changes in the rules were also made.*

*The Ludo board in the illustration below was used in an English television broadcast in December 1959, and is signed by members of the studio staff.*

*In the Royal Navy, Ludo is known as Ucker and is a gambling game. The board reproduced here is an early twentieth century Ucker board of inlaid woods, with a metal ring on the back for hanging it on the mess-room wall when not in use.*

**PLAYERS**
Two, three or four.

**PIECES**
One set of four for each player.
(See equipment sheet.)

**SCORING**
One cubic die.

**AIM**
A race to get one's pieces round and off the board.

**ORIGIN**
United Kingdom, 1896.

RULES
1. Ludo can be played by two, three or four players.

2. Each player throws the *die* to determine the order of seating around the board; the highest throw indicating the *senior* player who opens the game.

3. Play proceeds clockwise around the board; the second highest thrower sitting on the *senior* player's left, and the lowest on his right.

4. At the start of the game the pieces are in their own coloured 'yard'. A throw of six is needed to introduce a piece onto the track.

5. A throw of six gives another turn; further throws of six are similarly rewarded. The six may be used either to introduce another piece onto the track, or to advance a piece already on it.

6. A piece reaching a square occupied by another player's piece sends the first occupant back to his 'yard'. Pieces can only be re-entered onto the track with a throw of six.

7. If a player has two or more pieces on the same square, no opposing piece can pass or send them back to their 'yard'.

8. A player whose piece is blocked by an opponent's 'double' on a square loses the throw unless he can use it for another piece.

9. A throw must be used, if possible, even though it may be to the player's disadvantage.

10. An exact throw is required for a piece to enter the home triangle. If the throw is too high and no other piece can move, the piece moves into 'home' and then back out, as many spaces as the number is in excess of that required.

11. The first player to get his four counters round the board, down the centre squares of his own colour, and into 'home' wins the game.

12. The other players may play on to determine the order of losing.

*'Signalling' by Christian Symonds, nineteenth century.*

113

# Crown and Anchor & Chuck-a-Luck

K & C LONDON

MA

Crown and Anchor is popular among British seamen and the fishing fleet. The players sit around a board, usually made of cloth, divided into six sections, each one painted with one of six symbols – Heart, Spade, Diamond, Club, Crown or Anchor. Three special cubic dice are used, each face carrying one of the six devices on the board. One player is the banker. As the game is heavily weighted in favour of the bank, each player should have a turn as banker. The advantage to the banker is worked out as follows: there are two hundred and sixteen possible combinations with the three dice; on average, a hundred and twenty singles, ninety doubles and six triples. If each space on the layout is covered with one unit and two hundred and sixteen throws are made, six units are wagered two hundred and sixteen times making a total of one thousand, two hundred and ninety-six units. In a hundred and twenty throws, the gains and losses are three units and three units, coming out even. On ninety throws with a pair, five hundred and forty units are wagered. Two hundred and seventy units are returned on the doubles at two to one, and a hundred and eighty units on the third number at evens, a total of four hundred and fifty units and a gain of ninety units. On the six triplets thirty-six units are wagered, but at three to one only twenty-four units are returned at a gain of twelve units. The total gain of a hundred and two units out of one thousand, two hundred and ninety-six units gives a percentage in favour of the banker of a hundred and two multiplied by a hundred and divided by one thousand, two hundred and ninety-six, which equals approximately eight percent. You have been warned!

## Chuck-a-Luck

Chuck-a-Luck, a very similar dice-game to Crown and Anchor was once known in England as Sweat-Cloth. This gambling game appeared around 1800 in the United States of America where it was called Sweat, later Chuck-Luck and eventually Bird-Cage. This was a reference to the wire cage in which three cubic dice, each numbered one to six, are tumbled. A cloth has the corresponding numbers (one to six) marked out in the segments of a hexagon (see figure) and bets are placed on the segments. The rules are the same as for Crown and Anchor and the figure may be drawn on paper instead of being painted on cloth. The 'bird-cage' may be replaced by a dicing-cup.

**PLAYERS**
Any number.

**PIECES**
Gaming chips or coins.

**SCORING**
Three special cubic dice. (See equipment sheet.)

**AIM**
Gambling to beat the odds.

**ORIGIN**
United Kingdom.

**RULES**

1. Any number of players can take part and they place their bets on the board on the symbols of their choice. Betting units may be any commodity from matches to currency.

2. The banker throws the three dice from a cup. He pays evens on singles (one symbol appearing on a *die*), two-to-one on pairs (if two dice bear the symbol) and three-to-one on triples (the symbol appearing on all three dice).

3. The bank should pass to each player in turn, since the banker's advantage is considerable.

4. Rules for the banker:
a. If one unit is put on each of the six numbers on the board, and three different dice are thrown, the banker wins three units and loses three units, breaking even.
b. If two dice show the same number, the banker pays two units on the double, and one unit on the single, and collects four units, gaining one unit.
c. If a triple is thrown, the banker pays three units to the winner, and collects five units from the losers, a profit of two units.

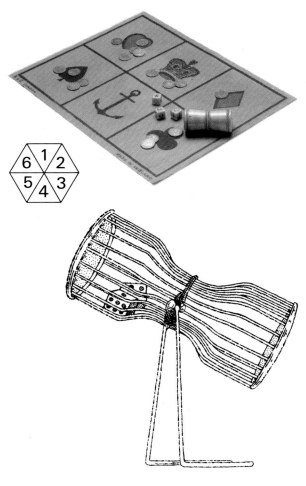

# Ringo

**PLAYERS**
Two.

**PIECES**
Four white for one side and seven black for the other.
(See equipment sheet.)

**AIM**
White tries to capture six black pieces; Black tries to move two pieces into the citadel.

**ORIGIN**
Unknown.

RULES
1. White places his four defenders on the green spaces of the innermost ring of the board.

2. Black places his seven attacking pieces on seven of the eight spaces of the outer ring, leaving the 'neutral zone' empty.
(See figure below.)

3. Only one piece may occupy a space, except for the 'citadel' at the moment of a Black victory.
(See Rule twenty-two.)

4. The pieces of both sides can make either simple moves or *jumps* from ring to ring, along the radiating segments.

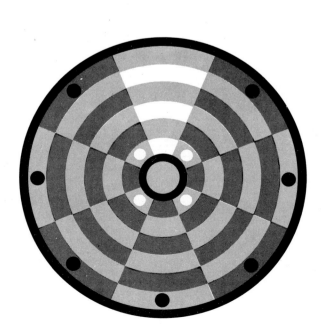

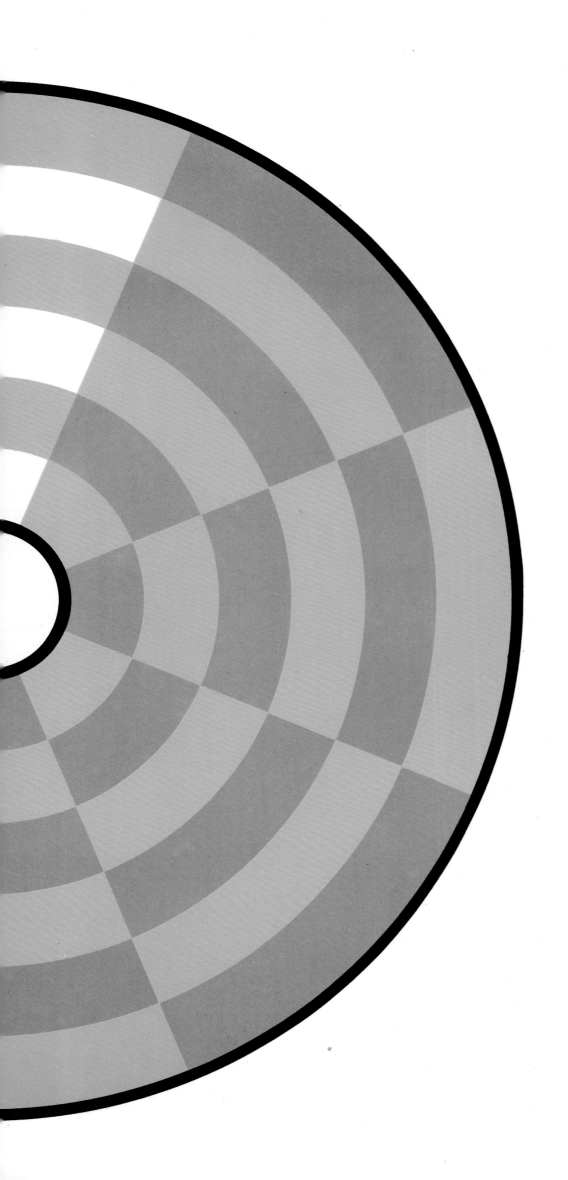

5. Black's pieces can only move one space at a time, always in the same direction – towards the centre, the pieces landing on white and black spaces alternately.

6. In the 'neutral zone' the pieces move from white to grey spaces.

7. White's pieces also move from one ring to the next along a radiating segment, but they can move either forwards or backwards.

8. Pieces of either colour can *jump* within a radiating segment across a ring over an opposing piece, landing on a vacant space immediately beyond. This is by a *short leap* onto an empty space of the same colour. The opposing piece is thereby captured and removed from the board.

9. Pieces of either colour can also land on a space already occupied by an opposing piece. The earlier arrival is then removed from the board Note the exception in Rule sixteen.

10. Only one piece may be captured in a turn of play.

11. Capturing a piece at risk is not compulsory.

12. Pieces may move from one segment to the next along the ring on which they stand. Black pieces can only move to the adjacent space, but White's pieces can move any number of empty spaces along a ring. White can also make a *long leap* over a black piece to land immediately beyond, removing the black piece from the board. Note Rules thirteen, fourteen, fifteen and sixteen which limit this movement.

13. Pieces of either colour can move into the 'neutral zone', but have to wait for another turn of play before leaving it. The 'neutral zone' acts as a barrier to white pieces making a complete circular movement around the board.

14. The 'neutral zone' provides a safe place for Black to organize an attack.

15. A piece may make a capture while moving into a 'neutral zone'.

16. Captures are not permitted by either Black or White when leaving the 'neutral zone'.

17. A piece in the 'neutral zone' is safe from attack.

18. Black is only permitted to have the same number of pieces in the 'neutral zone' as White has left on the board.

19. White is not permitted to move pieces into the 'citadel'.

20. White tries to leave one piece on the innermost ring to defend the 'citadel' or else to capture any single black piece within it by *jumping* over it.

21. A black piece moving into the 'citadel' may capture a white piece by *jumping* over it on the way.

22. Black wins the game if he moves two of his pieces into the 'citadel'. A single black piece in the 'citadel' is vulnerable to attack from a white piece *jumping* over it it from one side of the inner ring to the other, except from the 'neutral zone'. (See Rule sixteen.)

23. White wins the game if he captures six of the seven black pieces.

# Jungle

The board and pieces for this modern Chinese game are shown in the illustration below with the pieces laid out in the opening position. The pieces for one side are marked in blue and for the other in red. Each player has a set of eight animals of graded strength expressed as a numerical value. Three pieces – the rat, the lion and the tiger – have special powers, described in Rules six, seven, eight and nine.

**PLAYERS**
Two.

**PIECES**
Eight animals for each side – elephant, lion, tiger, panther, dog, wolf, cat, rat. (See equipment sheet.)

**AIM**
Penetration of the opponent's territory.

**ORIGIN**
China.

PIECES VALUE
An elephant's value is eight.
A lion's value is seven.
A tiger's value is six.
A panther's value is five.
A dog's value is four.
A wolf's value is three.
A cat's value is two.
A rat's value is one.
Any trapped animal's value is zero.

RULES
1. Only one piece can occupy a single square.

2. Blue has first move.

3. Each player, alternately, moves a piece one square along any straight line in any direction except the diagonal.

4. An animal may be 'killed' and removed from the board by any animal stronger than itself moving onto its square. The only exception is that the rat can 'kill' the elephant by running into its ear and gnawing into its brain.

5. If animals of the same kind meet, the animal moving onto the square destroys the one already there.

6. A rat can swim and move as if it were on dry land on the water-squares. No other animal can move onto a water-square; so a rat is safe from attack there. However, the rat cannot attack the elephant from a water-square.

7. If both rats meet in the water, the moving piece eats the stationary one.

8. On the following move, after arriving at a square on the edge of the water, both lions and tigers can *jump* over the water. They make this *jump* in any direction in a straight line, except the diagonal, to reach the nearest land-square on the other side. Any weaker animal that already occupies such a square is destroyed.

9. The leap is blocked if there is a rat of either colour on a water-square in the line of the *jump*. This makes it impossible for the lion or tiger to spring over the water.

10. Three traps are set around each den and the player's own animals may move on and off trap-squares without hindrance. If a hostile animal occupies a trap-square, however, it loses all its power and becomes weaker than any defending piece. As soon as an animal moves out of a hostile trap, it regains its full strength. Animals of either colour may enter or leave traps at will.

11. No animal may enter its own den.

12. The first player to manoeuvre one of his animals into the opponent's den wins the game.

# Coiled Snake

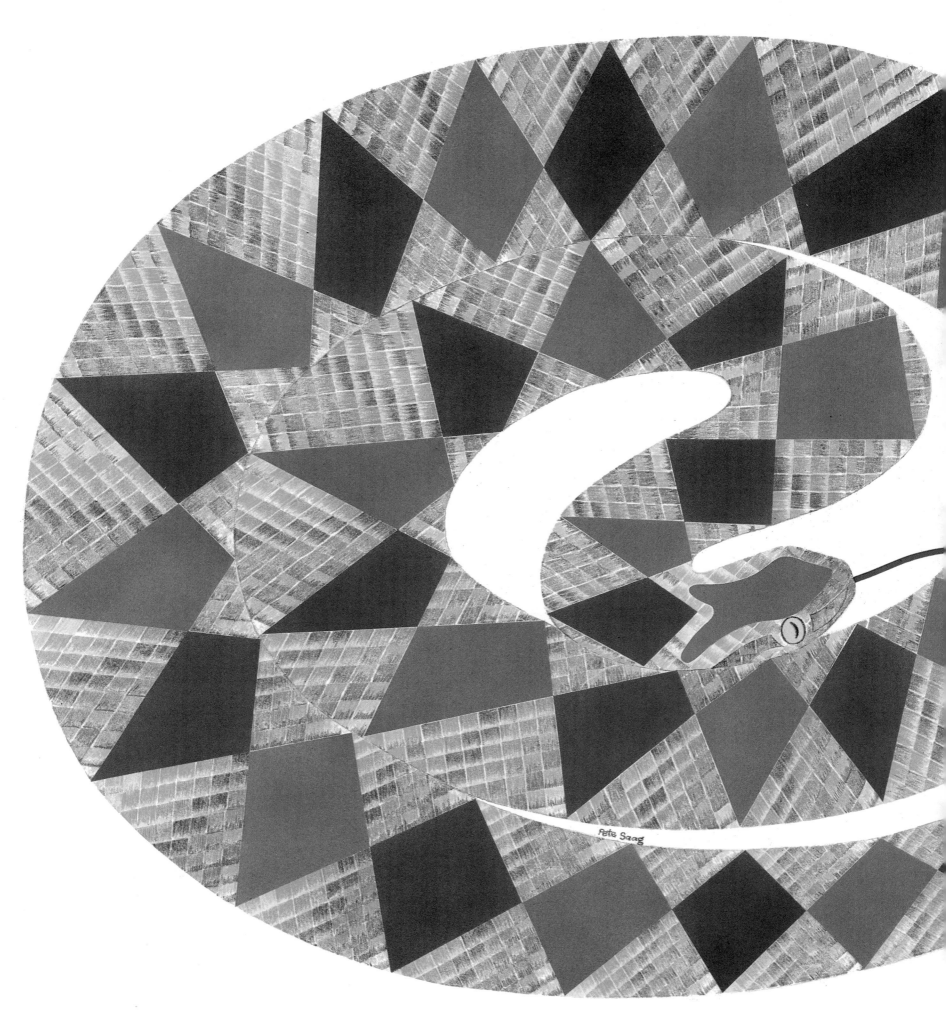

A Coiled Snake game is painted on the wall of a tomb dating from the third dynasty of Ancient Egypt c.2868–2613 B.C. Actual boards have been found in tombs of a later date and are of two types, either with a central stand, or as a flat slab with a hole at one side for hanging up on a wall. The scene on the tomb wall-painting shows an equipment box containing six sets of six marbles together with six animal figurines.

In Egyptian mythology a snake swallowing its own tail was a symbol of eternity, so this game may have had a ritual importance and originally been used for fortune-telling rather than for entertainment.

No rules have survived, but it is here suggested that up to six players can take part, using one set of six marbles and each having an animal figurine as a marker for his progress along the spiral towards the centre of the board. Six small coins or buttons may be substituted for the marbles.

**PLAYERS**
**Two to six.**

**PIECES**
**Animal marker for each player. (See equipment sheet.)**

**SCORING**
**Six marbles (or coins or buttons).**

**AIM**
**Race along the spiral to reach the centre of the board.**

**ORIGIN**
**Egypt, 2868–2613 B.C.**

RULES
1. Every player takes his turn in a clockwise direction around the board.

2. The first player picks up the six marbles and holds them behind his back. After shuffling them he holds out both fists to a challenger, who touches one of the fists, guessing aloud how many marbles it contains.

3. If the challenger is correct it becomes his turn to hide the marbles and the previous player loses his turn.

4. If the challenger is incorrect the opening player moves his marker along the scales of the snake by the difference between the call and the true number. For example, if his fist held five marbles, and the challenger called three, the player would move his marker on by two divisions. Then after shuffling the marbles behind his back, he would present his closed fists to the next player in a clockwise direction around the board.

5. Play continues in this way until the first player loses the turn by one of the other players guessing correctly the number of marbles in his closed fist.

6. The successful challenger becomes the next player, and the new challenger is the player on his left.

7. If a player's marker reaches an occupied space, it is placed on the next vacant scale towards the centre of the board.

8. Should the score give a player more points than he needs to reach the centre of the board, he must move his marker back the excess number.

9. The first player to reach the centre of the board wins the game.

# Snail

Far removed in time and surroundings from the Ancient Egyptian game of Coiled Snake, though similar in appearance, is the Snail game of the Victorian nursery for six or less players.

Each player has a distinctive marble or marker and the game is played with a dicing cup and cubic "die" on a square wooden board. There are fifty shallow depressions or sections arranged in a spiral, the first and last being painted red, the others cream and numbered from two to forty-nine.

**PLAYERS**
**Up to six.**

**PIECES**
**One marker for each player (see equipment sheet).**

**SCORING**
**One cubic die.**

**AIM**
**To reach the central space.**

**ORIGIN**
**England, nineteenth century.**

RULES
1. Each player throws the *die* in turn, the player with the highest score beginning the game. If two or more tie for the highest score, these players throw again.

2. The opening player throws the *die* and moves his marker to the indicated space.

3. The *die* and cup are then passed to the player on his left, who throws and moves his marker in the same way.

4. Should a player's marker land on an occupied space he announces 'You go back!' and takes his opponent's piece. The displaced marker has to start again at the beginning of the spiral.

5. Any player throwing a higher number than is required to reach the central space must go back as many spaces as the number thrown or, should this space be occupied, then one further back. Other players' pieces are not sent off the board by a marker travelling in the wrong direction.

6. The owner of the first marker to rest in the central space wins the game. If desired the other players can continue playing to determine the order of losing.

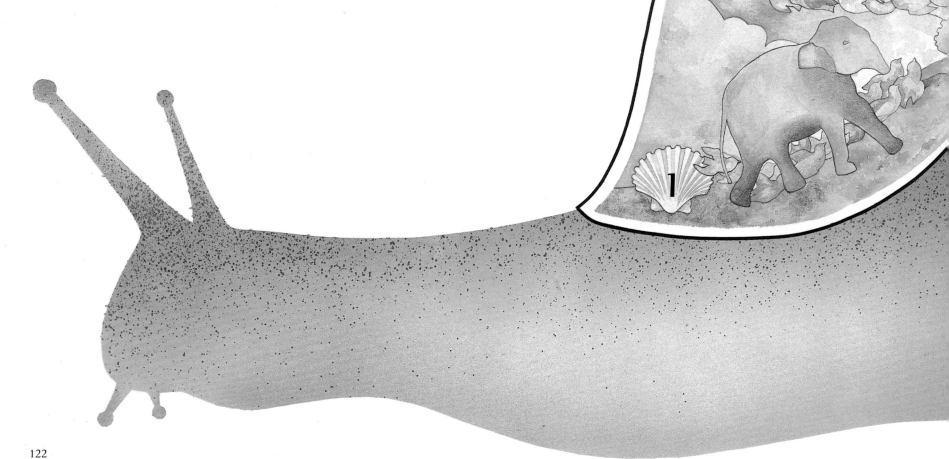

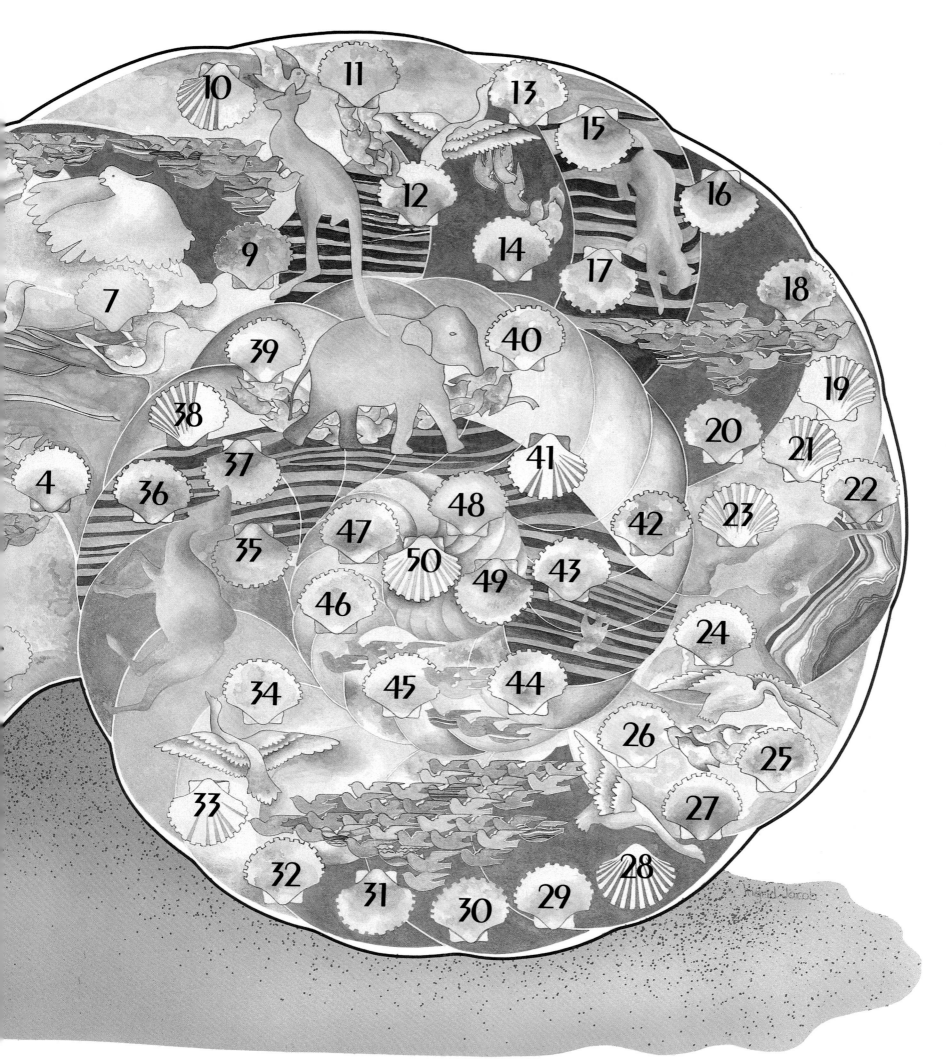

# Go

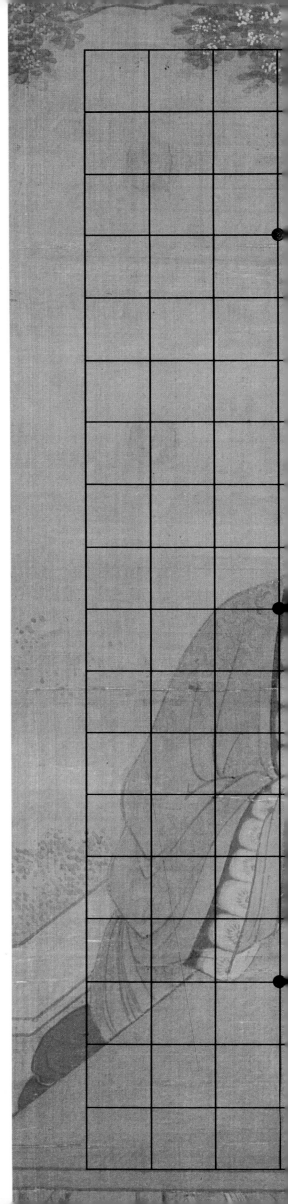

Go is a contraction of I-go, which was how the game was known when it first reached Japan about 500 A.D. Originating in China c.2000 B.C., the game was called Wei-ch'i and is first mentioned in writings from about 625 B.C. A white porcelain Wei-ch'i board still exists which dates from the Sui Dynasty (581–618 A.D.). The eighteen by eighteen squares on this board are hollowed out which suggests that the game must have been played on the squares and not the intersections, as later became the rule. The first books on the game appeared during the T'ang Dynasty (618–906 A.D.).

Before the eleventh century Go was played only within Japanese court circles, but by the thirteenth century the game had become very popular with the Samurai or warrior class. Boards and stones were regarded as essential articles of military equipment and were taken on active service. As soon as fighting was over, Go contests began.

In Japan to promote the game and several master-players were installed as professors. Private schools appeared and professional players toured the country playing matches and teaching pupils. The lowest degree in Go was 'Shodan', and the highest or ninth was 'Kudan', an honour very rarely granted. A strict system of handicapping was also devised.

The game prospered during the first half of the nineteenth century and the painting on glass reproduced here dates from this period. The Shogunate fell in 1867, state control of the game ceased and the Academy was disbanded, but there was a revival about 1880. Today there are over four hundred professionals and some eight million Go players in Japan; Wei-ch'i is played widely in China and is also very popular in Korea where it is known as Pa-tok.

The Go board is marked out with thin black lines into a grid of eighteen by eighteen squares, forming three hundred and sixty-one intersections or "points". Nine of these are marked to assist in handicapping and in rapid orientation. Japanese Go boards are traditionally made of a solid block of wood about half a metre (one and a half feet) square, mounted on short, detachable feet only about seven centimetres (three inches) high. The players sit on the floor facing each other across the board.

The underside of this board is hollowed out to lighten it and increase its resonance. When the pieces are placed on it they make a pleasant clicking sound. In Korea, wires are sometimes stretched under the board, so that as the stones are placed, they produce a musical note.

The stones for each player are contained in bowls: a hundred and eighty white stones for one and a hundred and eighty-one black for the other. The white stones of the best sets are shells from particular provinces in Japan, while the black are made from a special kind of slate. Cheaper modern sets use glass or plastic counters and folding-boards may be made of hinged lightweight wood, or even cardboard.

The rules for Go are quite simple, but the game is very subtle and fascinating. Although the pieces never move on the board, there is a continual shift in territorial strength. The game may be divided into three phases: the first, in which the territorial limits are staked out, is the intuitive stage. The second phase comprises the middle game during which occupied areas are contested, stone-to-stone, and the fighting involves a logical analysis. The end-game is the third phase when the final moves are calculated and also the value of the defined territory.

Go has been compared to five simultaneous Chess games (see pages 18–21)—one at each corner of the board and the fifth in the centre—with the added interest of the pieces in one area influencing those in the other four. Casual games last from one to three hours and professional matches can take up to three days.

Beginners are advised to play on only one quarter of the board by masking off the rest. If possible, it is a good idea to join one of the many Go centres and further information can be obtained from the reference books given in the Bibliography.

**PLAYERS**
**Two.**

**PIECES**
**One hundred and eighty white for one side; one hundred and eighty-one for the other. (See equipment sheet.)**

**AIM**
**Capture of the most territory.**

**ORIGIN**
**China, c.2000 B.C.**

## RULES

PHASE ONE
1. The board is empty at the beginning of the game.

2. Black plays first by putting a piece on any *point* including those on the edge of the board—a privilege granted to the weaker player as this gives a slight advantage.

3. Play then alternates, each player placing only one piece at each turn.

4. Once played the pieces cannot be moved and remain in position until the end of the game unless they are captured, when they are lifted from the board and retained by the captor.

5. The object of the game is to gain as much territory as possible by controlling vacant *points* and prevent them falling to the opponent. It is easiest to gain territory at the corners of the board or at the sides, and most difficult at the centre.

PHASE TWO
6. Single pieces or a group of closely connected pieces, surrounded by opposing pieces on adjacent *points*

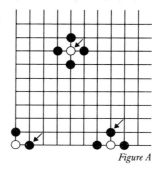

*Figure A*

# Go & variants

(connected only along the marked lines and not diagonally), are considered 'dead' and removed from the board. This area or territory is then left ringed by the captor. (See figures A and B.) The variety and excitement of the game is increased by capturing pieces, although it is not the primary objective.

*White stones will be 'dead' if black occupy arrowed points.*

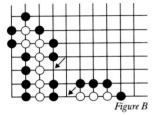

*Figure B*

7. Capture cannot be made if there are any 'liberties' or unoccupied *points* in the centre of a surrounded group of pieces. (See figure E.)

8. Captured pieces give the captor, at the end of the game, two extra points, one for the liberated territory and another for the forfeited piece.

9. On the edge of the board, capture is made by surrounding a piece, or closely connected group of pieces, on three sides only. (See figures A and B.)

10. A player cannot play a piece into 'atari' or put it at risk, sometimes referred to as 'suicide', by entering a *point* completely surrounded by hostile pieces, unless in doing so he also makes a capture. (See figure C.) A piece cannot occupy the last free *point* of one of its own group.

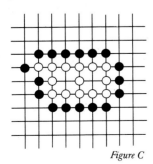

*Figure C*

either, unless enemy pieces are thereby captured. (See figure D.)

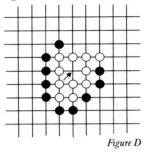

*Figure D*

11. Vacant *points* controlled by pieces of one colour are called 'eyes' and a group with two 'eyes' is safe from attack. (See figure E.)

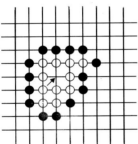

*Figure E*

12. A group of pieces not in adjacent contact may contain empty *points*, but the disconnected stones can be attacked and the formation destroyed. These empty *points* may form temporary or 'false eyes'. (See figure F.)

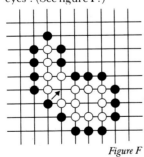

*Figure F*

13. A player may place a stone on any vacant *point* except when contravening Rule ten. Similarly, when a piece has just been captured in a situation which involves the possibility of unending capture and recapture, known as a 'ko', (see figure G), the opponent must first

play elsewhere on the board before returning to attack. This avoids perpetual position and a drawn game.

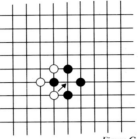

*Figure G*

14. When fighting for a vital 'ko', players try to find a threatening move elsewhere which the opponent will be forced to defend, allowing the first player to recapture the 'ko'. A 'ko' ends either when one player runs out of threats or a threat is ignored in order to fill the 'ko'.

15. If there are three 'ko' positions on the board at the same time, the game is drawn.

16. 'Seki' or a stalemate position occurs when opposing pieces are interlocked in such a way that neither player can attack the opponent's pieces without losing his own. (See figure H.) These positions, even though without eyes, are left until the end of the game when the free *points* within them are considered neutral and do not count as territory for either player.

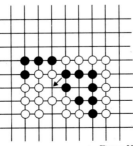

*Figure H*

**PHASE THREE**

17. A game ends when the players can neither seal off any more territory nor make any captures which will affect the final score.

18. Isolated vacant *points* between opposing formations at the end of the game are neutral. They are filled in by either player.

19. Pieces not surrounded, but which could have become prisoners, are 'dead' and are removed from the board without further play.

20. When the neutral *points* have been filled in and the 'dead' pieces removed, each player places captured pieces on vacant enemy *points*, reducing the opponent's score by the number of pieces captured. The interiors of territorial areas are arranged in rectangles of up to ten *points* long, (see figure I) to make scoring easier.

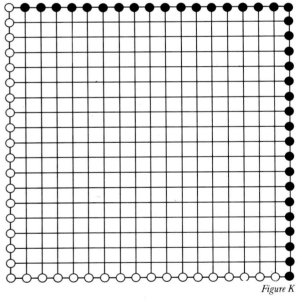

*Figure I*

21. The *points* left vacant within each territorial area are added together and the difference between the two sides is the final score.

22. Players of equal strength play Black alternately, but if one player wins three consecutive games, he usually gives his opponent a handicap of two pieces. The nine 'stars' on the board are indications for placing handicap pieces. (See figure J.)

23. The better player is always White and the handicap stones given to Black are worth about ten points each. If White continues to win, the black handicap pieces are gradually increased.

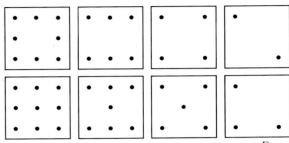

*Figure J*

## Ming Mang

*This game can be played on an eight by eight checkered board like those used for Chess (see pages 18–21) and Draughts/Checkers (see pages 26–29). In Tibet, where the game originated, it is usually played on an uncheckered one similar to the Go board and using Go pieces (see pages 124–125). The opening position of the pieces is shown in figure K below.*

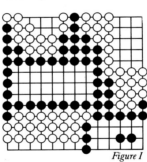

*Figure K*

**PLAYERS**
**Two.**

**PIECES**
**One hundred and eighty white counters and one hundred and eighty-one black. (See equipment sheet.)**

**AIM**
**To capture opposing pieces.**

**ORIGIN**
**Tibet.**

**RULES**

1. Each player places his pieces on adjacent sides of the board, on the intersections of the lines, or *points*.

2. The players move one piece in alternate turns of play to any vacant *point* in a straight line in any direction except diagonally. *Short leaps* or *jumping* are not permitted.

3. A piece is captured if it is trapped between two enemy pieces along any straight line except for the diagonal. Two or more pieces may be captured in continuity along the same line, or along different lines in the same turn of play. (See figure L.)

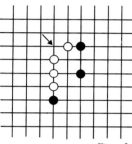

*Figure L*

4. All trapped pieces are removed from the board and replaced by pieces of the player's own colour.

5. A piece placed between two hostile pieces in any straight line, except the diagonal, is safe from capture. If, however, one of the opposing pieces is moved away and then returned to the square, on the next move, the trapped piece is captured. (See figure M.)

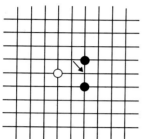

*Figure M*

6. Pieces on corner squares are safe from capture because they cannot be trapped between enemy pieces in a straight line. The corners are crucial and their loss is likely to result in defeat.

7. In the final stages of the game, care should be taken not to trap the weaker player's last piece in a corner, causing stalemate.

8. The player losing all his pieces loses the game.

*A modern Go board in traditional Japanese style.*

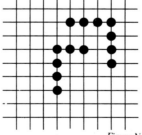

*Above: Chinese painting of two men playing Go.*

## Renju

*Renju means 'to-link-round-stones' in Japanese and is more popularly known as Gomoku-Narabe, which translated is 'five-small-round-pieces-put-side-by-side'. Renju was introduced into Europe about 1885 and is known in England as Spoil Five. In this version the pieces are placed on the squares and not on the "points". The board and pieces used for Renju are the same as those used for Go (see pages 124–125).*

**PLAYERS**
**Two.**

**PIECES**
**One hundred and eighty white counters and one hundred and eighty-one black. (See equipment sheet.)**

**AIM**
**Formation of a line of five in any direction.**

**ORIGIN**
**Japan.**

RULES
1. The board of nineteen by nineteen *points* is empty at the beginning of the game and the players place their pieces in alternate turns of play on any unoccupied *points*.

2. Pieces are not moved after they have been placed on the board.

3. The construction of open-ended forks whose branches consist of three pieces each is not allowed. Forks of three and four, or four and four, are permitted. (See figure N.)

4. The first player to form a continuous line of five pieces in a *column*, *row* or diagonal wins the game.

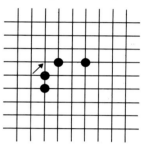

*Figure N*

## Ninuki Renju

*The literal translation of the name for this Japanese game is 'two-(pieces)-to-take-away-two-chain-stones'. The game is played with a Go board and pieces (see pages 124–125).*

**PLAYERS**
**Two.**

**PIECES**
**One hundred and eighty white counters and one hundred and eighty-one black. (See equipment sheet.)**

**AIM**
**Either to form a continuous chain of five stones; or to capture ten of the opposing pieces.**

**ORIGIN**
**Japan.**

RULES
1. Black starts by placing a piece on any point on the board.

2. White follows and the game continues with the players placing pieces alternately.

3. Once placed the pieces do not move, except under Rule six.

4. There are two methods of winning: either a continuous chain of five pieces in a *column*, *row*, or diagonal is formed as in Renju; or ten of the opponent's pieces are captured. (See Rule six.)

5. A player can capture and remove from the board any pair of the opponent's pieces trapped between two of his own. (See figure O.)

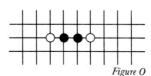

*Figure O*

6. A player is not permitted to place a piece on the board which will form two or more chains of three pieces simultaneously and under this three and three chain rule is included a chain of three stones with a vacant point between. (See figure P.) Compare Rule eight.

7. Only if it prevents an opponent from forming a four or a five stone chain is forming a three and three chain permitted.

8. A chain of more than five stones is 'over-ripe', or invalid, and does not give the player the game.

*Below: nineteenth century Japanese vase showing an open-air game of Go.*

*Figure P*

# Conspirators

This game was probably invented in France and dates perhaps from the Revolution in the eighteenth century. This was a period of feverish political activity with factions conspiring against each other. Conspirators is a game for two or four and the pieces are placed on the intersections or "points". Thirty-nine of the sixty-four "points" along the edge of the board are marked as sanctuaries, as shown below, while at the centre of the board a rectangle of thirty-two squares represents a secret meeting place. If two players take part, each has a set of twenty pieces and if four players, each has ten pieces, distinctively coloured.

**PLAYERS**
**Two or four.**

**PIECES**
**Twenty each for two players or ten for four players. (See equipment sheet.)**

**AIM**
**Survival: the first player to get all his pieces to a hiding-place wins.**

**ORIGIN**
**France, probably after the Revolution of 1789.**

RULES

1. Black begins by placing one of his pieces on any of the forty-five *points* within the marked central rectangle. White replies and the players continue to place their pieces alternately.

2. As soon as all the pieces are in position for their secret conference, one of the players gives a warning shout that they have been discovered and the conspirators scatter to try and find hiding-places.

3. The players take turns to move their pieces towards one of the thirty-nine sanctuaries marked on the edge of the board. Only one piece may be moved in a turn, one *point* in any direction – forwards, backwards, sideways or diagonally (note that the last direction is not along a marked line).

4. A piece is allowed to *jump* over any other piece if there is a vacant *point* immediately beyond. Also a piece may make a series of *short leaps* in any direction within the same turn of play.

5. The first player to succeed in getting all his pieces to sanctuary is the winner.

# Pope Joan

The traditional board for this game, as illustrated, consists of a wooden circular tray divided into eight compartments, each having a label: Pope, Matrimony, Intrigue, Ace, King, Queen, Knave and Game. Pope is the Nine of Diamonds. Matrimony is the Queen and King of "trumps", in the same hand. Intrigue is the Queen and Knave of "trumps", in the same hand.

The tray on the actual board revolves on a central pillar with a compartment in the centre of the board to hold the counters. Any number of players can take part and each receives thirty of these counters at the beginning of the game. A fifty-two card pack completes the equipment. The rare Pope Joan, illustrated here, both open and shut, is Chinese and dates from the middle of the nineteenth century. The revolving tray with eight compartments of the standard set has been replaced by papier mâché dishes. The counters are of mother-of-pearl; the cards, made by Hunts & Sons, have plain backs, square corners with no indices and the Knave of Hearts carries a feather instead of a baton. The tax paid on the pack was one shilling, which dates the cards between 1825 and 1860. They are probably the original pack sold with the set.

*Below: the card players – a German engraving.*

**PLAYERS**
Any number.

**PIECES**
Thirty counters for each player. (See equipment sheet.) One fifty-two pack of cards.

**AIM**
Either to be first to play all the cards of a hand; or to win the most counters by playing certain cards.

**ORIGIN**
England, early nineteenth century.

RULES
1.  The dealer removes the eight of Diamonds from the pack to form a stop before Pope, the nine of Diamonds. (Aces count low.)

2.  Each player including the dealer *dresses* the board by placing fifteen counters from his own store in the compartments on the board: six counters on Pope; two each on Matrimony and Intrigue and one counter each on Ace, King, Queen, Knave and Game.

3.  The player on the dealer's right shuffles the pack.

4.  The cards are dealt to each player, with an extra hand in the centre of the table. Any cards left over in the deal are added to the central stack.

5.  The last card of the pack is turned up to decide the *trump* suit.

6.  If the turn-up is the Nine of Diamonds (Pope), or an Ace, King, Queen or Knave, the dealer wins the counters in the relevant compartment of the board.

7.  The player on the dealer's left leads and names the card he places as he does so.

8.  The holder of the card in the same sequence and immediately above it follows. This continues until no one is able to play – either the King of the suit has been reached, or the wanted card is in the extra hand, or the card has already been played, or it is the eight of Diamonds.

9.  When the Knave, Queen, King or Ace of *trumps* is played during the game, the player wins the counters in the appropriate compartment and if he can play Knave-and-Queen, or Queen-and-King, he wins the counters in Intrigue or Matrimony as a bonus.

10.  The first to play all his own cards wins the counters in Game. He also takes one counter for each card held by every player except for the holder of an unplayed Pope card who is exempt from this fine.

11.  Pope can only be played when the holder has the lead.

12.  When no one can follow a card led, the player of it leads any other card he wishes.

13.  Unclaimed counters in each compartment are left to accumulate for the next game. Sometimes counters in Intrigue and Matrimony may remain unclaimed throughout the session.

14.  At the end of the game, unclaimed counters are distributed by dealing a final round to the players, face upwards and without a surplus hand. Those receiving Pope, Ace, King, Queen and Knave of Diamonds receive the counters in the respective compartments. The holder of the Queen also takes half the counters in Intrigue and Matrimony the other halves being taken by the holders of the Knave and King.

*A Chinese version of Pope Joan in the form of a lavishly lacquered box with moveable trays and mother-of-pearl pieces.*

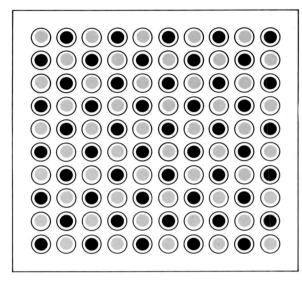

*Death of Captain Cook on Hawaii.*

Several stone Konane boards have been found on prehistoric Hawaiian sites, dating from before the arrival of Europeans. Captain Cook mentioned in his 'Voyage to the Pacific' 1776–80 that the Hawaiians played a game resembling Draughts/Checkers (see pages 26–29) played on the squares. The playing pieces were stored in a deep wooden bowl – black stones of close-grained basalt and white stones made from branching coral. The boards seem to have varied in size, and the board shown is a reconstruction based on two in the Bernice P. Bishop Museum in Honolulu. One of these consists of a lava flat with ten by ten depressions cut into it containing black and white pebbles. The other is made of wood with ten by thirteen depressions. The teeth embedded in the lava board are purely for decoration and have no significance in the game.

*Volcano Park, Hawaii: source of the volcanic basalt used in the past for Konane boards.*

**PLAYERS**
Two.

**PIECES**
Fifty black for one side; fifty white for the other. (See equipment sheet.)

**AIM**
Capture or immobilization of opposing pieces.

**ORIGIN**
Hawaii.

**RULES**
1. The game is for two players who face each other across the board.

2. Each player has fifty pieces, one set being dark and the other light. All the spaces on the board are filled with their pieces arranged alternately black and white.

3. One player then picks up one piece of each colour, shuffles them behind his back and brings his closed fists back in front of his body for his opponent to choose from. The piece chosen will be that player's colour.

4. Black always starts first.

5. The two pieces used to decide the players' colours are returned to their spaces on the board.

6. Black must begin by lifting either one of the two central black pieces, or one from a corner of the board. This piece is placed off the board in front of his opponent.

7. White then lifts a white piece which must be adjacent to the space made by the removal of the first piece – either one of the two central white pieces, or one next to the vacant corner space. The white piece removed is placed in front of the opening player.

8. The game continues by alternate turns of play.

9. After the first two moves, all the following are made by *jumping* over an opponent's piece onto a vacant space immediately beyond by a *short leap*—forwards, sideways or backwards. *Jumping* diagonally is not permitted.

10. More than one *jump* can be made in a turn of play as long as movement continues in the same direction, but a change of direction is not permitted.

11. When making more than one capture in a turn of play the captured pieces must be in a straight line and each piece separated by one vacant space from its neighbour.

12. If a player can capture more than one piece in a turn of play he may choose how many to capture and need not include them all. There is no *huffing*.

13. As pieces are removed from the board, *jumping* becomes more difficult. If a player is unable to *jump* when it is his turn to play he loses the game.

14. If a player loses all his pieces the game is over and his opponent has won. Drawn games cannot occur.

15. At the end of every game the players exchange pieces, their new pieces having accumulated in front of them during the preceding game.

16. A match consists of the best of several games, the exact number being agreed at the start of play.

133

# Snakes and Ladders

This popular children's race-game is derived from 'Moksha-Patamu', a game used in India for religious instruction. The Hindu sages taught that 'pap' (good) and 'punya' (bad) exist side by side and that virtuous behaviour, represented by the ladders, helped the individual to progress towards ultimate perfection or 'Nirvana'. Wickedness, symbolized by the snake, led to reincarnation into a lower, animal form.

In the original Indian game, each square from which a ladder rose specified a particular virtue: Faith (square twelve), Reliability (square fifty-one), Generosity (square fifty-seven), Knowledge (square seventy-six) and Asceticism (square seventy-eight). Conversely, the snake heads signified vices: Disobedience (square forty-one), Vanity (square forty-four), Vulgarity (square forty-nine), Theft (square fifty-two), Lying (square fifty-eight), Drunkenness (square sixty-two), Debt (square sixty-nine), Murder (square seventy-three), Rage (square eighty-four), Greed (square ninety-two), Pride (square ninety-five), and Lust (square ninety-nine).

It is interesting to note that vices outnumber virtues and the two most disastrous evils were murder (square seventy-three) and Lust (square ninety-nine).

In the West, the Snakes and Ladders board has lost its religious connotations and is merely an exciting obstacle race. However, the board reproduced here, published about 1935 (note the L.N.E.R. Silver Link class engine on squares thirty-eight and seventy-eight), retains an educational intention, although of a more secular kind, being designed to teach children how to avoid the dangers and difficulties of travel. For example, square fifty-eight where the boy plays with the door handle and falls out onto the track (snake fifty-eight to twenty-five). The makers of this board did not appreciate the symbolism involved in the snakes and have made the players travel from their harmless tails to their dangerous heads.

The track starts at square one and follows a path along the rows running from left to right and right to left alternately, ending at square one hundred, the winning point.

*Ritual snake stones near Madras, southern India.*

## PLAYERS
Any number.

## PIECES
One marker for each player.
(See equipment sheet.)

## SCORING
One die.

## AIM
A race to reach square one hundred.

## ORIGIN
India, imported into England, mid nineteenth century.

## RULES
1. The players each throw the *die* once, the player with the highest score has the first turn. They sit around the table in a clockwise order of play, the caster with the lowest score sitting to the right of the opening player.

2. Before a player can start he must throw a six. He then throws again, moving his marker the number of squares indicated by his second throw.

3. If a marker lands on a square showing the bottom of a ladder the marker climbs to its top.

4. If a marker lands on a square where there is the tip of a snake's tail, it slides down to its head.

5. If a player throws a six he moves his marker on, possibly taking it up a ladder or down a snake and then has a second throw.

6. The first player to reach square one hundred wins the game and the others continue playing for places.

7. An exact throw is needed to win. If the number thrown is more than is required, the marker is moved backwards from square one hundred for each unwanted point.

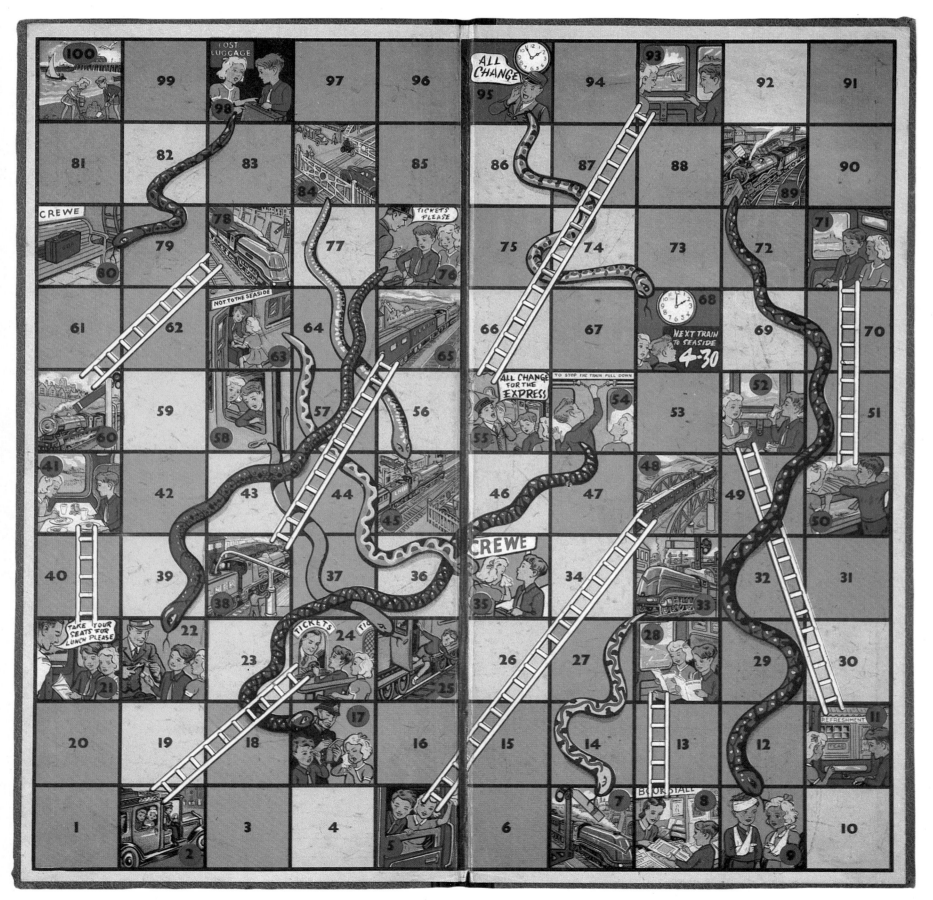

# Rithmomachia

*Rithmomachia, a game of calculation, and the game called Zodiac (loose fold-out sheet) based on astrology, were both popular for several centuries during the Middle Ages and then passed into oblivion.*

*The first mention of Rithmomachia was by Hermannus Contractus, who lived from 1013 to 1054 A.D., and several other descriptive manuscripts exist, written between the eleventh and fourteenth centuries. The game appears to have originated in Byzantium or Alexandria and was based on the Pythagorean philosophy of numbers. The intelligentsia of the Middle Ages became fanatical players of Rithmomachia and even regarded it as superior to Chess. Today it is as forgotten as the number theory on which it was based. However, those with an interest in mathematics will find the principles of the game's construction explained in Discovering Old Board Games, by R. C. Bell.*

*The board has eight by sixteen plain squares and the two players have pieces in the shape of Rounds, Triangles, Squares, which combine to form Pyramids. These pieces are white for one side and black for the other, also referred to as 'evens' and 'odds' respectively, according to the numbers inscribed on the round pieces. Dots below the numbers serve to distinguish six from nine, eighteen from eighty-one etc.*

*The initial arrangement of the pieces is shown in the figure below. The players move their pieces alternately, Black having the first move. Rounds move onto any adjacent empty space, Triangles move three empty spaces in any direction and Squares four spaces in any direction. The Pyramids move in the same way as any of the layers of which they are composed.*

## PLAYERS
Two.

## PIECES
Twenty-nine for White – ten Rounds, ten Triangles and nine Squares; and twenty-eight for Black – nine Rounds, ten Triangles and nine Squares. (See equipment sheet.)

## AIM
Capture of opposing pieces according to agreed arithmetical combination; or formation of pieces in agreed numerical combinations within opponent's territory.

## ORIGIN
Eastern Mediterranean, before the eleventh century.

## RULES
1. The players sit facing the longer sides of the board.

2. No piece can *leap* over any other piece.

3. The object of the game is – by means of various methods listed below – to capture the opponent's pieces to form some desired combination; or, in games between very skilled players, to achieve particular formations of pieces within the opponent's territory. (See Proper Victories.)

## METHODS OF CAPTURE
4. 'Meeting'. If White's Triangle twenty-five, by advancing three spaces, can land on Black's Round twenty-five, White does not move his piece, but captures and removes his opponent's piece instead.

5. 'Assault'. If a smaller number, multiplied by the number of vacant spaces between it and the larger one, equals the larger one, then the smaller number can take the larger. For example, White's Round five can capture Black's Square forty-five if nine vacant spaces separate them.

6. 'Ambuscade'. If two pieces whose sum equals the number on an opponent's piece can move onto the spaces on either side of it, the latter is ambuscaded and removed. For example, if White's Rounds four and eight move on either side of Black's Triangle twelve, the latter is *borne off*.

7. 'Siege'. If a piece is surrounded on all four sides by enemy pieces, it is captured and removed.

8. Each player has one Pyramid. The total value of ninety-one for White is built up of two Squares, thirty-six and twenty-five, two Triangles sixteen and nine, and two Rounds four and one. Black's Pyramid of a hundred and ninety is built up of two Squares sixty-four and forty-nine,

| 1 | 2 | 3 | 4 | 5 | 6 | 7 | 8 | 9 | 10 | 11 | 12 | 13 | 14 | 15 | 16 |
|---|---|---|---|---|---|---|---|---|---|---|---|---|---|---|---|
| 49 | 28 | 16△ | | | | | | | | | | | 81△ | 153 | 289 |
| 121 | 66 | 36△ | | | | | | | | | | | 49△ | 91 (Pyramid) | 169 |
| 12△ | 9○ | 3○ | | | | | | | | | 8○ | 64○ | 72△ | | |
| 30△ | 25○ | 5○ | | | | | | | | | 6○ | 36○ | 42△ | | |
| 56△ | 49○ | 7○ | | | | | | | | | 4○ | 16○ | 20△ | | |
| 90△ | 81○ | 9○ | | | | | | | | | 2○ | 4○ | 6△ | | |
| 225 | 120 | 64△ | | | | | | | | | | | 25△ | 45 | 81 |
| 361 | 190 | 100△ | | | | | | | | | | | 9△ | 15 | 25 |

two Triangles thirty-six and twenty-five, and one Round sixteen. Pyramids are rarely captured except by siege.

9. Pyramids are therefore considered vulnerable whenever one of their constituent layers is attacked by any of the four methods of capture. A ransom is permitted – an equivalent piece to the layer being attacked is offered instead. If no such piece is available, due to previous capture, any other piece is given that the opponent will accept.

10. As the Pyramids cannot be captured if their total numbers of ninety-one and a hundred and ninety are considered,

capture is permitted if a successful attack is made on the base square, namely thirty-six (White) or sixty-four (Black).

11. The object of the game is to gain a 'victory' by capturing the opponent's pieces. The players agree before beginning a game which type of 'victory' is to be achieved. Five of the 'victories', known as 'Common Victories' are suitable for beginners and the other three or 'Proper Victories' are for skilled players.

COMMON VICTORIES
12. 'De Corpore'. The players agree at the beginning of the game upon a particular number of pieces to be captured. As

soon as either player captures the number of pieces agreed on, he wins.

13. 'De Bonis'. This depends on the value of the captured pieces. If a winning number of a hundred and eighty is decided on, as soon as one player's captured pieces add up to a hundred and eighty or more he has won.

14. 'De Lite'. This depends on the value of the pieces and the number of digits inscribed upon them. If a winning total of a hundred and sixty is chosen, a further stipulation requires the total number of digits on the pieces to be some small number, such as eight. A player then tries to capture

pieces like fifty-six, sixty-four, twenty-eight and fifteen, totalling a hundred and sixty and having eight digits. The numbers a hundred and twenty-one, nine, and thirty, also totalling a hundred and sixty, would not suffice as there are only six digits.

15. 'De Honore'. This 'victory' depends on the number of the pieces and their value. If a hundred and sixty is the agreed number for the sum of the values, some other number like five is chosen for the number of pieces to be captured. Assembling sixty-four, thirty-six, thirty, twenty-five, and five provides a 'De Honore Victory', while fifty-six, sixty-four, twenty-eight

and twelve, or a hundred and twenty-one, nine, and thirty would not, as both conditions are not fulfilled.

16. 'De Honore Liteque'. The players agree on a hundred and sixty for the value, five for the number of pieces, and nine for the number of digits. Black can satisfy these conditions and win with the capture of sixty-four, thirty-six, forty-two, sixteen and two; or White with sixty-four, thirty-six, thirty, twenty-five and five.

PROPER VICTORIES
The 'proper victories' sought by expert players depend on combinations related to arithmetic, geometric and harmonic progressions. In these

'victories' the pieces, one of which must belong to the opponent, are arranged in a selected progression on the opponent's side of the board.

17. 'Victoria Magna'. This consists of an arrangement of three counters in any one of the three basic progressions. There are forty-one possible combinations in arithmetic progression. The possibilities are greater for White in the arithmetic, for Black in the geometric, and equal in the harmonic progression. One of these arrangements, in harmonic progression, is (six, eight, twelve).

18. 'Victoria Major'. This consists of a combination of any two progressions: arithmetic and geometric; geometric and harmonic; harmonic and arithmetic. This 'victory' is obtained by bringing four pieces in to line in the enemy's territory, two of which must belong to one of the selected progressions and two to the other. For example, (two, three, four, eight) is a 'Victoria Major' for either Black or White. This is because (two, three, four) are in arithmetic progression and (two, four, eight) in geometric, where (two, four, eight) are White's pieces and three is Black's piece. There are sixty-one such double progressions, all of which are available to Black and all but one to White.

19. 'Victoria Excellentissima'. This is the most difficult and desirable of all the 'victories', requiring four numbers in a row embodying all three progressions. There are only six possible solutions: (two, three, four, six), (four, six, eight, twelve), (seven, eight, nine, twelve), (four, six, nine, twelve), (three, five, fifteen, twenty-five) and (twelve, fifteen, sixteen, twenty).

# Music Masters

This game, published in Nuremburg, south Germany in the nineteenth century and now in the Victoria and Albert Museum, London, England, relates to the cultivation of music among the middle classes of the period. The playing of a musical instrument was always one of the accomplishments expected of fashionable ladies, but in the nineteenth century many more people learnt to play. One of the causes for this was the Romantic Movement that spread through European culture at this time, with its emphasis on the emotional appreciation of the arts. Also, as the prosperity and numbers of the middle class increased it was considered improper in those circles for women to take part in business activities or public life, and they were encouraged to devote their abundant leisure to amateur artistic pursuits.

Any number of players can take part in this nineteenth century game printed in Nuremburg, Germany, and now in the Victoria and Albert Museum, London, England. Each player starts the game with fifteen counters or tokens.

The player who gains mastery of the violin position wins the game.

**PLAYERS**
Any number.

**PIECES**
Fifteen counters for each player. (See equipment sheet.)

**SCORING**
Two cubic dice.

**AIM**
To win all the counters on the board.

**ORIGIN**
Germany, nineteenth century.

1. After placing an agreed number of tokens in the *pool* at the centre of the board (marked with a figure one), players throw the two dice to determine which player starts first.

2. The players throw the dice in turn. When the same score as one of those marked on the inner circle of the board is thrown, the player places the equivalent number of tokens on the musician portrayed above that score.

3. If a position already has tokens placed on it, the second player to score the same number withdraws the tokens from this particular music master.

4. Only exact throws are used; for example, if eight is thrown, each *die* must show four pips. Eight tokens are then placed on the trumpeter. Other scores than those on the board are not valid and the dice pass to the next player.

5. The player who scores two (one and one), landing on the Chinese bell player, cannot withdraw any tokens but must place two tokens on the position even if it is already occupied.

6. Only the player who scores twelve (six and six), landing on the violinist, can take the tokens placed on the Chinese bell player. Moreover he wins all the tokens placed anywhere on the circle and in the centre *pool*.

7. If, however, a twelve (six and six) is thrown, and the Chinese bell player position is empty, then the throw wins nothing and the player who has scored this number must place two tokens on the Chinese bell player, twelve tokens on the violinist, and also one token into the *pool*. So, only if the Chinese bell player already carries two tokens, can the player who scores twelve be the winner.

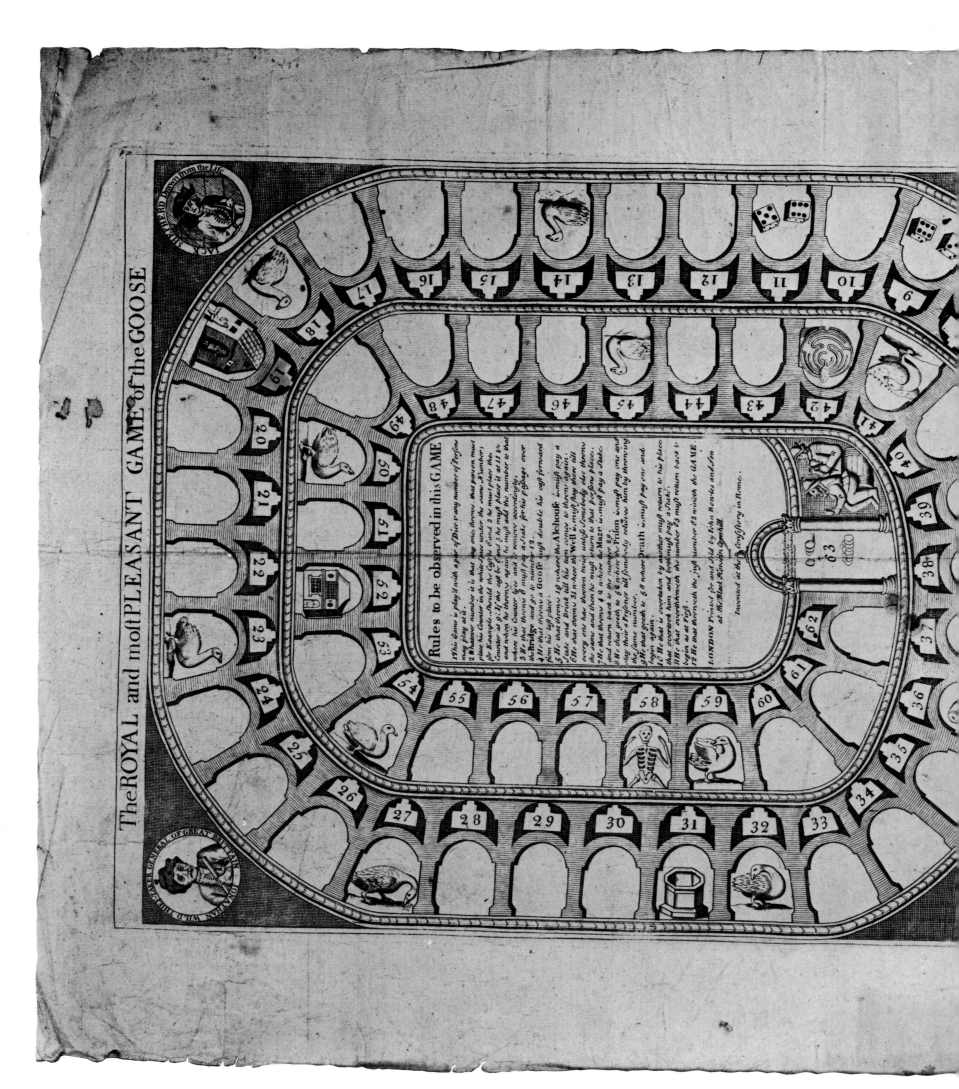

The ROYAL and most PLEASANT GAME of the GOOSE

Rules to be observed in this GAME

The Royal and most Pleasant Game of the Goose.

This game, originally known as 'Giuoco dell'Oca', or Game of the Goose, was invented in Florence at the time of Francesco dei Medici (1574–87) who sent it as a gift to Philip II of Spain. It reached England in 1597 when John Wolfe entered 'the neue and most pleasant game of the Goose' in the Stationers' Register, on the day of June 16, 1597.

Originally the Game of the Goose was simply an amusing journey with adventures and pieces moved along according to the throw of dice. The recurring squares decorated with a goose rewarded the player landing on them with another turn.

The copper-plate engraving shown here was found in a Northumbrian farm-house between the pages of a large atlas published in 1720. It bears insets of Jack Shepherd, a thief executed at Tyburn on November 16, 1724 and Jonathan Wild who betrayed him. On the board Jonathan Wild is described as 'Thief-taker General of Great Britain', but after being arrested for receiving a piece of stolen lace he was tried at the Old Bailey and afterwards hanged at Tyburn on May 24, 1725. So this copy of the game would appear to have been printed between these two dates.

The rules given in quaint English in the central panel are here reproduced in a more modern form. The space before the starting square shows a Fool and in very small script, the following:

'Fortune is the Changling Diety of fools,
Against ill luck all cunning foresight fails,
Whether we're wise or not nought avails.'

On the last or winning square, number sixty-three, a complimentary couplet is written:

'On not small Accidents Depends our fate . . .
While Chance not Prudence makes us fortunate . . .'

**PLAYERS**
Two or more.

**PIECES**
One marker and twenty counters for each player.

**SCORING**
Two cubic dice.

**AIM**
A race round the board to reach the last square.

**ORIGIN**
Italy, 1574–87.

**RULES**

1. The players take turns to throw the pair of dice and place their marker on the numbered squares of the board. For example, on a throw of six and five, the marker is placed on eleven, etc. On the following turns, the number scored is added to the figure on which the marker rests and the marker is moved accordingly.

2. If a player throws six, he pays a forfeit of one counter for his passage over the 'Bridge' and goes to number twelve.

3. On landing on a 'Goose' the player doubles his score and moves forward from his last place.

4. If a player throws nineteen, which is the 'Ale-house', he forfeits one counter to pay for his drink until it is his turn to throw again.

5. If the throw is thirty-one, which is the 'Well', the player stays there for two turns unless somebody else lands on the same place allowing him to move back to the position from which the second player arrived.

6. If a player throws forty-two, which is the 'Maze', he pays a counter and returns to twenty-nine.

7. If a player goes to fifty-two, which is the 'Prison', he pays one counter and stays there until somebody relieves him by throwing the same number.

8. On scoring fifty-eight, which is 'Death', the player pays one counter and begins again.

9. If a player is overtaken by another, the first returns to the place of the one who overtook him and both pay one counter.

10. If on approaching sixty-three the score exceeds it, the player returns to begin at the first square.

11. The player who manages to score an exact throw and reaches sixty-three, wins the game and wins the *pool*.

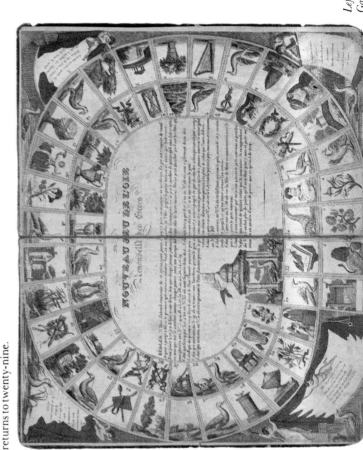

*Left: nineteenth-century French Game of Goose.*

141

# Nine Men's Morris

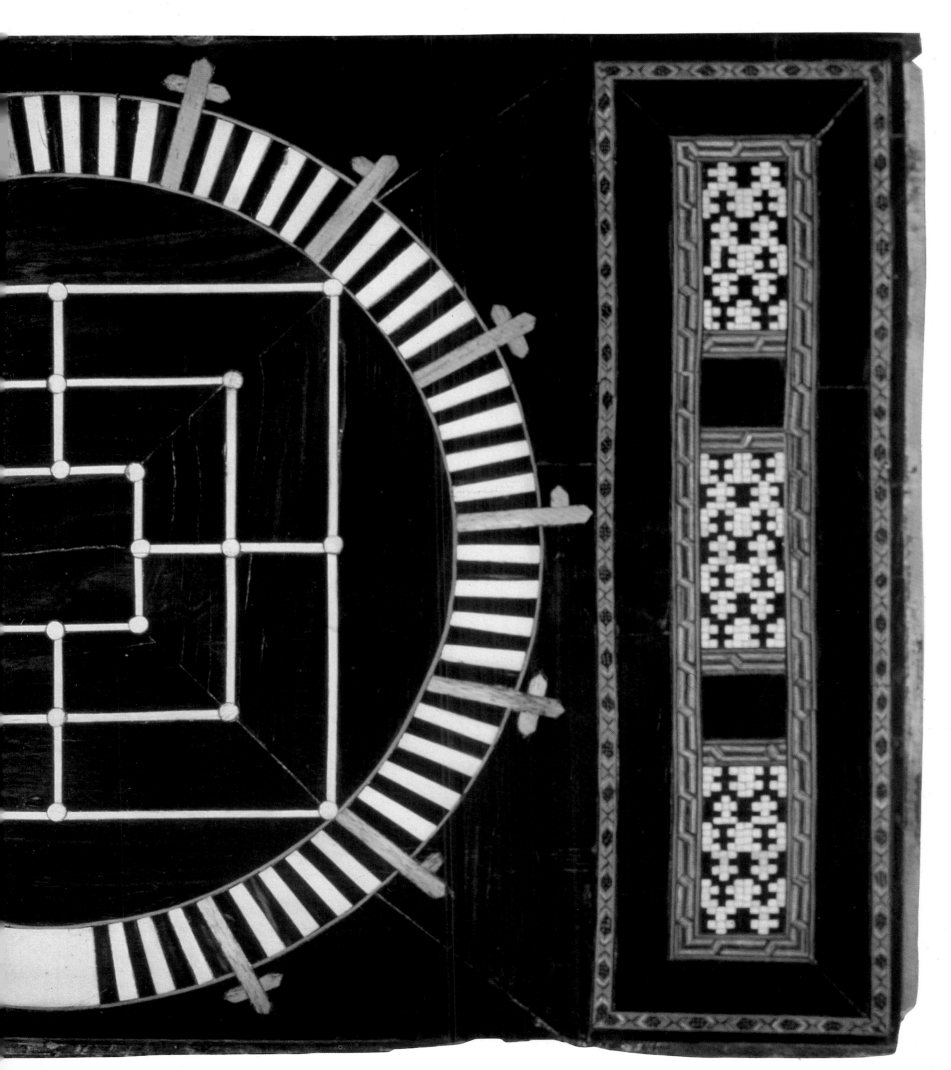

# Nine Men's Morris & variants

Outlines for the game of Nine Men's Morris have been found carved into the roofing slabs of the ancient Egyptian temple at Kurna, c.1400 B.C. Two similar boards were cut into the great flight of steps up to the shrine at Mihintale in Ceylon, built during the reign of Mahadathika Maha-Naga, 9–21 A.D.

In Europe traces of the board have been found on objects from the first city of Troy, and also at a Bronze Age burial site in County Wicklow, Ireland, where the game was possibly introduced by Greek or Phoenician traders. In Norway part of a Nine Men's Morris board was found among the royal burial hoard on the Gokstad Viking ship, c.900 A.D.

**PLAYERS**
Two.

**PIECES**
Nine men or pieces for each side. (See equipment sheet.)

**AIM**
To reduce the opponent to two pieces or immobilize him.

**ORIGIN**
Egypt, c.1400 B.C.

**RULES**
1. At the start of the game the board is empty, each player holding nine pieces of his own colour. The game is played in two phases.

**PHASE ONE**
2. A game for two players who draw lots for the advantage of starting.

3. Each player enters his nine pieces, one at a time, onto any vacant *point* on the board in alternate turns of play.

4. Each time a player forms a row of three men along a line, known as a *mill*, he removes one of his opponent's pieces from the board. Pieces in a *mill* are exempt from attack.

5. When all the pieces have been placed on the board the game enters the second phase.

**PHASE TWO**
6. The turns of play continue with the players moving one man to an adjacent vacant *point* along any line, attempting to make a *mill* and remove an opposing piece.

7. A *mill* can be made and broken any number of times, an opposing man being removed each time a *mill* is formed.

8. If a player makes a *mill* and all the opponent's pieces are safely in *mills*, play continues without loss to the opponent.

9. Double *mills* are five pieces so placed that each time a *mill* is broken, another is formed, with a capture being made at every turn. (See figure below.)

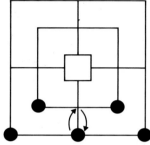

10. When a player has only three men left on the board and these are in a *mill*, if it is his turn to move he must break the *mill*, even if it means losing a piece and the game at his opponent's next move.

11. There are two ways of winning the game:
a. By reducing the opponent to two pieces.
b. By blocking all the opponent's pieces so that they cannot move.

## Twelve Men's Morris

Nine Men's Morris (see pages 142–143) reached its peak in the fourteenth century, and superb illustrations of the game are contained in the codices of the north Italian academies, manuscripts intended for use at court. About this time a variant of the game appeared in which diagonal lines were added to join the corners of the squares. Early English settlers took this game called Twelve Men's Morris to North America.

**PLAYERS**
Two.

**PIECES**
Twelve for each side.

**AIM**
To reduce the opponent to two pieces or immobilize him.

**ORIGIN**
Probably Italy, fourteenth century.

**RULES**
1. The game is played by two players, each having twelve pieces.

2. *Mills* are constructed in straight lines or diagonally.

3. Otherwise the game is played with the same rules as Nine Men's Morris.

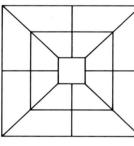

*The Romance of Alexander, a medieval manuscript, shows a couple playing 'Merells', as the game was then known.*

*An emigrant typical of those who sailed to America on the mayflower.*

## Dicing Men's Morris

The thirteenth century A.D. manuscript compiled for the Spanish King Alfonso X describes a variant of Nine Men's Morris (see pages 142–143) using three cubic dice, unlike other games of this type.

**PLAYERS**
Two.

**PIECES**
Nine for each side.

**SCORING**
Three cubic dice.

**AIM**
To reduce the opponent to two pieces or immobilize him.

**ORIGIN**
Spain, thirteenth century.

RULES
1. During the entry phase, throws of six and five and four, or six and three and

three, or five and two and two, or four and one and one permit the caster to break into an opposing *mill* and capture a man or piece at the same time as introducing one of his own pieces onto the board.

2. If a *mill* is formed with this piece the player removes another of his opponent's pieces. With any other throw a piece is entered onto the board only.

3. When all the pieces have been entered, the dice are discarded and the game continues as already described.

## Tic-Tac-Toe

A board found cut into the roofing slabs of the temple at Kurna in Upper Egypt, c.1400–1333 B.C. was probably used for playing a game similar to Tic-Tac-Toe as it is now called.

Known as Luk Tsut K'i the same game was played in China at the time of Confucius, some five hundred years before the birth of Christ. In Africa, under the name of Achi, Ghanaian school children play the game by marking out a board on the dusty ground. Little sticks are used as pieces, three with the bark left on for one player and three peeled for the other.

Ovid mentions Tic-Tac-Toe in his 'Ars Amatoria' (Art of Love) written more than a thousand years after the Egyptian temple was built. The Roman boards were usually of wood or stone. A good example of a stone one was found recently at the Roman military station of Corbridge, in northern England.

The game was most popular in England in the fourteenth century. Boards were cut into the cloister seats of the cathedrals at Canterbury, Gloucester, Norwich, Salisbury and Westminster Abbey, providing a frivolous pastime for monks during the long hours spent at their devotions.

*Game of Nine Men's Morris cut into the West Walk at Westminster Abbey.*

**PLAYERS**
Two.

**PIECES**
Three for each player of contrasting colours. (See equipment sheet.)

**AIM**
To achieve three pieces in a row.

**ORIGIN**
Known in Egypt c.1333 B.C.; China 500 B.C.

RULES
1. Each player has three pieces of his own colour and enters them in turns of play on any vacant *point* on the board.

2. When all the pieces are on the board the game continues with the players making alternate moves, one *point* at a time, until one player succeeds in placing his three pieces in a straight line.

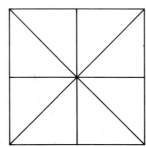

## Line of Three

The same Tic-tac-toe board is used by Egyptian children for an unrecorded game in which each player has three pieces of his own colour, placed on the board at the beginning of the game. (See figure below.)

**PLAYERS**
Two.

**PIECES**
Three for each side.

**AIM**
To make a 'line-of-three' with the pieces.

**ORIGIN**
Egypt.

RULES
1. Each player places his three pieces on his back row.

2. In any turn of play a piece can move one square in any direction (the king's move in Chess).

3. The players take turns to move a single piece.

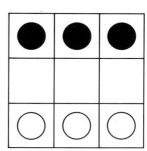

4. Each tries to make a 'line-of-three' of his pieces anywhere on the board except on his own back row. There are seven possibilities.

5. The first to make a 'line-of-three' wins the game.

## Noughts & Crosses

This variant of Tic-Tac-Toe requires a very simple board which can be used for several games. A Noughts and Crosses grid (see figure below) can easily be drawn on a sheet of paper or cardboard.

**PLAYERS**
Two.

**PIECES**
Five for each side.

**AIM**
To achieve three pieces in a line before the opponent.

**ORIGIN**
Unknown.

RULES
1. Each player has five pieces of his own colour.

2. One player places a piece on any square on the board.

3. The other player does the same and they play alternately, each trying to arrange three of their own pieces in any straight line or diagonally.

4. If a player succeeds in making a 'line-of-three' he wins the game, otherwise it is drawn.

# Alquerque

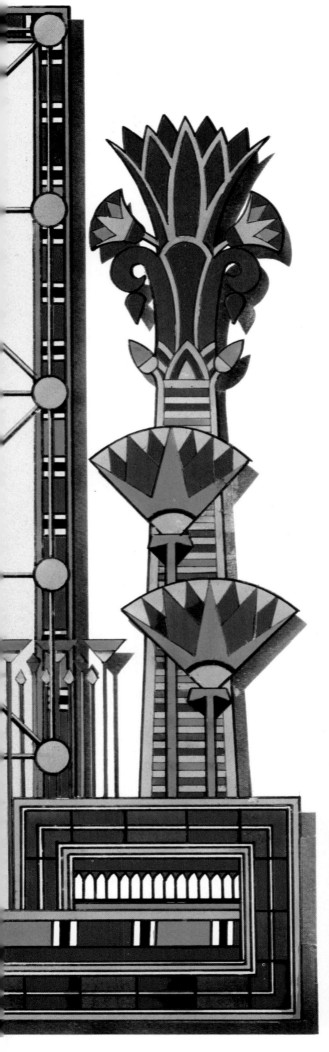

The game of Alquerque was first introduced into Spain by the Moors who called it 'el-qirkat'. It is mentioned in a tenth century Arabic work, 'Kitab al-Aghani' and there is a later description of it in the 'Book of Games', written during the reign of King Alfonso of Castile (1251–1282 A.D.). This book collected together all the known games of the time, under the personal supervision of King Alfonso whose wide scholarship inspired the popular title of 'El Sabio' or 'The Learned'. He considered that games were an important and pleasant aspect of life. However, the game itself dates back as far as the fourteenth century B.C., if not earlier, as there is a replica of a quadruple Alquerque board engraved on the roofing slabs of the temple at Kurna, Thebes, on the western side of the Nile, which was begun by Rameses I (1400–1366 B.C.) and completed by Seti I (1366–1333 B.C.). The board appears to have been cut by the stone masons working on the temple who probably played on it. When the slabs were finally placed in position they had to be trimmed and three of the boards were partially cut away.

The four by four squared Alquerque board provides the basic structure for many other battle games which have been developed along similar lines all over the world–such as Zamma (pages 148–149). There is no record of the rules followed by the Egyptians but we do know the rules which were used in Spain. Alquerque is also an early form of Draughts/Checkers (pages 26–29). In Alfonso's 'Book of Games' it is described as a game 'played with the mind'.

**PLAYERS**
Two.

**PIECES**
Twelve for each player. (See equipment sheet.)

**AIM**
To capture or immobilize all the opponent's pieces.

**ORIGIN**
Middle East before 1400 B.C.

RULES
1. The two players each have a set of twelve pieces of distinctive colour which are arranged on the board before play starts, as shown in the illustration below.

2. A piece may move from any *point* to any adjacent empty *point* along a line.

3. If an adjacent *point* is occupied by one of the opponent's pieces and the next *point* on the line beyond is empty, the player's piece can make a *short leap* over it and the opponent's piece must then be removed from the board.

4. If another piece is then threatened the player's piece may make a second *jump* in the same or a different direction. Two or more captures are permitted in the same turn of play.

5. If a piece can make a capture, it must do so, or be *huffed* and removed from the board.

6. When one player has captured all the opposing pieces the game is over and he has won.

*Below: a game of Alquerque at the start of play, as shown in King Alfonso's manuscript.*

# Zamma

*Zamma comes from the Sahara and is derived from a game played in the times of the Pharaohs. The modern form is played on a quadruple Alquerque board, modified by the second, fourth, sixth and eighth rows and columns being omitted, which reduces the power of movement of the pieces from these "points". The board is usually drawn in the sand, the pieces representing men being short lengths of stalk, while pellets of camel-dung are used to represent women. Just as in Draughts/Checkers (pages 26–29) a piece become a king, so in Zamma it can become a 'mullah'. This term is used in the Islamic world for a religious leader. A 'mullah' may be a reciter of the Koran, a teacher in a religious school, an expert in Islamic law, or a prayer leader. Although not ordained priests in the Christian sense, 'mullahs' are usually graduates of a 'madrasa' (Islamic college), and their learning brings them a great deal of influence among their congregations.*

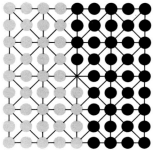

**PLAYERS**
Two.

**PIECES**
Forty men on one side and forty women on the other. (See equipment sheet.)

**AIM**
Capture of all the opponent's pieces.

**ORIGIN**
Sahara, North Africa.

RULES

1. Each player starts with forty pieces arranged as shown in the figure (See figure to the left.)

2. The player having the men (black) always plays first.

3. The pieces move only one *point* at a time, directly or diagonally forwards.

4. The pieces capture by a *short leap* in any direction, straight or diagonally forwards or backwards or sideways.

5. Capturing when possible is compulsory, under penalty of the piece being *huffed*.

6. When a piece reaches the opposite back row it is promoted to being a mullah and is distinguished either by some mark or by turning the piece onto its reverse side.

7. A mullah moves any distance along any marked line through the *point* it occupies, and in any direction.

8. A mullah captures by a *short* or a *long leap*, but the captured pieces are not lifted from the board until the completion of the move. The mullah is not permitted to *jump* over a piece a second time. This rule restricts the otherwise enormous power of promoted pieces.

9. The game is won by one player capturing all the opposing pieces.

*Muslim religious leader.*

# Fanorona

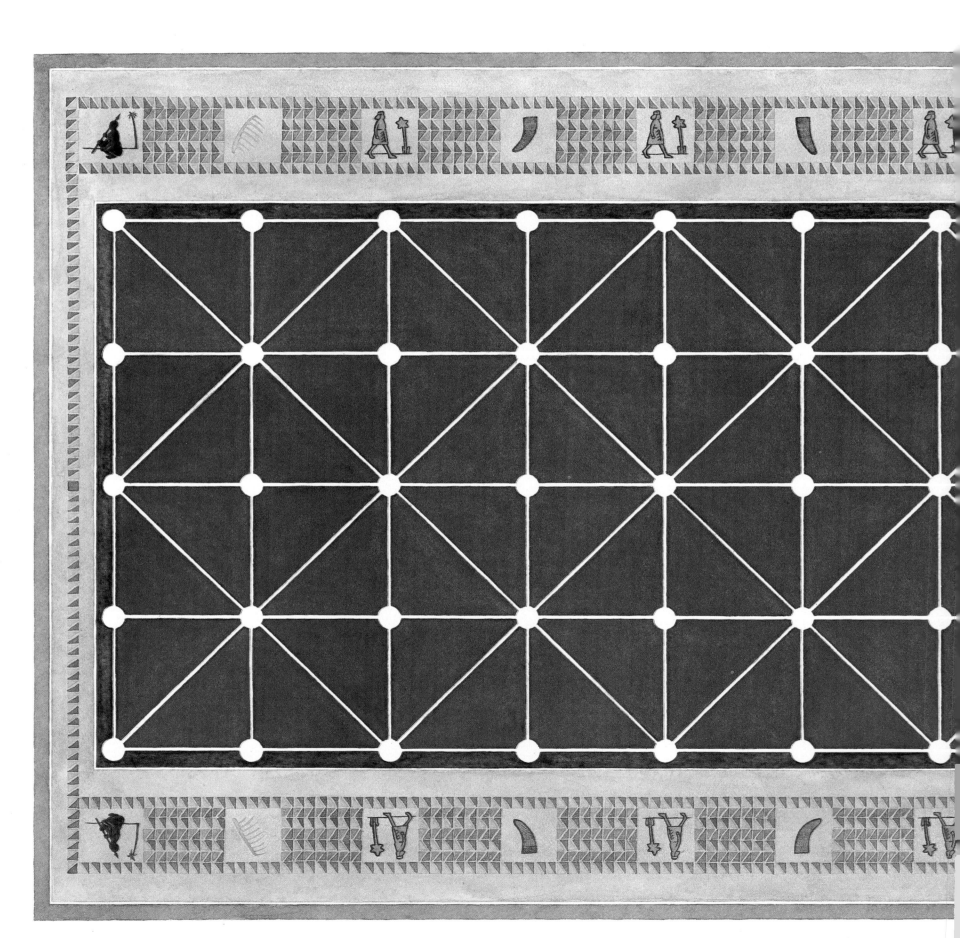

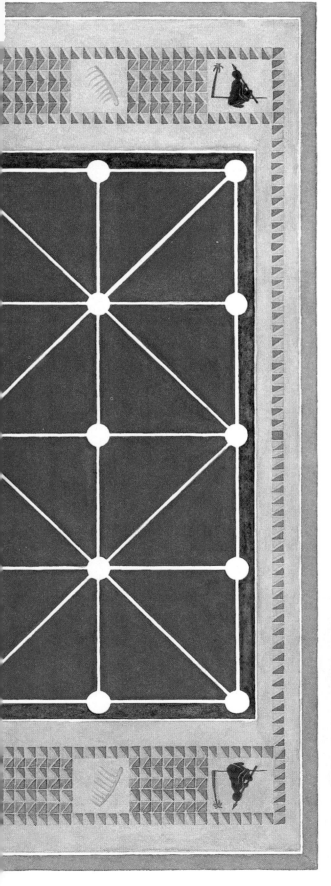

Fanorona comes from the island of Madagascar and dates back to about 1680 A.D. It was developed from the older Arabic game of Alquerque (see pages 146–147) and is more elaborate than its predecessor, being played on a board twice as large and with forty-four instead of twenty-four pieces. The method of capture is also different. The game has a ritualistic quality and was, it appears, invested with divinatory properties by the Malagasi. The last queen of Madagascar, Queen Ranavalona III (her name means 'The-Lady-who-has-been-folded', like a garment) was a frail creature, only five feet tall. She was crowned when only twenty-two and married forcibly to her fifty-nine year old prime minister. One of her predecessors, Queen Rasoherina, who reigned twenty years earlier, had superstitiously refused to allow any locks to be placed on the palace doors, and had also insisted that her architects avoid all dimensions including the numbers six or eight in their buildings. It is not surprising, therefore, to learn that when the French attacked the capital of the island in 1895, the equally superstitious Ranavalona III and her councillors allowed their military tactics to be influenced by the results of an official match of Fanorona – with disastrous consequences. The French conquered the island; the monarchy was abolished and Ranavalona sent into exile, first to the island of Réunion and later to Algeria where she died in 1917, aged fifty-six. Later, in 1938, her remains were returned to Madagascar.

Queen Ranavalona III.

**PLAYERS**
Two.

**PIECES**
Twenty-two for each side. (See equipment sheet.)

**AIM**
To capture all the opponent's pieces and win a majority of games in the match.

**ORIGIN**
Madagascar, c.1680.

RULES
1. There are two distinct types of opening which are played alternately. A match consists of an agreed number of games.

PHASE ONE
2. White begins by moving a piece along any line to an adjacent empty *point*.

3. If a move ends on a *point* in contact with a *point* or *points* beyond in the line of movement occupied by enemy pieces in an unbroken sequence, these are captured and removed. Such capturing is by *approach*.

4. Capture may also be by *withdrawal*. If a player's piece moves away from a *point* next to a *point* or *points* occupied by the opponent's pieces in the same line of movement, these pieces are captured and *borne off*.

5. Capturing is compulsory, but in the first move by each player only one group can be taken.

6. In later moves a player may make several captures, either by *approach* or *withdrawal*, but each move must be along a different line, the piece changing direction to make each capture.

7. If a player's piece can take enemy pieces in two directions, the player can choose to capture pieces in either direction, but not in both. He is not obliged to capture the larger number.

8. The phase ends when one player has captured all the other's pieces.

PHASE TWO
9. The second phase is played in a different manner. The defeated player starts, and the previous winner sacrifices piece after piece until he has lost seventeen. During this 'vela' play the winner refrains from making any captures, and his opponent may only capture one piece at each move.

10. When seventeen pieces have been captured normal play is resumed using the Rules 1 to 7.

11. The third phase is played as the first, and the fourth is a 'vela' phase, each type of opening being played alternately.

12. The player who gains the majority of games in a match (consisting of an agreed number of games) is the winner.

*Opening position for phase one.*

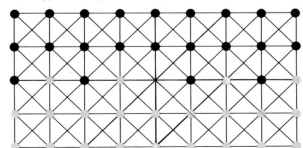

# Dablot Prejjesne

This is a Lapp game from Frostviken. The first Lapps reached the area they now inhabit, the zone running across the north of Scandinavia from Norway to the Kola Peninsula in the Soviet Union, before the first century A.D. It is mainly flat tundra with mountains in the centre. At first the Lapps survived by hunting the wild reindeer, but in time they learnt to domesticate these animals and kept them in herds. They still retain their nomadic way of life, however, since if their herds stay in one area they soon exhaust the sparse vegetation. The Lapps invented the art of skiing to help them move through the snow, which covers the country for much of the year.

In the first millenium of the Christian era, the Finns arrived and forced the Lapps out of the southern, more fertile part of the country. The influence of the Finns was so great that the Lapps now speak a form of Finnish, but there was an inevitable conflict between the settled agricultural way of life of the Finns and the nomadic herding of the Lapps. Dablot Prejjesne reflects this conflict. It is played on a board of thirty squares with their diagonals, making seventy-two "points". The pieces of one side represent a tribe of nomadic Lapps and the other a community of farmers settled on the land. One player has twenty-eight Lapp warriors with pointed helmets, a Lapp prince who is slightly larger and the Lapp king who is larger still.

The other player has twenty-eight tenant farmers with horned helmets, the landlord's son and the landlord who is the same size as the Lapp king. The opening position of the pieces on the board is shown in the figure on the right, with tenant famers on "points" one to twenty-eight, the landlord's son on thirty-three, and the landlord on thirty-nine. The Lapp warriors are on forty-five to seventy-two, the Lapp prince is on forty and the Lapp king on thirty-four.

*Traditional Lapp dress and method of travel.*

**PLAYERS**
Two.

**PIECES**
Thirty for each side: twenty-eight tenant farmers, landlord and landlord's son; twenty-eight Lapp warriors, Lapp king and Lapp prince.
(See equipment sheet.)

**AIM**
Capture or immobilization of all the opponent's pieces.

**ORIGIN**
Lapland.

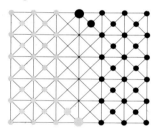

**RULES**
1. Every piece may move to the nearest unoccupied *point* on any straight line, forwards or backwards. A *short leap* may be made (but never combined with the above move) over an enemy piece onto a vacant *point* beyond, the former being removed from the board. A series of *short leaps* in any

direction may be made by a piece in one turn of play, each enemy piece being removed from the board as it is captured.

2. Capture is not compulsory and if a number of captures is possible, it is not necessary to make them all.

3. Lapp warriors and tenant farmers are of equal power and can take each other, but they cannot attack the opposing leader.

4. The Lapp prince and the landlord's son can capture each other, or minor pieces, but cannot attack the opposing leader.

5. The Lapp king and the landlord can capture each other, or any opposing piece. Their power of movement, however, is the same as the other pieces: they can move to the nearest vacant *point* in any direction, or make a *short leap* over an enemy piece onto a vacant *point* beyond. There may be a series of such *leaps* in one turn of play.

6. The game ends when one player is overwhelmed and resigns.

7. If one player has only a major piece left, and the other has several minor pieces, the latter can win by surrounding the former and depriving him of the power to move. This is winning by immobilization.

8. If both players are left with a single piece each of equal power, one of them calls for 'Single Combat'. The pieces then move towards each other in direct confrontation, and the player who has the next move will capture the other player's piece and win the game.

9. Rule eight does not apply if only the Lapp king and the landlord are left on the board, in which case the game is declared drawn.

# Chinese Checkers

This game for three, four, or six players is a modern derivation of Halma (see pages 30–31), but is played on the intersections or "points" of a board shaped as a six pointed star. Each player has ten marbles or pieces of his own colour. The plywood board reproduced here was found a few years ago at Kaslo in Central British Columbia. It is one of the first Hop Ching Checker boards made by J. Pressman & Co., New York, and was patented in America around 1870–1880.

**PLAYERS**
**Two, three, four or six.**

**PIECES**
**Six sets of ten pieces.**
**(See equipment sheet.)**

**AIM**
**A race, between single players or teams, to move move all their pieces into the opposite camp.**

**ORIGIN**
**Nineteenth century.**

RULES
1. The players of this game place their pieces on the *points* of the star at the start of the game. The method of play is the same as for Halma.

2. Each player moves one piece in turn, passing clockwise around the table.

3. Pieces may move in any direction along the marked lines.

4. Pieces are moved either one *point* at a time, or they *jump* in *short leaps* over their own or other pieces, and may make several *leaps* in one turn of play.

5. Players are not allowed to combine moves of one *point* and *jumps* in a single turn.

6. The first player to occupy all the positions in the opposite camp to his own is the winner.

7. The other players play on for second, third, fourth fifth and last place.

*Chinatown in San Francisco during the 1880s.*

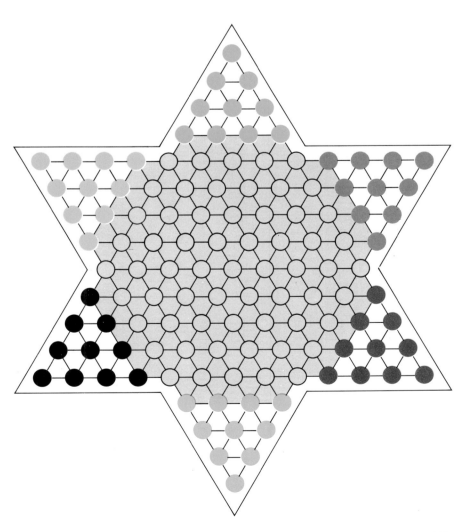

# Bibliography

Arnold, P. — *The Encyclopedia of Gambling*, New Jersey, 1974.

Ashton, J. — *The History of Gambling in England*, London, 1895.

Austin, R. G. — 'Roman Board Games', *Greece & Rome*, IV, (1934–35).

Bell, R. C. — *Board & Table Games from Many Civilizations*, Vol I, 2nd Edn., and Vol II, London, 1969.

*Discovering Old Board Games*, Aylesbury, 1976.

*Discovering Backgammon*, Aylesbury, 1975.

*Discovering Chess*, Aylesbury, 1976.

Cotton, C. — 'The Compleat Gamester', *Games & Gamesters of the Reformation*, London, 1930.

Culin, S. — *Chineses Games with Dice and Dominoes*, Washington, 1907.

'Hawaiian Games', *American Anthropologist*, New Series, I (1899).

*Korean Games*, Philadelphia, 1895.

*Chess and Playing Cards*, Washington, 1895.

*Games of the North American Indians*, Washington, 1907.

Dawson, L. H. — *Hoyle's Games Modernised*, London, 1923.

Falkener, E. — *Games Ancient and Oriental*, London, 1892.

Finn, T. — *Pub Games of England*, London, 1975.

Fiske, W. — *Chess in Iceland*, Florence, 1905.

Forbes, D. — *History of Chess*, London, 1960.

Foster, R. F. — *Encyclopedia of Games*, London, 1901.

Friedman, W. — *Casino Games*, New York, 1973.

Gardner, M. — *The Unexpected Hanging and other Mathematical Diversions*, New York, 1968.

Grant, M. — *Erotic Art in Pompeii, The Secret Collection of the National Museum of Naples*, English Edn., London, 1975.

Grunfield, F. V. — *Games of the World*, New York, 1950.

Hammond, A. — *The Book of Chessmen*, London, 1950.

Hedges, S. G. — *The Home Entertainer*, London, (Undated).

Hoerth, A. J. — *Gameboards in the Ancient Near East*, M.A. Thesis, University of Chicago, Illinois, 1961.

Hyde, T. — *De Historia Nerdiludii*, Oxford, 1964.

H——, G. — *Hoyle's Games Improved*, London, 1853.

Iwamoto, K. — *Go for Beginners*, Harmondsworth, 1976.

Jones, C. — *Hoyle's Games Improved*, London, 1786.

Kambayashi, H. — *Go Game for Beginners*, Japan Publication Trading Co., 1964.

King, T. — *Twenty-one Games of Chance*, London, (Undated).

Lane, E. W. — *An Account of the Manners and Customs of the Modern Egyptians*, Minerva Library, 1890.

La Roux, M. — *The Complete Draughts Player*, London, 1955.

Lasker, E. — *Go and Go-Moku*, New York, 1960.

Laurent, M. — 'Tessères en os du Musée d'Athens', *Le Musée Belge*, VII (1903) quoted in *Pompeii A.D. 79*, published by Imperial Tobacco Ltd., 1977.

Linneus, C. — *Lachesis Lapponica*, London, 1811.

Marin, G. — 'Somali Games', *Journal of the Royal Anthropological Institute*, LXI, London, 1931.

Murray, H. J. R. — *History of Chess*, Oxford, 1913.

*A History of Board Games other than Chess*, Oxford, 1952.

Parker, H. — *Ancient Ceylon*, London, 1909.

Petrie, F. — *Objects of Daily Use*, British School of Archaeology in Egypt, 1927.

Quinn, J. P. — *Fools of Fortune*, Chicago, 1892.

Richard, W. L. — *Complete Backgammon*, 1st English Edn., London, 1938.

Robinson, J. A. — *Time of St. Dunstan*, Oxford, 1923.

Sapper, K. von — *Boas Anniversary Volume*, New York, 1906.

Scarne, J. & Rawson, C. — *Scarne on Dice*, Harrisburg, Pa., 1946.

Smith, A. — *The Game of Go*, Vermont, 1958.

Strutt, J. — *The Sports and Pastimes of the People of England*, 3rd Edn., London, 1845.

Takagawa, K. — *How to Play Go*, Japan, 1956.

Whitehouse, F. R. B. — *Table Games of Georgian and Victorian Days*, London, 1951.

Wong, W. F. — *Chinese Chess*, Hong Kong, 1971.

Woolley, Sir C. I. — *Ur of the Chaldees*, London, 1929.

*Ur; The First Phases*, London, 1946.

## OTHER WORKS BY R.C. BELL

*Commercial Coins 1787–1804*, Corbitt & Hunter, 1963.

*Copper Commercial Coins 1811–1819*, Corbitt & Hunter, 1964.

*Tradesmen's Tickets & Private Tokens 1785–1819*, Corbitt & Hunter, 1966.

*Specious Tokens & those struck for General Circulation 1784–1804*, Corbitt & Hunter, 1968.

*Unofficial Farthings 1820–1870*, Seaby Publications, 1975.

*Building Medallets of Kempson & Skidmore 1796–1797*, Frank Graham, 1978.

*Tyneside Pottery*, Studio Vista, 1971.

*Potteries of Tyneside*, Frank Graham, 1973 (with M. A. V. Gill).

*Diaries from the Days of Sail*, Holt, Rinehart & Winston, 1974.

*The Use of Skin Grafts*, Oxford University Press, 1973.

# Acknowledgments

1–7 R. C. Bell Collection/Tessa Traeger
8 Mary Evans Picture Library
10(t) Bethnal Green Museum, London/
Dennis Rolfe
(b) Pollocks Toy Museum/Denis Rolfe
11 R. C. Bell Collection/Con Putbrace
12(1) Peter Taylor
(r) Museum Rietberg, Zurich/Dr
Eberhard Fischer
13(1) Peter Taylor
(tr) R. C. Bell Collection/Robert Golden
14 R. C. Bell Collection/Robert Golden
15 R. C. Bell Collection/Robert Golden
(b) British Museum, London/Peter
Clayton
16(t) Agencia Salmer/Bevilacqua
(bl) R. C. Bell Collection/Robert Golden
(br) John Carrod
17 R. C. Bell Collection/Robert Golden
19 R. C. Bell Collection/Con Putbrace
20 Bodleian Library, Oxford
21 (1) Bulloz/Petit Palais, Paris
(r) India Record Office, London
22 Mary Evans Picture Library
23 Raymond Benson
24 Vicky Fisher
26 Mary Evans Picture Library
27 R. C. Bell Collection/Con Putbrace
28 R. C. Bell Collection/Robert Golden
29 Mary Evans Picture Library
30 R. C. Bell Collection/Con Putbrace
31 R. C. Bell Collection/Con Putbrace
32 R. C. Bell Collection/Con Putbrace
33 Daily Telegraph/Westair
34 Ann Ronan
35 John Thompson
36 Western Americana
37 R. C. Bell Collection/Robert Golden
38–39 Anna Pugh
39 Stephen Johnson
40–41 Patrick Egan
42 (c) Ian Beck
43 Pam Raithby/Robert Golden
44 (bl) R. C. Bell Collection/
Robert Golden
44 (r) R. C. Bell Collection/
Con Putbrace
45 (t) R. C. Bell Collection/
Robert Golden
(b) Carnarvon Collection, Metropolitan
Museum of Art, New York/Ian Beck
46–47 John Camm
47 Barnaby's Picture Library
48 R. C. Bell Collection/Robert Golden
(r) Lindsey Blow
49 Lindsey Blow
50 R. C. Bell Collection/Robert Golden
50–51 Victoria and Albert Museum,
London/Dennis Rolfe
52 Mary Evans Picture Library
52–53 Spears/Con Putbrace
54 R. C. Bell Collection/Robert Golden
55 Mary Evans Picture Library/tinting
Patrick Egan
56–57 Mick Brownfield
57 R. C. Bell Collection/Ian Beck
58–59 R. C. Bell Collection/
Con Putbrace
59 R. C. Bell Collection/Con Putbrace
60 R. C. Bell Collection/Con Putbrace
61 Barnaby's Picture Library
62 R. C. Bell Collection/Con Putbrace
63 Peter Taylor
64 John Gorham
65 Dover Publications/Pat Hodgson

66 Anne Morrow
68–69 R. C. Bell Collection/
Con Putbrace
70 Western Americana
70–71 R. C. Bell Collection/rubbings,
Julie Staniland
71 R. C. Bell Collection/Robert Golden
72–73 Kevin Maddison
74 Ian Beck
74–75 R. C. Bell Collection/
Con Putbrace
76–77 Tony Spaul
78–79 Just Games/Robert Golden
80 John Strange/Con Putbrace
81 Viva/Deluc
82–83 Ch'en-Ling
83 (cr) Peter Clayton
(br) R. C. Bell Collection/Robert Golden
84–85 R. C. Bell Collection/Con Putbrace
86 Picturepoint
86–87 R. C. Bell Collection/
Con Putbrace
88–89 Victoria and Albert Museum,
London/Dennis Rolfe
91 (1) R. C. Bell Collection/
Robert Golden
(r) Preussicher Kulturbesitz
92–93 R. C. Bell Collection/
Con Putbrace
93 R. C. Bell Collection/Robert Golden
94 Stephen Johnson
94–95 R. C. Bell Collection/
Con Putbrace
96 Iain Stuart
97 Picturepoint
98–99 R. C. Bell Collection/
Con Putbrace
100 (bl) R. C. Bell Collection/
Robert Golden
100–101 Medals and envelopes:
C. S. Holder Collection/Robert Golden
102–103 R. C. Bell Collection/
Con Putbrace
104 Ian Beck
104–105 Patrick Egan/The Castle
Museum, York
105 Ian Beck
106 Malcolm English
107 (t) Pat Hodgson
(bl) R. C. Bell Collection/Robert Golden
(bc) Jerry's Club, London/
Robert Golden
108 (t) Report of the U.S. National
Museum 1896/Culin, plate 29
108 (b) Ian Beck
109 R. C. Bell Collection/Con Putbrace
110 Radio Times Hulton/Bert Hardy
110–111 R. C. Bell Collection/
Con Putbrace
112 R. C. Bell Collection/Robert Golden
113 Mary Evans Picture Library
(r) R. C. Bell Collection/Robert Golden
114–115 R. C. Bell Collection/
Con Putbrace
115 (t) R. C. Bell Collection/
Robert Golden
(b) Ian Beck
116–117 Patrick Egan
118 R. C. Bell Collection/Robert Golden
118–119 R. C. Bell Collection/
Con Putbrace
120–121 Pete Saag
122–123 Ingrid Jacob
124–125 Giraudon/Nationale Art
Orientale, Rome

127 (t) British Museum, London
(bl) Courtesy of the London Go Centre
(br) Private Collection/Robert Golden
128–129 Matthew Wurr
130 R. C. Bell Collection/Con Putbrace
131 (bl) Mary Evans Picture Library
(tc), (bc), (cl) R. C. Bell Collection/
Con Putbrace
132–133 Bill Dare
133 (c) Magnum/Dick Rowan
(r) Mary Evans Picture Library
134 (l) Stephen Johnson
(bc) Robert Harding
134–135 R. C. Bell Collection/
Con Putbrace
136–137 Michael Farrell
138 Mary Evans Picture Library
138–139 Victoria and Albert Museum,
London/Dennis Rolfe
140 R. C. Bell Collection/Con Putbrace
141 Pollock's Toy Museum, London/
Dennis Rolfe
142–143 Victoria and Albert Museum,
London/Dennis Rolfe
144 (r) Pat Hodgson
(1) Bodleian Library, Oxford
145 (c) Woodmansterne Production
(b) Ian Beck
146 Concha Latapi
147 Escorial, Madrid/Toby Molenaar
148 Jon Wells
149 Mansell Collection
150–151 Iain Stuart
151 Mansell Collection
152–153 Raymond Benson
153 Radio Times Hulton
154–155 R. C. Bell Collection/
Con Putbrace
155 Western Americana
158–159 Index, Jenny Kane
*Fold out sheets*
Basket of Fruit: Bethnal Green Museum,
London/Dennis Rolfe
Cottage of Content: Bethnal Green
Museum, London/Dennis Rolfe
Game of Genius: R. C. Bell Collection/
Con Putbrace
Hare and Tortoise: R. C. Bell Collection/
Con Putbrace
Journey through Life: Pollock's Toy
Museum, London/Dennis Rolfe
Railway Game: Giraudon
Tour through Europe: R. C. Bell
Collection/Con Putbrace
Zodiac: Escorial, Madrid/Toby Molenaar
Endpapers: illustration, Peter Hill
Equipment sheet: Alan Aldridge assisted
by Jubilee Graphics/Harry Willock
Slipcase: design, John Strange/
R. C. Bell Collection/Mary Evans
Picture Library/Con Putbrace
We would also like to thank the following
for their assistance: Face, Quicksilver,
Slingers, Spectrographic, Summit Art,
Topic, TRP Slavin, Tradespools.

The author and publishers wish to thank
Oxford University Press and Shire
Publications Limited for allowing
material previously published by them in
*Board and Table Games*, Vol I and Vol II,
and *Discovering Old Board Games*
respectively, to be included in this work.

# Index

*Game-boards and their countries of origin are in bold type and main references to the boards and rules are indicated by numerals in italics.*

158

# Glossary

*This glossary contains words with a special meaning in a games context. Terms used only in a particular game are not normally included as they are explained in the relevant text.*

**Approach**  See *capture.*

**Bear Off**  Remove pieces from the board and out of the game.

**Capture**  See *approach—withdrawal* below.

Approach  If a move ends on a *point* in contact with a *point* or *points* beyond in the line of movement occupied by enemy pieces in an unbroken sequence, these are captured and removed.

Custodian  Capture by trapping one player's piece between two of the opponent's pieces placed on either side in a straight line.

Intervention  Capturing two opposing pieces by occupying the *point* immediately between them.

Long Leap  A *jump* by one piece over another to capture it and land beyond. Vacant spaces may intervene on either side of the captured piece.

Replacement  Capture made by a piece moving onto a space occupied by an enemy piece and removing it from the board.

Short Leap  Capture made by a piece *jumping* over an enemy piece on an adjacent space to land on the vacant space immediately beyond.

Withdrawal  If a piece moves away from a *point* or *points* occupied by enemy pieces in the same line of movement, these are captured and *borne off.*

**Column**  A straight line running from top to bottom of a board at right angles to a *row* or *rank.*

**Custodian**  See *capture.*

**Die**  The singular of dice.

**Doublet**  1. The same number shown on two dice, or the number shown by a throw of the *die* or dice is doubled.

2. Uniting two markers and moving them in the game as one piece.

**Dress**  Dealer or 'banker' in a gambling game lays out the board, usually with cards, in preparation for the bets to be placed.

**Elder**  The opening or first player in order of play.

**File**  See *column.*

**Grace**  An extra turn.

**Huff**  Confiscation of a piece for infringing a rule.

**Intervention**  See *capture.*

**Jump**  Move one piece over another to an adjacent *point* or square.

**Long Leap**  See *capture.*

**Mill**  Three or more pieces placed in a line of adjacent *points* or squares.

**Point**  The intersections of lines on which pieces are placed instead of on the spaces or squares in between. In the case of Backgammon, pointed lines or columns on which pieces are placed.

**Pool**  A kitty into which players pool their counters or coins at the start of play or during play.

**Rank**  A line running at right angles to a *column* or *file* across the board from one side to the other.

**Replacement**  See *capture.*

**Row**  The same as *rank.*

**Senior**  The same as *elder.*

**Short Leap**  See *capture.*

**Singleton**  Isolated single piece, often vulnerable to attack.

**Teetotum**  Originally a *die* composed of a four sided disc which rotated like a top on a spindle passing through the centre. Each of the four sides was inscribed with

a letter and the one which appeared uppermost at the end of a spin decided the player's fortune. *T-totum* combines the Latin word *totum,* meaning 'all', with the initial by which it was represented on one side of the disc. This was also spelled out as *teetotum,* and sometimes abbreviated to *totum.* The other letters on the disc were also the initials of Latin words: S for *sufer,* 'take away the stake'; D for *depone,* 'deposit the stake'; N for *nihil,* 'nothing'. Later, the initials of English words were used: T for 'take all'; H for 'half'; N for 'nothing' and P 'put down a stake equal to that placed at the beginning of the game.' On the equipment sheet, a variety of *teetotums* has been included to replace cubic and other dice of more than two sides.

**Triplet**  The same number shown on three dice.

**Trumps**  Every card of the suit temporarily chosen in rank above all others.

**Withdrawal**  See *capture.*

**Younger**  Second or last player in order of play.